Balanced Literacy

for English Language Learners, K–2

Linda Chen
Eugenia Mora-Flores

HEINEMANN
Portsmouth, NH

KH

Heinemann
A division of Reed Elsevier Inc.
361 Hanover Street
Portsmouth, NH 03801–3912
www.heinemann.com

Offices and agents throughout the world

© 2006 by Linda Chen and Eugenia Mora-Flores

Library of Congress Cataloging-in-Publication Data
Chen, Linda, 1970–
    Balanced literacy for English language learners, K–2 / Linda Chen, Eugenia Mora-Flores.
        p.   cm.
    Includes bibliographical references and index.
    ISBN 0-325-00880-9 (acid-free paper)
    1. English language—Study and teaching—Foreign speakers.   2. English language—Study and teaching (Primary)   3. Language acquisition.   4. Bilingualism.
I. Mora-Flores, Eugenia, 1975–.   II. Title.
    PE1128.A2C446 2006
    428.6′4—dc22
                                                2006010853

Editors: Harvey Daniels and Kate Montgomery
Production: Patricia Adams
Typesetter: Publishers' Design and Production Services, Inc.
Cover design: Lisa Fowler
Cover and interior photographs: Denise Ascencion
Manufacturing: Jamie Carter

Printed in the United States of America on acid-free paper
10 09 08 07   EB   3 4 5

2/7/08

To our parents who came to this country and successfully navigated through a new culture while learning English and instilled in us a passion for seeing the world through two languages.

—L. C., E. M. F.

Contents

Introduction

*F*or the past eight years we have had so many conversations about how best to teach our second language learners. As classroom teachers we were exposed to a variety of methods and practices used to teach English learners (ELs). The most effective methods we implemented were those in which the students were able to use their primary language to learn and to facilitate second language learning. We taught in dual language and waiver programs, where instruction was delivered part of the day in the students' primary language and the other part of the day in English, and we were amazed at the progress our students were making in both English and Spanish or English and Chinese. There were still questions that lingered when it came to the instructional time of day when students were taught in English. We wondered, "Are we doing this right? Are we teaching them content and language properly?" This led to conversations about how to improve our instructional time in English. We thought about the rich teaching practices employed during primary language instruction as well as the quality, theoretically sound methods we had learned in our teacher education programs—methods such as workshop models and the use of real reading and writing experiences to help students learn. We thought, "How can we use those methods with students when teaching them in a second language?" A real marriage of second language acquisition theory and linguistics with literacy instruction began to surface in our conversations. This was an exciting time for us, when we would talk about our teaching, look at our students' work, and make informed decisions about what was working and what we could do better to develop language and literacy.

After years of working directly with English learners as classroom teachers, our roles changed to professional developers, and we currently work as an administrator and a professor of teacher education. We began to see so many changes in the field, with new mandated literacy programs, policies that prohibited primary language instruction, and the fear of standards and accountability, all of which had a huge impact on teaching and learning. We began to see very structured programs where students would sit and listen as the teacher talked most of the day; we saw classrooms where English learners were pulled aside during whole-group lessons, programs that emphasized phonics over reading authentic literature, and so many other variations. We started to ask ourselves, "What is happening in these classrooms, in our classrooms? Are English learners receiving a quality program? Are they actually developing language in rich contexts? How can we go about providing them the best possible program?" These questions began our journey toward writing this book. We knew what we had used as classroom teachers and we knew what it meant to teach under so many mandates and restrictive policies, so we wondered how we could help teachers of ELs meet the needs of their students within these contexts.

Before we continue to talk about how this book was developed and organized, we want to clarify our own personal beliefs about how best to teach English learners. We strongly believe that bilingual programs where students can develop and utilize their primary language as they learn a second language is the best way to teach ELs. Our work in this book is not meant to replace that type of teaching. What we want to do is provide teachers with suggestions for quality, theoretically and practically sound methods for teaching English learners in contexts where they are not able to use their primary language directly in the classroom. These contexts include structured English immersion classrooms as well as bilingual classrooms during "English time." That is, when students are being taught in English, teachers can utilize these methods and strategies to support language and literacy development. Also, the intent is not to present our ideas as a program. Parts of the book might be useful for your classroom, and others may not. English learners are not a monolithic group and there will be variations in how best to meet their needs. However, we do hope this book demonstrates what our expectations are for ELs as proficient readers and writers of English and shows how certain methods can help develop those proficiencies. Chapter 2 introduces you to the *essential elements* that all students need to become proficient, lifelong readers. We want teachers, future teachers, administrators, professional developers, and teacher educators to see our book as a beginning, as a place for conversations and further questions. We hope you will ask yourself every year with every new group of students you are blessed with teaching, "What are my expectations for my students as readers and writers? What am I currently doing in my language arts program that helps my students meet those expectations? What is missing in my program? How can I fill the void in my program so that *all* of my students have opportunities to learn beyond my expectations and beyond the classroom?" This book offers suggestions for expectations as well as methods and classroom activities that can help fill those voids in our programs.

Organization of the Book

In order for teachers to become better decision makers in their practice, it is important for them to have a fundamental knowledge of how learners learn and develop language and literacy. We begin with an overview of language and literacy development in Chapters 1 and 2. Now be prepared: These first couple of chapters are a bit heavy in theory and terminology. We toyed with these chapters so much, wondering if they were too academic, and then we realized that we wanted you to see where the methods and practices we present came from. We wanted to be sure that we shared with you our understanding of language and literacy and how theory supports what we believe about how children develop both. When reading Chapters 1 and 2, it might take you back to your teacher preparation program courses on language development and reading methodology. It's almost like a crash course or a review session.

Following the heavy reading, Chapter 3 guides you through how instruction is organized with attention to theory, essential elements, levels of support for students (whole groups, small groups, and individuals), and instructional methods. These all work together to provide a comprehensive and balanced program for English learners. Sample class schedules are offered to further demonstrate how these can all fit within the mandated three hours of language arts instruction in kindergarten, first-grade, and second-grade classrooms. Your day may look different; we just wanted to share some suggestions since we are always asked during workshops and seminars, "How can we possibly fit this all into a day?" You will make decisions as to what your classroom needs to create a quality program.

Chapters 4–9 are organized by methodologies (interactive read-aloud, emergent storybook read-aloud, shared reading, independent reading workshop, writing workshop, and guided reading). They present the how-to for each of the methods with theoretical support and in-action pieces that give you a look inside a classroom that is implementing the method. Each in-action piece is reflected upon with attention to English learners' development of language alongside literacy. We wanted to show you how students were thinking, learning, and developing English. There are a variety of classroom resources available to further your knowledge base about each of the methods.

Finally, Chapter 10, "Word Work," is organized a bit differently. Because it is not a single method, we present an overview of what is involved in word work, followed by a number of classroom activities.

We hope that this book provides for you a resource for developing, organizing, and implementing a comprehensive language arts program for your English learners. We strongly believe that they deserve quality programs that support their second language needs while maintaining high expectations and academic rigor. You will find that most of the practices we suggest in this book are beneficial for all students, but they are essential for English learners because they are developing literacy while juggling more than one language.

Acknowledgments

Although we did not know it at the time, the seeds for this project were planted during our first year after moving to New York City, when we taught first grade together in Manhattan. Under the leadership of our principal, Jorge Izquierdo, we had the privilege of working with an amazing first-grade team—Sally Mamdouh and Eugenia Wu. Our staff developers, Laurie Pessah and Kristin Eagleburger, from Teachers College Reading and Writing Project, provided us with the first glimpses of the infinite possibilities for English learners in reading and writing workshops. Since that year, we have individually embarked on different experiences, all the while living parallel professional lives (now on opposite ends of the country) immersed in literacy and best practices for English learners.

To all of the teachers and students at Corona Ave. Elementary who welcomed us into their classrooms—Belen Pichardo, Thea Lebeouf, Rosalba Guevarra, Lily Chow, Ivan Parra, and Danny Rodriguez—we thank you for all you have taught us about how children learn. A special thank-you goes to Angelica Mora-Machado for all of her feedback on drafts and for being so flexible and accommodating when we needed to work with students and access materials. Angelica is truly a gifted teacher who dedicates countless hours to children and believes in providing all students a rigorous and high-quality education. To the wonderful leaders at Corona Ave. Elementary, Viola Wyman, John Olguin, and Jack Baumann, thank you all for your support and trust in me (Eugenia) to work alongside your teachers in helping them meet the language and literacy needs of their English learners.

I (Linda) would like to thank various mentors in my career who have ignited my steadfast journey of seeking equity for all children in our schools—John Morefield, Jorge Izquierdo, Ruth Swinney, Brenda Steele, and Marilyn Ruda. I see this book as part of that journey. My ever-growing vision for how we can forge better learning opportunities for children and their teachers stands on the shoulders of their insight and collective spirit. I thank Kate Montgomery, Katherine Bomer, and Randy Bomer for encouraging me to write and Leah Mermelstein, Gaby Layden, and Mary Ann Colbert for their support in reading early drafts. I also thank the various professional learning communities I have had the privilege of being involved in over the years. I will never forget my roots at Hawthorne Elementary in Seattle with Venise Jones-Poole (I know you're constantly looking out for me from above), Jeanne Farmer, Evelyn Beeler, Leslie Sager, Marion Vinson, and Patti Salerno. After moving to New York, I had the privilege of learning alongside Lucy Calkins, who has an extraordinary ability to push everyone around her to be smart and forge unknown territories in literacy. Our brief writing partnership also caused me to envision the possibilities for this book. I also thank Lucy for believing in our passion for working with English learners and allowing Miriam Swirski-Lubin and me to begin the Teachers College Reading and Writing Project's first leadership groups on English language learners. For two years, Miriam and I had the privilege of learning alongside Anita Adolphus, Ronit Fisch, Irene Guzman, Rebeca Madrigal, Jaime Maiello, Robin Newman, Ivelisse Rojas, Amy Sell, Marcella Trotta, and Pamela Wen. At the Project, conversations with various think tanks and study groups were always invigorating and greatly influenced some of the thinking in this book—thanks to Carl Anderson, Lydia Bellino, Mary Ann Colbert, Kathy Collins, Gaby Layden, Ginny Lockwood-Zisa, Leah Mermelstein, Isoke Nia, Laurie Pessah, Hannah Schneewind, Kathleen Tolan, and Cheryl Tyler. I also want to thank the students, teachers, and principals of schools that I worked with as a staff developer.

In our journey we had the pleasure of learning and growing as writers from our editors, Kate Montgomery and Harvey "Smokey" Daniels. Thank you both for believing in our work and the need for more texts on how to address the needs of English learners. Our passion for the important work of providing English learners with quality educational programs could not have been realized without your ongoing support and patience. Thank you both for your positive words and hopeful attitude. You made this process not only bearable, but possible.

A very, very special thank-you to our families—we could not have finished this book without your patience, love, and support. And John and Rudy, thank you both for putting up with us through it all, the long nights of writing, take-out dinners, and trips back and forth from New York to Los Angeles. We love you guys!

1 Language Development

A word devoid of thought is a dead thing and a thought unembodied in words remains a shadow.

—L. S. Vygotsky

*F*rom the day babies are born, they begin to acquire language. As they try to make sense of the world around them, they learn to communicate through sounds and gestures. Eventually, they learn to use words and sentences to convey meaning. This development of language happens naturally as children simply pick up words or ways of speaking. They are not taught formal rules; they just hear others speak and use what they hear to communicate. This acquisition of language becomes more complex and continues over a lifetime. Every day children are exposed to new words and new ways of expressing themselves to communicate. As children interact with their environment (family, community, school), they are exposed to diverse, rich, and complex systems of language. They also learn language formally in school through language arts instruction. This instruction helps students understand the language they have acquired as well as further develop their ability to communicate effectively through both oral and written forms.

All students, whether English is their first, second, or even third language, bring to school a foundation in language. They have learned to communicate orally in a primary language. This development of language becomes a tool to help students learn in school. However, for students whose primary language is not English, the ability to use their primary language to learn in school may not be an option. Though numerous studies have proven the effectiveness of the use of a child's primary language as a tool to facilitate second language acquisition, many English learners are being denied this theoretically sound practice. They encounter the difficult task of learning a new oral language system while trying to learn content at the same time.

For some English learners school may be their first exposure to English; for others they may hear English at home only when listening to the radio or watching television. There are still other English learners who grow up in predominantly English neighborhoods and pick up English when they are traveling out in the community. These different ways in which children are exposed to the English language also include differences in the manner in which they learn to speak. The accent, sentence structure, word choice, purposes, and rules for communicating will differ from one community to the next and even across families within that community. These differences among children's social and cultural backgrounds influence how they learn to communicate (Vygotsky 1962).

The Components of Language

Every language has a common, socially agreed upon structure for communicating in a variety of contexts. Children will understand, speak, read, and write a language through their exposure to the language. They begin to acquire a complex, organized language structure. This structure will include *phonology*, *orthography*, *syntax*, *morphology*, *semantics*, *pragmatics*, and *discourse*. These seven terms are referred to as the parts or components that make up a language. We briefly review these components here and refer to them throughout the book. A conscious awareness of what is involved in learning a language helps us teach more explicitly toward second language acquisition.

Phonology is the sound system of a language. The ways that sounds are created, articulated, and produced determine the phonological system of the language. For example, in English we pronounce the letter *f* by placing our lower lip between our teeth and blowing. Or you might even say we slightly bite down on our lip to produce the sound. Each language has a unique, set number of sounds. This helps us understand why English learners sometimes have a difficult time creating certain English sounds. For example, in Spanish the /th/ sound does not exist. For this reason we often hear Spanish-speaking ELs pronouncing the /th/ sound like a *d*. As teachers, we need to show them that to create the /th/ sound, they should place their tongue between their teeth and blow. This will help them create the sound.

Think about the teaching of phonemic awareness. We are teaching children to hear, recognize, identify, and create the sounds of the English alphabet. We are teaching and developing children's English *phonology*.

We then teach children the connection between those sounds and our written language system, the alphabet. This written language system is the English language *orthography*. So when we teach children the letters of the alphabet, we continue to develop their English language. They are developing important language skills that will be used for literacy development. They will learn how to decode those letters and sounds as they begin to read text.

Syntax is the grammatical structure of the language. When we learn to speak, we naturally develop our syntactic knowledge (Chomsky 1959). We hear people speak, and we start to distinguish between proper and improper grammatical formations. For example, we quickly acquire the ability to produce a standard sentence such as "He went home." We don't say, "He goed home." We know what sounds right and what doesn't. This is a very difficult component of language for English learners to develop if they are not exposed to English or do not have opportunities to practice speaking English. During read-alouds, think-alouds, pair-shares, and independent reading, English learners are exposed to English syntax and will learn what sounds right. Also, there are many overlaps between English and Spanish syntax that students can call upon as a resource when learning English. To help facilitate this transition, we can also highlight those syntactical rules that are different.

Semantics is the study of words and their meaning. This includes both the denotations (dictionary definitions) and connotations (implied or social meanings) of words in and out of context. Part of semantics is the study of how words are formed for meaning. This is referred to as *morphology*. Morphology is the study of word parts and their meaning. This includes prefixes, suffixes, base words, and roots. Developing students' knowledge of word parts will improve their vocabulary. For instance, we teach children that the prefix *re-* means "to do again or repeat." This then helps them understand the meaning of a variety of words that contain the *re-* prefix, such as *rewrite*, *revisit*, and *reteach*. Close to 60 percent of the words we know can be understood by breaking them down into their individual word parts (Lehr, Osborne, and Hiebert 2005).

Pragmatics involves communicative competence; it is the understanding of how language is used in a variety of contexts, including which words to use, how to form our sentences, in what tone to speak, and how to engage in conversation (the rules of conversation). Let's take a look at how phonology, syntax, and semantics are all affected by context. When you are talking to your friends about a movie you have just seen, you might say, "Wow, you should see this movie. It's awesome. I mean the best. It had it all. Action. And oh, you know who was in it? That girl from, what's that movie again, oh yeah, that one day we went to the movies and we saw it, what was her name?" However, if you were talking about the same movie in a formal critique of the film, it might sound something more like this: "The latest feature by acclaimed writer and director John Singleton highlights the ever changing family structure. With seasoned actors such as . . ." What you might notice is that the words used (semantics), the sentence structure (syntax), and, as much as we can tell, the tone and phonology were all altered depending on the setting and purpose for using language. In school we remind students that there is a proper way to speak when they are in class and it may differ from how they speak to their friends on the playground. When teaching writing we also focus students' attention on pragmatics. We ask them to think about audience and purpose, which affect word choice, sentence structure, and voice. All of this practice with and attention to how and in what way language is being used is part of language development.

The final component, *discourse*, is the study of language beyond a simple sentence. It is how longer stretches of language (both written and oral) are organized. Students consider discourse when they are writing within a particular genre. It is the style, characteristics, and organization of the entire piece. In oral language it also includes our knowledge of turn taking in conversation.

All of these components or levels of language continue to develop over a lifetime. In school, students have opportunities to engage in discussions and dialogue to practice their English. They are exposed to models of English through books and from teachers and peers. They are also presented minilessons that explicitly highlight components of the English language. All of these experiences present opportunities for ELs to develop English.

Second Language Acquisition

Students who are learning English in school come with a foundation in *a* language. The challenge arises when the words, sounds, and sentence structure they have acquired are not like the language of school, English. While their English-only classmates continue to use their language skills to advance their literacy development, many English learners have to learn the English language *and* literacy simultaneously. What helps English learners are the *common underlying proficiencies* (CUP) between their primary language (L1) and their second language (L2). In the course of learning one language, a child acquires a set of skills and implicit metalinguistic knowledge that can be drawn upon when working in another language. So if a child has already learned to read in his primary language, he can utilize what he knows about reading, the process and the skills, and apply them to reading in English. Conceptual knowledge developed in one language helps to make input in the other language comprehensible. This is referred to as the Linguistic Interdependence Model (Cummins 1991). A child can use the conceptual, cognitive proficiencies known and understood in her primary language to develop and comprehend English.

The surface language—what we actually say in conversation—is referred to as *basic interpersonal communication skills* (BICS) (Cummins 1984). Students will begin to develop their BICS in order to express what they already know and understand in their primary language. Their common underlying proficiency makes it possible for English learners to understand what they are being taught, and they will then just need to attach the new English label (semantics) to the concept at hand. For example, a child who learned to count objects in his primary language can still count the same items but will now have to learn the English words for numbers (*one, two, three*, etc.). He doesn't need to relearn the concept of counting; he just needs to learn how to express himself when counting in English. But in order for their common underlying proficiencies to surface, ELs need to understand what is being taught and asked of them. This academic language of school is referred to as *Cognitive Academic Language Proficiency* (CALP).

Jim Cummins (1992) explains that in school, children engage in two different kinds of tasks: cognitively demanding and cognitively undemanding. These tasks are taught in one of two types of contexts: embedded or reduced. A context-embedded task is one where the student has access to a range of additional visual and oral cues to comprehend the information at hand. A context-reduced setting would be one in which there are few to no additional cues besides oral language for comprehension. This would be the case during a lecture. In order for the students to understand the information given in a lecture, they would have to be able to comprehend the English language. Remember, English learners may not have the English input or output to follow the teacher's oral language explanation, but they can still learn if the information is presented in a more comprehensible, creative way.

Let's suppose the learning objective for a lesson was to help students *understand the concept of air pollution*. In a context-reduced setting, the teacher might read aloud a definition with examples. The only cue from the environment that students can rely on to comprehend air pollution is what the teacher is saying, purely oral language. On the other hand, in a context-embedded setting, the teacher might present a variety of images that showed polluted areas in the students' city, along with a brief caption for each. When she reads the captions, she can use facial expressions to signify disgust at the images. The students may then begin to paint a mental image, perhaps even utilize their common underlying proficiencies from their understanding of the images in their primary language, to connect to the term *air pollution*. The additional cues of images, short, simple sentences (captions), and expressive language make the lesson more comprehensible. With the additional cues, ELs will understand the information and continue to develop their conceptual knowledge base while learning the new English words to later communicate their knowledge.

English learners also need a *language-rich classroom*. We often hear about print-rich or literacy-rich classrooms, but we must understand the importance of a language-rich classroom. A language-rich classroom would be buzzing with conversation and oral communication. In order for students to successfully develop oral language, teachers must provide opportunities for dialogue (Gibbons 2002). Children learn to organize and focus their ideas during oral conversations and discussions (Lyle 1993). Learning is not accomplished by simply receiving information in a teacher-centered model, but by participating in intelligent inquiry and thought through talk and dialogue (Gibbons 2002; Stabb 1986). This understanding that language is a social process requires opportunities for children to interact with one another at school. Children in the primary grades have the chance to keep developing oral abilities and skills by consulting with each other, raising questions, and providing information in varied situations (Genishi 1998). Students should be given opportunities to talk in partnerships, in small groups, and to the entire class.

A language-rich classroom utilizes all its resources. The teacher serves as a model of language and must speak in a manner that is comprehensible to the students. This may include speaking in shorter sentences at first, with clear articulation and slowed speech. The teacher can offer additional models of language by putting labels on items around the room and whenever possible including a variety of visual cues with lengthy written explanations. A well-stocked library with a variety of genres and book levels is also important to provide models of how language is used for many purposes and genres. This language-rich environment will present opportunities for students to acquire English and further develop their language skills through purposeful language learning.

In addition to providing a learning environment that is rich in contextual and linguistic cues, there are other theories about second language acquisition that we need to explain so you will understand how the methods presented throughout the book help English learners develop language and literacy. Stephen Krashen's (1981) input comprehension hypothesis and affective filter hypothesis help us understand the type of learning environments and experiences English learners need in order for language development to occur.

Input (Comprehension) Hypothesis

Second language acquisition is possible in classes taught in the second language if the student can understand what is going on in the class; that is, when input is comprehensible. Comprehensible input can include the use of visuals, gestures, films, pictures, dialogue and discussion, adjusted speech by the teacher, and other forms of visual and audible media.

Students can acquire language by "intaking" and understanding language that is a "little beyond" their current level of competence (Krashen 1981, 103). Krashen refers to this as the $i + 1$ model, where the i stands for the language the child already knows and the $+ 1$ is the language presented that is slightly above what the child can produce on his own. For example, if a child understands when the teacher says, "Good morning, class, please take out your math books," the teacher may begin to develop the child's language by now saying, "Good morning, class, isn't it a beautiful Monday morning? Please take out your math books for today's lesson." This elaborated sentence construction along with the use of adjectives and proper nouns is a little beyond what the child understands, so there is potential for language learning to occur. Krashen's $i + 1$ model is similar to Vygotsky's (1962) zone of proximal development (ZPD), where a child's potential for learning falls between what he already knows (background knowledge) and what the intended objective or goal is. A student can learn within his ZPD with the help of a more knowledgeable other. This mirrors Krashen's theory further in the role of a more knowledgeable or proficient user of the language. The teacher and peers can serve as models of language for English learners to acquire and develop their English language skills.

Affective Filter Hypothesis

In order for the language input to be understood and retained by a learner, the affective filter must be low. The affective filter is an imaginary screen that blocks the information from being received. When a child is in a stressful, high-anxiety setting, the affective filter is high, so the input will not get through. When the student is in an environment that is comfortable and encouraging, the affective filter is low and there is a greater chance that learning will occur. This is a critical piece in second language acquisition. Because an English learner is trying out a new language, she needs to feel it is safe to take risks and make mistakes. In an environment where perfection is demanded and mistakes can lead to laughter and ridicule, an EL will not want to speak. The goal is to establish a communal classroom environment where students are engaged in talk and share a common understanding that everyone is a language learner. Cultural sensitivity plays a key role in the affective disposition of many English learners. Get to know students, their personal needs, their need to be understood, their communicative preferences, and their views of school and learning.

Stages of Second Language Acquisition

The best way to plan instruction and determine comprehensible input is to understand what students are able to do and understand at different stages of second language acquisition. Each learner will progress through the stages at her own rate, and the stages may vary depending on the task or language function at hand. It is common to find a classroom full of students at different levels of second language acquisition. For this reason it is important to continuously assess students' language development to adjust instruction accordingly. We can assess students' language proficiency by providing opportunities for dialogue and discussion. Conversations produce comprehensible input, and they allow us to judge what level the student is at in second language acquisition.

There are different ways proficiency levels are discussed and understood across the country. You may hear them referred to as English language development levels or second language acquisition levels. In either case the important thing is that they are used to make instructional decisions to move English learners further in language. Throughout the book we refer to English learners' levels of proficiency by the stages of second language acquisition listed and described here.

Stage I: Preproduction or Silent Stage

Children are exposed to a new language for the first time and are trying to make sense of their new surroundings. They understand a few words in the second language but will mainly communicate through miming, pointing, and drawing. This stage often involves a silent period because students are trying to first comprehend the input from their environment, and until they have built up the confidence to try out the new language, they may not speak. We must be careful not to presume that the students are not paying attention or learning; on the contrary, ELs at this stage are active listeners, acquiring the sounds and words they are hearing. Allow the students to express their knowledge through a variety of expressive strategies such as pointing to an object, picture, or person, performing and acting, nodding or using gestures. In addition to students communicating through these means, teachers should also use similar strategies when teaching children at this stage. When students are in the silent period we should provide a lot of modeling with pictures, realia, and simplified language with short, articulate sentences and a common vocabulary.

> *Theory in Action (Stage I): Vy just moved to America from Vietnam. In her first weeks of kindergarten, she is hearing English for the first time and continually looks all around her, soaking in the environment, the new sounds, the new faces. When her teacher asks her which sticker she wants, the bear or the dog, Vy points to the one she wants. During writing workshop, she looks around and pays close attention to what all the other students are doing. She sees that they take a pencil and put pictures and marks on the page. She then mimics what she sees them doing and soon has a picture of a chicken on her paper. You will notice that she is absorbing everything around her quickly even though she is not producing any language.*

Stage II: Early Production Stage

During the second stage, students are understanding more oral language and can usually speak in one- or two-word phrases and simple sentences related to social, everyday events. They can demonstrate their comprehension of new material by giving short answers. We can help students with their new oral language skills by asking questions that can be answered using simple vocabulary such as yes/no, either/or, and who, what, when, and where questions. At this stage students should have opportunities to engage in role playing, labeling, and the use of realia.

> *Theory in Action: A few weeks after Vy's arrival, she is orally communicating with her teacher and her peers, but in limited ways. She is able to say, "Bathroom please," and "Mommy here."*

Stage III: Speech Emergence Stage

At the third stage, English learners can begin to understand abstract concepts when they have opportunities to engage in conversations and dialogue. They can create simple sentences on their own and understand written English in rich contexts. It is important that information is always presented in context to enhance their comprehension and, in turn, language development. The focus will be on communication and sharing ideas. ELs are not ready for constant correction of their form or sentence structure because they are trying to develop their oral fluency and the confidence to try out longer stretches of language. Students engage in dialogues and their syntax may contain errors that interfere with communication, but in a supportive learning environment they will continue to practice and eventually start to fix up their language. Students are able to compare and contrast, make predictions, describe, and ask how and why questions. We can use lists, charts, and other graphic organizers to record and organize language.

> *Theory in Action: Rahim is a child who speaks only Arabic outside of school. It is just a few months into the school year and he interacts more regularly with other students than he did at first, but he is speaking mostly in short phrases such as "Give me ball."*

Stage IV: Intermediate Fluency Stage

At the intermediate stage of second language acquisition, students can express their thoughts and feelings orally and in writing. Students are beginning to make complex statements, state opinions, ask for clarification, share their thoughts, and speak at greater length. Students will show proficiency in writing essays, literary analysis, and analyzing charts and graphs. We can further support students' language development through a variety of prewriting activities and more complex problem-solving tasks, preferably in cooperative groups. An English learner often arrives at this stage quickly (one to three years) and may even sound fluent because her social communication skills (BICS) are highly proficient. During this stage and the next, we might be quick to assume that our students are fluent in English; however, they need to continue to develop the academic language (CALP) of school.

At this stage we can use specially designed academic instruction in English (SDAIE) strategies (see Figure 1–1). SDAIE is the bridge that connects students' English language abilities and the cognitively challenging subject matter that involves and develops critical thinking. These strategies can include text-structure analysis, vocabulary front-loading, previewing or background-knowledge-building activities, and the use of visuals and other media.

Stage V: Nativelike Fluency Stage

English learners can understand advanced concepts in their second language and use it to perform higher-order thinking skills such as analyzing, interpreting, inferring, and evaluating. Students are able to produce oral and written language using a variety of grammatical structures and vocabulary comparable with their English-only peers. It can take students from five to seven years to reach this level of proficiency. We can further develop students' second language by integrating content area and language objectives.

The second language acquisition levels described here can help teachers understand how best to plan instruction for ELs and choose

- Using manipulatives, miniature objects, and real items
- Using visuals with labels (photos, pictures, drawings)
- Using body movement, pantomime, gestures, and facial expressions
- Using clear expression and articulation
- Placing an emphasis on intonation
- Stressing key nouns and verbs
- Using high-frequency vocabulary
- Using personalized language, such as nouns instead of pronouns
- Reducing idiomatic expressions
- Providing more description through synonyms
- Repeating, restating, and summarizing
- Using shorter sentences, with longer pauses at natural breaks
- Allowing time to think about and answer questions (silent four-second count)
- Allowing adequate time for transitions between activities
- Having clear objectives and legible instructions
- Connecting new information to previously learned material (background knowledge)
- Creating authentic and communicative activities
- Introducing key vocabulary and concepts (previewing)
- Focusing on topics, concepts, and meaning
- Using creative ways to check comprehension
- Giving a thorough review at the end of a lesson or unit
- Creating a low-anxiety environment
- Encouraging risk taking

FIGURE 1–1: Components of Contextualized (SDAIE) Instruction (Handheld Education 2004)

techniques for making content more comprehensible. They are also helpful in understanding the linguistic output of English learners. What are they able to communicate in oral and written language?

Also, when focusing specifically on language development, teachers can pair students up by their level of proficiency in English (see Figure 1–2). Pairing a student with a partner who is just slightly beyond her level of second language acquisition can help lower her affective filter and provide models just slightly above her linguistic abilities

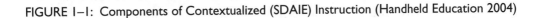

Preproduction--Speech Emergent

Preproduction--Intermediate Fluency

Early Production--Speech Emergent

Early Production--Intermediate Fluency

Speech Emergent--Intermediate Fluency

Speech Emergent--Nativelike Fluency

Intermediate Fluency--Native English Student

Nativelike Fluency--Native English Student

FIGURE 1–2: Possible Partnerships Across Levels of Second Language Acquisition

($i + 1$). You would not want to discourage children from trying out or comprehending English by giving them a partner who was too advanced. At the same time, partnerships should be flexible so that all students have opportunities to serve as models as well as learners in partnerships.

Language Functions and Forms

Language functions, also referred to as language genres, are the reasons for using language. They are the purposes for which we use language. It is important to give explicit instruction and attention to the language necessary to participate and understand lessons in order to meet the linguistic needs of English learners. Language forms, also referred to as sentence frames, are the way we produce language to accomplish a task (Dutro and Moran 2003). For example, if a child is able to compare and contrast (language function: comparing), we should be aware of the forms (sentence frames and vocabulary) associated with making comparisons, such as *is or is not, can or cannot, similar, different from, in contrast to,* and *as opposed to.* Books, teachers, and peers will be models of these forms throughout the school day when students engage in formal and informal conversations.

During a shared reading lesson, a teacher asks her students to compare the two main characters from the story, John and Jamie. She asks students to turn and talk with a partner about John and Jamie. While the students are talking, the teacher listens in on their conversations, listening for how her students are using oral language to make comparisons. Once the students have had time to talk with a partner, the teacher asks pairs to share out their comparisons. Some students share, "John is tall but Jamie is short. John can jump high but Jamie can't." As the students share out their comparisons, the teacher records them on chart paper. Later in the day, the students are comparing animals during science. The teacher asks them to write in their science journal how mammals are different from reptiles. The teacher notices many of her students referring back to the chart the class created during shared reading (comparing John and Jamie) when writing their animal comparisons. She sees sentences such as "A mammal is warm blooded but a reptile is cold blooded. A mammal can use its fur or hair to stay warm but a reptile can't because they don't have hair." You can see similar sentence frames being used. The attention to the language of comparing during shared reading helped the students learn how to talk and write when asked to compare during science.

These frames are just a starting point for English learners to become active users of the English language. Once they continue to hear other models and examples of language, they will develop more complex syntactic and semantic English skills. For instance, in the previous example, the frames the teacher presented are not the only forms of language we use when making comparisons, but they are examples of common terms, sentence structures, and word order that we use when making oral or written comparisons. The attention to functions and forms is a starting point to help ELs become active participants and communicators of English. Appendix A provides a list of language functions and forms that students utilize in school. Though frames are important for helping students understand how language is organized for a specific purpose, you should not present them unnaturally or as the only way to organize language. The models should come from the students, the teacher, and texts through real and purposeful discussions.

Conclusion

English learners have the difficult task of having to acquire and learn English language and English literacy simultaneously. This includes exposure to and instruction in English phonology, orthography, syntax, semantics, morphology, pragmatics, and discourse structure. In order to support English learners in this process, it is imperative that we provide an instructional program that is comprehensible both linguistically and academically in a risk-free environment. By understanding students' levels of proficiency in the second language, teachers can plan comprehensible instruction that fits within students' zone of proximal development, or $i + 1$ level. With careful attention to the varied purposes and contexts for using language in school (functions and forms), teachers can plan instruction that will develop both literacy and language.

Professional Literature on Language Development

Brown, Douglas H. 2000. *Principles of Language Learning and Teaching.* 4th ed. White Plains, NY: Addison Wesley, Longman.

Cook, Vivian. 2001. *Second Language Learning and Language Teaching.* 3d ed. New York: Oxford University Press.

Diaz-Rico, Lynne T., and Kathryn Z. Weed (contributor). 2006. *The Crosscultural, Language, and Academic Development Handbook: A Complete K–12 Reference Guide.* 3d ed. Boston: Pearson Education.

Freeman, David E., and Yvonne S. Freeman. 2004. *Essential Linguistics: What You Need to Know to Teach Reading and ESL, Spelling, Phonics, and Grammar.* Portsmouth, NH: Heinemann.

Gibbons, Pauline. 2002. *Scaffolding Language, Scaffolding Learning: Teaching Second Language Learners in the Mainstream Classroom.* Portsmouth, NH: Heinemann.

Gibbons, Pauline. 1993. *Learning to Learn in a Second Language.* Portsmouth, NH: Heinemann.

Krashen, Stephen D. 1992. *Fundamentals of Language Education.* Columbus, OH: Laredo.

Richards, Jack C., and Theodore S. Rodgers. 2001. *Approaches and Methods in Language Teaching.* 2d ed. Cambridge: Cambridge University Press.

2 Literacy Development

To understand is to discover or reconstruct by rediscovery, and such conditions must be complied with if in the future individuals are to be formed who are capable of production and creativity and not simply repetition.

—Jean Piaget

*I*n order to teach English learners effectively, it is not enough to just know about language development, but it is essential to understand literacy development as the learners are acquiring both simultaneously. Literacy is a complex process of meaning making that develops over a lifetime. Children begin their development of literacy with a curiosity of how to make sense of the images and symbols in their environment. You hear children say "McDonald's" when they see the golden arches. They ask for cereal, pointing to the picture of the Trix rabbit on television. We even see the beginnings of writing as toddlers scribble on paper, books, and even walls, pointing to their masterpiece while saying "Mommy" or "flower." Children begin to connect meaning to everything they experience and encounter in their environment. They demonstrate the basic understanding that print (i.e., images, pictures, symbols, and text) conveys meaning. These early literacy experiences that children demonstrate are the beginning of a journey into the world of text and meaning.

Our goal in this chapter is not to present a full explanation of literacy development and learning theories, but to provide a background of terms and concepts that we refer to throughout the book. We hope these brief descriptors will help you understand how we understand language arts instruction, literacy development levels, and what it means to develop proficient readers and writers.

Domains of Literacy

Becoming literate means becoming able to understand, speak, read, and write in a language. In school we refer to these abilities as the domains of language arts instruction (listening, speaking, reading, and writing). Many students begin school with a strong foundation in understanding and speaking in a language. Some children may even begin school able to read and write, but many will begin their formal instruction for reading and writing in school. Regardless of the variations in children's literacy development prior to entering school, all children will continue to develop all four domains upon entering school. Children will learn to listen, speak, read, and write on many levels. They begin with basic skills and comprehension and develop sophisticated abilities to critically analyze and evaluate information.

Listening, speaking, reading, and writing a language are further taught in school through specific *components of literacy*. We teach children phonemic awareness, phonics, comprehension, writing, vocabulary, and fluency as a way to equip them with the tools necessary to develop literacy.

Phonemic awareness is the ability to understand and manipulate sounds orally. Children learn to identify the sounds of the English language and begin to rearrange those sounds to create words. Phonemic awareness begins with the recognition of any sound, such as the sound of a fire truck or a doorbell. This helps children become aware of sounds. They are then introduced to the specific sounds of the English alphabet. They identify the sounds at the beginning, middle, and end of words. Ultimately, children will be able to rearrange sounds in words to create new words orally. Marilyn Adams (1990) found that phonemic awareness is a strong predictor of early reading success. Students who are instructed in phonemic awareness have a smoother transition to becoming early readers, acquiring the ability to decode and understand words in and out of context.

Phonics is the next step in a child's reading development. Once they are able to identify the sounds of the English alphabet, we begin to teach students the symbols, or letters, that are associated with those sounds. Phonics begins with a simple connection of one sound to one letter and builds in complexity to include one sound for a group of letters. For example, children will first learn that the sound /a/ like in *cake* is spelled *a_e*. Later they will learn that the same sound can be spelled *ai*, *ay*, and *eigh*. Phonics instruction can help children decode words (sound them out) to aid in their reading and writing.

Comprehension involves teaching children the skills to make sense of what they are reading. It involves a variety of skills and strategies to create meaning from text. Children generally begin to comprehend what they read or hear at a basic level; they get the gist of it. This level of comprehension, as referred to in Bloom's Taxonomy of Cognition (1984), is knowledge. Children can answer basic who, what, when, and where questions. Ultimately, the goal is to help children become critical thinkers and evaluators of all they hear and read. In Bloom's taxonomy, this is the highest level of cognition, which he refers to as evaluation. Appendix B provides the additional levels of comprehension and the skills children may demonstrate within each level. It is important to note that as children interact with texts at various levels of difficulty, they will move flexibly from basic to more complex levels of understanding.

Writing helps children organize their thinking. Writing instruction involves a variety of skills. Children are taught how to form the letters of the alphabet, connect those letters to write words, connect words to create sentences, and simultaneously connect their sentences to tell stories or relay information. Children are taught how to generate ideas and how to write them clearly and articulately. They learn the grammar of the English language to ensure clarity and flow of ideas. They learn to spell correctly and use words properly, depending on the context and situation. Writing further involves the challenge of learning to organize ideas differently depending on the genre or audience.

Vocabulary is an integral part of all components of literacy. Children must learn the meaning of words and how to use them properly when speaking and writing. They need to learn multiple meanings of words to understand how words are used within and across texts. The more children read and encounter words, the larger their vocabulary will become (Stanovich 1986; Krashen 2004). Further, with a stronger vocabulary, children possess a greater resource to express their ideas when writing.

Fluency instruction helps children learn how to read and write with ease and meaning. Children will learn to read through a passage strategically with expression and intonation while understanding what they read. They will learn to write with fluidity in a way that makes sense to the reader.

All children need instruction in all components of literacy to develop their listening, speaking, reading, and writing abilities. Ultimately, the goal is that children will become proficient, independent readers. You may be asking, "What does it mean to become a proficient, independent reader? What does it look like?" To help you better understand how to help children become proficient readers, we have created a conceptual framework of what a proficient reader is able to do. We call this framework the *essential elements of literacy*.

The intent of presenting these essential elements is to better understand what we are doing as teachers of literacy and what we will ultimately come to expect of children. Every lesson we conduct and every objective we set during language arts instruction is a building block for children to develop and demonstrate the essential elements of a proficient, literate person. In the chapter that follows, we explain how the essential elements can be used and taught within a balanced literacy program. You will notice that these essential elements of literacy reflect both receptive and expressive modalities.

Essential Elements of Literacy

1. Learners construct meaning from visuals, actions, objects, and symbols in their environment. [Receptive Comprehension]
2. Learners hear and manipulate the sounds of a language (English phonemes) in order to connect them to the written symbols (English alphabet). [Receptive Comprehension and Phonemic Awareness]
3. Learners decode the symbols of the language (English alphabet) with automaticity, phrasing, and expression. [Receptive Decoding and Fluency]
4. Learners understand how meaning is created and affected by context (pragmatics, discourse). [Receptive and Expressive Pragmatics]
5. Learners understand and use words to convey and receive meaning. [Receptive and Expressive Vocabulary]
6. Learners understand and use words appropriately in the culture and context in which the words are being used. [Receptive and Expressive Comprehension and Pragmatics]
7. Learners generate meaning and communicate it in written form. [Expressive Comprehension and Writing]
8. Learners form ideas and communicate them purposefully and effectively. [Expressive Comprehension, Writing, and Speaking]
9. Learners understand that reading is a valuable tool for learning in school, beyond school, and in life. [Lifelong Value]

Throughout our book, we also hold fast to a constructivist view of teaching and learning. There must be ample opportunities for children to interact with one another and their environment. Lev Vygotsky (1962) explains that instruction should be responsive to help students learn within their zone of proximal development. The zone of proximal development is described as the child's potential for learning with the proper supports. It involves understanding what a child is able to do alone without the help of a "more knowledgeable other," referred to as the zone of actual development (ZAD), and understanding what we want the child to learn (the goal or objective). The child's ZPD is then the potential for learning between the ZAD and the goal or objective. Vygotsky further emphasizes that in order for learning to occur within a child's ZPD, the child must have support from a more knowledgeable other. This can be the teacher, but it can also be a classmate. Based on the ZPD theory, interaction is key to learning. This theory parallels Krashen's comprehensible input hypothesis (see Chapter 1), in which he states that language develops within a child's $i + 1$ level. That is when the input is slightly above what the student can do alone.

$$\text{ZPD with Support}$$
$$\downarrow$$
$$\text{ZAD } (i)\text{-------------------------------------Knowledge: Goal/Objective } (i{+}1)$$

Literacy Development Levels

There are different ways literacy development levels are identified and defined across the country. What is important is that they are understood in terms of how a child develops as a reader and writer—what a child can understand and do at different literacy development levels. This will help a teacher make informed instructional decisions to move children forward in literacy. Throughout the book we refer to the literacy development levels as those listed and described here. It is important to remember that we design instruction according to development levels rather than grade levels; however, to give you an idea, we list what literacy development levels are typically reflected by which grades.

Emergent Reader

Emergent readers use their oral language and knowledge of the world to read pictures, images, and text (Holdaway 1979; Snow, Burns, and Griffin 1998). They begin to understand that text conveys meaning. They rely heavily on contextual information provided by pictures. They are becoming familiar with how texts work and are organized. They begin to understand how to turn the pages of a book and what the markings (letters and punctuation) mean. Emergent readers begin to identify and distinguish between sounds they hear while learning how to create the letters that will make those sounds. They learn the names of letters and begin to read basic sight words. At this stage of reading, we should present many songs, poems, and chants containing rhymes and alliteration. Presenting children with a variety of opportunities to develop their fine motor skills (e.g., cutting, making letters with a variety of materials, finger painting, engaging in songs with hand gestures) will help children control their hand and fingers when learning to form letters on paper. We should point out the characteristics and parts of a book when reading to children and point out connections between words and pictures. Emergent readers need texts with familiar stories that have strong picture support. Typically, kindergarten students enter at this level. Please refer to Chapter 5 in particular for strategies that support emergent readers.

Early Reader

Early readers begin to make the connections between the sounds of the letters and their corresponding written form (Snow, Burns, and Griffin 1998). They use this knowledge to sound out words (decode) and begin to make strategic spelling decisions. They continue to learn sight words and will begin to read text with more lines. Early readers begin to use reading strategies such as rereading when they lose the meaning of the text. They begin to say to themselves, "That didn't make sense," or "That sounded weird," and reread to clarify the meaning of text for themselves. At this level of literacy, teachers should provide readers with many opportunities to read and reread books at their level to develop their fluency. We want to help early readers move beyond the skill of decoding to focus on making meaning while they read. Typically, kindergarten students end the year at this level and enter first grade at this level.

Transitional Reader

Transitional readers have developed a sense of automaticity. They can decode text with general ease and work on using a variety of sources of information when creating meaning from text. To maintain their fluency, beginning readers need to learn how to decode more complex word patterns and multisyllabic words. Though many books at this level will still contain pictures, transitional readers do not rely as heavily on picture clues to read the text (Clay 1991; Snow, Burns, and Griffin 1998). Their knowledge of the world has grown, their decoding skills have improved, they know more sight words, and they use this information to develop their reading fluency. Transitional readers begin to use the clues of text to read with expression and determine the mood of a story. At this stage they need continued support with their comprehension of text. At times, first graders enter this stage at the end of the year; however, this is typically a second-grade level.

Self-Extending Reader

Self-extending readers use all sources of information, skills, and strategies to maintain meaning when reading longer, more complex texts (Clay 1991; Snow, Burns, and Griffin 1998). Their automaticity has improved with longer words containing more complex spelling patterns, and their sight-word bank has grown tremendously. They become problem solvers as readers by attacking new information and challenging text. Self-extending readers use reading as a tool for acquiring new knowledge. They realize that the world has been opened up to them because they possess the ability to access information on their own. As teachers, we should continue to help self-extending readers deepen their comprehension of text and ultimately help them become critical consumers of information. We should help children transfer what they have learned about reading across texts, genres, and content areas. Typically, students enter this stage of reading sometime during second grade.

Within each level of literacy development, children will be exposed to literacy experiences and texts that are at different readability and comprehension levels. Throughout the book we refer to the range of ease and difficulty of text for readers by the levels explained in the following sections.

Independent Level

The independent level is the level at which a student can read a text without assistance. This includes the reader's ability to both decode the text and comprehend what he is reading. In order to build fluency, children need to read text at their independent level. When children select a text for independent reading time, teachers should be sure they are reading a text at their independent level. A text is considered to be at a child's independent level if the child is able to read the text with 95 percent accuracy or higher and comprehend the text with at least 90 percent accuracy during an assessment.

Instructional Level

The instructional level is the level at which a child can read a text with the help of a teacher. The reader can work through the text, but it will present challenges that will require her to learn new problem-solving strategies. When you work with children during shared and guided reading, the text should be at the students' instructional level. This will allow for teachable moments to build their literacy skills and strategies. A text is considered to be at a child's instructional level if the child is able to read the text with at least 90 percent accuracy and comprehend the text with at least 75 percent accuracy.

Frustration Level

The frustration level is the level at which a text is so difficult that the child cannot read it, even with help, and he may be turned off from reading the text. If a child is forced to read frustration-level texts, it will stifle his fluency and cause anxiety. But there is a place for the use of frustration-level texts in the classroom. During a read-aloud the teacher can read text to children that is above what they can read alone or with assistance. When reading text to children, you provide them access to information and stories they want to hear and enjoy but cannot yet access alone. When you have a mix of reading levels in your class, read-alouds are a great way to make sure students do not miss out on great stories because they are still developing as readers. As the teacher, you do the difficult task of decoding the text with ease and expression so that the children can focus on comprehending the text.

Conclusion

Literacy development is a process of creating meaning from one's environment (including text) that will develop over a lifetime. Children will begin with a basic understanding that print conveys meaning and will ultimately learn to become critical thinkers and users of information. This process is developed through intentional language arts instruction that includes the teaching of phonemic awareness, phonics, comprehension, writing, vocabulary, and fluency. This instruction must be presented through many, many opportunities for guided and independent practice.

Professional Literature on Literacy Development

Au, Kathryn H. 1993. *Literacy Instruction in Multicultural Settings*. Belmont, CA: Wadsworth/Thomson Learning.

Cambourne, Brian. 1998. *The Whole Story: Natural Learning and the Acquisition of Literacy in the Classroom*. Auckland, NZ: Ashton Scholastic.

Cambourne, Brian and Jan Turbill. 1991. *Coping with Chaos*. Portsmouth, NH: Heinemann.

Clay, Marie M. 1991. *Becoming Literate: The Construction of Inner Control*. Auckland, NZ: Heinemann Education.

Clay, Marie. 1998. *By Different Paths to Common Outcomes*. York, ME: Stenhouse.

Clay, Marie. 2000. *Running Records for Classroom Teachers*. Portsmouth, NH: Heinemann.

Garcia, Gilbert G. (ed.). 2003. *English Learners: Reaching the Highest Levels of English Literacy*. Newark, DE: International Reading Association.

Gibbons, Pauline. 2002. *Scaffolding Language, Scaffolding Learning*. Portsmouth, NH: Heinemann.

Goodman, Kenneth, Dorothy Watson, and Carolyn Burke. 1987. *Reading Miscue Analysis*. New York: Richard C. Owen.

Holdaway, Don. 1979. *The Foundations of Literacy*. Gosford, NSW: Ashton Scholastic.

Keene, Ellen and Susan Zimmermann. 1997. *Mosaic of Thought: Teaching Comprehension in a Reader's Workshop*. Portsmouth, NH: Heinemann.

Leslie, Lauren and Joanne Caldwell. 2005. *Qualitative Reading Inventory 4*. Boston: Allyn and Bacon.

Peregoy, Suzanne F. and Owen F. Boyle. 2001. *Reading, Writing, and Learning in ESL: A Resource Book for K–12 Teachers*. 3d ed. White Plains, NY: Longman.

Routman, Regie. 2002. *Reading Essentials: The Specifics You Need to Teach Reading Well*. Portsmouth, NH: Heinemann.

Wilde, Sandra. 2000. *Reading Miscue Made Easy*. Portsmouth, NH: Heinemann.

3

Putting the Essential Elements of Literacy in Place Across the Day

There is no single method or single combination of methods that can successfully teach all children to read. Therefore, teachers must be familiar with a wide range of methods for teaching reading and have a strong knowledge of the children in their care so they can create the appropriate balance of methods needed for each child. Further, these professionals must have the flexibility to modify those methods when they determine that particular children are not learning.

—*Using Multiple Methods of Beginning Reading Instruction*
International Reading Association

*I*n the previous two chapters we provided an overview of language and literacy theories. In this chapter, we transform those theories into practical frameworks for classroom instruction. The information contained in the previous chapters is similar to foundations that are taught in teacher preparation courses; however, as we work with teachers, we find that in the business of classroom work, we often forget about the deeper reasons that we teach in the ways we teach—especially when so many teachers are mandated to teach in particular ways.

Currently across the country, it seems that teachers are being told to teach either with very prescribed basal reading series or in fairly directed ways of implementing "balanced literacy." For those who are expected to implement basal anthologies, we want to offer you some different options that might be more meaningful and specifically targeted toward the students in your class. Often in these basal programs, the components of literacy are already preplanned and targeted for a monolithic audience with little opportunity to tailor instruction toward individual needs. For those who are expected to implement balanced literacy with a whirlwind of ten minutes here and twenty minutes there, we want to offer you an organized, meaningful approach that connects all the different snippets of time in a meaningful way.

In either approach or somewhere in between, we find there lacks a focus on specific language development. What we notice on a consistent basis, regardless of district and school mandates, is that teachers often lose sight of what we really want to teach students to do, why we want them to do that, and how we are going to effectively accomplish this. To a certain extent, theories remind us of what we need to do and why, but they don't clearly delineate how we might do these things. The various methods of teaching literacy that we outline in this book explore how we might put theory into practice to better meet the needs of our English learners.

Balancing Balanced Literacy

In recent years, balanced literacy, or comprehensive literacy, has become popular in elementary schools as an approach that includes aspects of literature-based instruction as well as phonics. This approach recognizes the complexities of the act of learning to read and the need to utilize multiple approaches because children learn differently. Reading requires the orchestration of simultaneous skills and strategies that are often unconscious to the mind. Marie Clay (1991) often refers to the "underground" strategies one utilizes in order to read. As proficient readers, we do many things automatically to comprehend a text by using different sources of information. *Visual*, or graphophonic, sources of information help us decode the words; *structural*, or syntactic, sources help us use our knowledge of the structure or grammar of the English language; and *meaning*, or semantic, sources help us monitor what makes sense in what we are reading. *Pragmatics* is a fourth cueing system that is often overlooked but helps us make sense of text by understanding the context in which meaning is taking place. Context has a great impact on meaning.

Children need direct instruction on how to use all sources of information (Figure 3–1) to help them comprehend what they read. Though all four cueing systems can be isolated for instructional purposes, they are interrelated. It is important to teach children how to use different sources of information when they read to provide a holistic repertoire

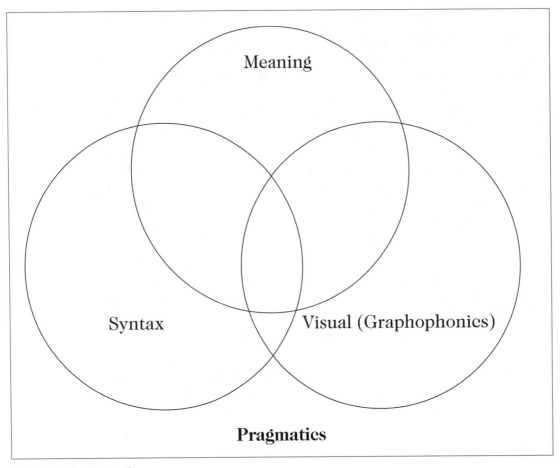

FIGURE 3–1: Cueing Systems

of strategies to use when reading. The use of all of our cueing systems makes us better readers because we can check or confirm our predictions of unknown words. Appendix C provides examples of how we can be good readers when using only one cueing system and evidence of how we can develop as accurate, strategic readers when we have the knowledge of how to use all four.

The less competent readers are, the more strategies they will need to draw from to be successful readers. If they are not successful using one cueing system, and we have taught them all four explicitly, they can call upon one of the others to read and comprehend the text. As Don Holdaway explains (1979), students need high redundancy and access to as many sources of information as possible when learning to read. Once students have been taught how to use their cueing systems, they will begin to subconsciously use them simultaneously and strategically when confronted with challenging text. The goal is to take them from the conscious learning of discrete skills to the subconscious acquisition of reading for meaning.

In order to illustrate this complex meaning-making process, during workshops with teachers, we often distribute a difficult reading passage and ask teachers to write down every possible thing they are doing in their mind to understand the passage. Commonly, teachers point out the following: need to decode or figure out some words and use context clues to connect the meaning; visualize part of the passage; determine importance. As we continue in the workshop, teachers often realize that the act of reading and comprehending is more complex than expected—as proficient readers, our minds do many things simultaneously without us being consciously aware of it.

The same can be said about helping teachers understand the strategies we use as language learners when trying to make sense of text. During workshops we use a similar activity with teachers; we distribute a passage written in Italian titled "Rapunzel." We do not tell the teachers that it is a version of the fairy tale "Rapunzel"; we simply ask them to read the passage and share with a partner what the text is about. We then discuss the strategies used to make sense of the text. Some of the strategies they use are semantic clues such as cognates (words that have similar spelling and meaning in English and, in this case, Italian) and syntactic clues such as identifying the names of the characters because of the use of capital letters; many use their prior knowledge of the "Rapunzel" story, and some use context clues by making reference to the pictures provided. In engaging in this activity, the teachers begin to identify the strategies English learners rely on to make sense of English text, how they utilize their primary language to support English comprehension and development, and the importance of providing text that contains language-rich cues so that students can use the strategies mentioned (semantics, syntax, background knowledge, and pictures). We also want teachers to see the value of giving children an opportunity to talk, so we ask the teachers to share what they think the Italian text is about with a partner prior to having the whole-group discussion. The reflections from this pair-share experience are powerful. We hear teachers sharing how their anxiety level (affective filter) was lowered because they could confirm their predictions with someone or gain a better understanding by hearing their partner's predictions. They overwhelmingly feel as if they have a better understanding of the Italian passage after sharing because their partner brought different experiences and sources of information to comprehend the text.

Balancing Through Various Levels of Support: *To, With, By*

Furthermore, if we were to break down how proficient readers came to know and utilize these strategies, we would find that they learned them through personal experiences that were scaffolded through various levels of support. In addition, they were presented through a variety of opportunities or methods of teaching. Margaret Mooney (1996) outlined this notion of various levels of support as *to*, *with*, and *by*.

In order to effectively learn to be literate, children need experiences in which teachers model the anticipated behaviors involved in reading or writing. When children are read *to*, they hear what reading is supposed to sound like (phonology and syntax), and the teacher models what she understands through thinking aloud strategies (semantics, pragmatics, discourse). When the teacher reads *with* children during shared reading, she might be asking the children to chime in with her at various points in the text so that the students can get a sense of the syntax or structure of the sentence to help them make meaning. When children are constantly immersed in experiences where they are read *to* and *with*, this helps them develop strategies and an internal sense of reading that support them when reading *by* themselves. We want to highlight the importance of students having ample time for independent practice (Cambourne and Turbill 1991; Krashen 2004). Without ample time to practice independently, students will not have opportunities to apply and reinforce what they have learned. When there are so many struggling readers, there is a sense of urgency to give them as much support as possible; however, in our well-intentioned efforts, we end up offering them imbalanced doses of *to* and *with* experiences without providing them with the much needed independent practice in order to apply what has been learned.

The goal of balanced literacy is for students to become independent. In the growing popularity of balanced literacy, teachers are bombarded with so many different methods that need to be implemented that the goal of independence is often lost. The different methods are meaningless if they do not strategically lead to independence. There should be ongoing assessment to measure whether or not the teaching is leading to a gradual release of responsibility to the individual reader or writer.

How Do We Teach All the Essential Elements of Literacy?

As the reading pendulum continues to swing right or left, phonics versus literature-based, what we truly need is a purposeful, strategic, and meaningful approach that proportionately includes all aspects of teaching literacy and language. Because the complexities of reading must be taught with multiple approaches, balanced literacy commonly addresses the essential elements of literacy (see Chapter 2) through methods that address differing levels of scaffolding—*to*, *with*, and *by*. We refer to these methods as

- interactive read-aloud
- emergent storybook reading
- shared reading

- independent reading workshop
- guided reading
- independent writing workshop
- word work

While these are common terms in the field, often there are varying definitions of what they mean and how they look in practice. There are other methods such as interactive writing and shared writing that are not listed in our book separately, but are instead embedded into the other practices listed. Calkins (2001), Cunningham (1999), Fountas and Pinnel (1996), and Taberski (2000) all outline similar methods of balanced literacy. In the subsequent chapters of the book, we specifically outline what these methods mean for us and how they serve as effective tools for helping English learners develop language and literacy. In general, these methods are organized and taught during segments of time across the day and specifically target differing aspects of literacy and language development. Because the emphasis is on independent reading and writing, more time is allotted to children having opportunities to practice on their own.

How Long Do These Methods Take and How Are They Arranged Throughout the Day?

The teaching of language and literacy can be organized by implementing different methods of instruction that take place across varying increments of time, depending on the literacy levels (see Chapter 2) of the students. While these literacy levels are not limited to grade-level designations, we make generalizations according to grade. Kindergarten students tend to be in the emergent and beginning stages of literacy; first graders tend to be in the beginning and transitional stages; second graders tend to be in the transitional and self-extending stages.

Each method differs in the time that it takes to implement into daily practice. In general, the methods that focus more specifically on independent practice tend to be longer, whereas the methods that involve more demonstration and practice through *to* and *with* strategies are shorter. As students move up in the grades and increase in their language and literacy skills, more time is devoted to content area instruction. You will notice that the literacy time tends to decrease in second grade because the expectation is that children are transitional to self-extending readers. Figure 3–2 outlines our recommended time allocations for each method, organized by grade level for kindergarten, first grade, and second grade. Please keep in mind that these are approximate times. Teacher judgment in determining the actual duration of instruction is imperative. We would like to caution, however, that significant time for independence must be set aside in order for students to practice what has been modeled to them by the teacher. In

STRUCTURE	KINDERGARTEN	FIRST	SECOND
Emergent Storybook Reading	15		
Interactive Read-Aloud	15	20	25
Shared Reading	20	20	15
Guided Reading	20	25	20
Word Work	20	20	20
Reading Workshop	40	45	50
Writing Workshop	50	50	50
Total Minutes	**180 minutes**	**180 minutes**	**180 minutes**

FIGURE 3–2: Number of Minutes Recommended for Literacy Methods

addition, the allocation of time for each method will change as students make progress across the year. Calkins (2001) also suggests that certain methods such as guided reading and aspects of emergent storybook reading can be embedded in the independent reading workshop.

We are often asked, "How can a teacher possibly get in all those methods during the day?" In general, we believe in an integrated approach to teaching where content areas such as science and social studies are woven throughout the literacy methods in order to create more cohesive learning experiences for English learners in particular. While each circumstance might vary, we offer some examples of daily schedules for each grade level. When first learning about the many different methods of instruction that take place across the day, one can become overwhelmed. If this is new to your teaching, we recommend that you introduce one method at a time into your teaching and gradually add on. You might want to begin with interactive read-aloud as it does not require significant changes in the management of the class. Next you might want to add writing workshop in addition to any word work you might already have. The ultimate goal is to implement all of these pieces on a consistent basis. Teachers often ask us if they can alternate days for reading workshop because there isn't enough time to do it all in one day. Part of the success of this type of instruction is the regularity of practice, with repetition each day. Young children become accustomed not only to the transitions needed in each method but also to receiving multiple exposures to various types of instruction at different levels of support.

A Possible Daily Schedule for Full-Day Kindergarten

8:30–9:05   Morning Meeting and Welcome
Shared Reading
Emergent Storybook Reading

9:05–9:25	Word Work
9:25–9:45	Guided Reading
9:45–10:00	Interactive Read-Aloud
10:00–10:40	Reading Workshop
10:40–11:30	Writing Workshop
11:30–12:15	Math
12:15–1:05	Lunch
1:05–1:45	Science or Social Studies
1:45–2:30	The Arts or Physical Education
2:30–3:00	Play-Based Centers

A Possible Daily Schedule for First Grade

8:30–9:00	Morning Meeting and Welcome Shared Reading
9:00–9:20	Word Work
9:20–9:40	Interactive Read-Aloud
9:40–10:25	Reading Workshop
10:25–10:50	Guided Reading
10:50–11:40	Writing Workshop
11:40–12:30	Lunch
12:30–1:30	Math
1:30–2:15	Science or Social Studies
2:15–3:00	The Arts or Physical Education

A Possible Daily Schedule for Second Grade

8:30–8:50	Morning Meeting and Welcome Shared Reading
8:50–9:10	Word Work
9:10–9:40	Interactive Read-Aloud
9:40–10:30	Reading Workshop
10:30–10:50	Guided Reading
10:50–11:40	Writing Workshop
11:40–12:30	Lunch
12:30–1:30	Math
1:30–2:15	Science and/or Social Studies
2:15–3:00	The Arts or Physical Education

To help you better see what you're doing and why, we have summarized the methods of instruction in the chart in Figure 3–3, aligned with the respective essential elements (Chapter 2) and components of language (Chapter 1). In the remaining chapters of the book, we focus on each method of instruction and how it supports literacy and language development.

ESSENTIAL ELEMENT OF LITERACY	COMPONENT OF LANGUAGE	METHOD OF INSTRUCTION
1—Construct meaning from visuals, actions, objects, and symbols in their environment. (Receptive Comprehension)	Semantics Pragmatics Discourse	Interactive Read-Aloud Emergent Storybook Reading Shared Reading Guided Reading Independent Reading Workshop
2—Understand how meaning is created and affected by context (pragmatics, discourse). (Receptive Comprehension and Pragmatics)	Semantics Pragmatics Discourse	Shared Reading Writing Workshop Word Work
3—Decode the symbols of the language (English alphabet) with automaticity, phrasing, and expression. (Receptive Decoding and Fluency)	Phonology Orthography Syntax	Interactive Read-Aloud Shared Reading Independent Reading Workshop Guided Reading Writing Workshop Word Work
4—Hear and manipulate the sounds of a language (English phonemes) in order to connect them to the written symbols (English alphabet). (Receptive and Expressive Phonemic Awareness)	Phonology Orthography Morphology	Interactive Read-Aloud Shared Reading Guided Reading Independent Reading Workshop Writing Workshop
5—Understand and use words to convey and receive meaning. (Receptive and Expressive Vocabulary)	Syntax Morphology Semantics	Interactive Read-Aloud Emergent Storybook Reading Shared Reading Guided Reading Independent Reading Workshop Writing Workshop Word Work
6—Understand and use words appropriately in the culture and context in which they are being used. (Receptive and Expressive Comprehension and Pragmatics)	Pragmatics Discourse	Interactive Read-Aloud Emergent Storybook Reading Shared Reading Guided Reading Independent Reading Workshop Writing Workshop
7—Generate meaning and communicate it in written form. (Expressive Comprehension and Writing)	Orthography Morphology Semantics Pragmatics	Writing Workshop
8—Form ideas and communicate them purposefully and effectively. (Expressive Comprehension, Writing, and Speaking)	Orthography Morphology Semantics Discourse	Writing Workshop

ESSENTIAL ELEMENT OF LITERACY	COMPONENT OF LANGUAGE	METHOD OF INSTRUCTION
9—Understand that reading is a valuable tool for learning in school, beyond school, and for life. (Lifelong Value)		Interactive Read-Aloud Emergent Storybook Reading Shared Reading Guided Reading Independent Reading Workshop Writing Workshop Word Work

FIGURE 3–3: The Essential Elements of Literacy Within a Balanced Program

Conclusion

Now that we have linked theory and how it is applied during the day, we will use the remainder of the book to describe each of the methods we outlined in this chapter. Our hope is that in understanding the purpose of each method, and how it helps develop proficient readers and writers, teachers will be able to see how these methods can fit within their language arts programs. Regardless of the specific reading programs used in individual classrooms, teachers need to ask themselves how the work they are doing is helping English learners develop language and literacy, how their lessons address the essential elements and help students progress through the levels of second language acquisition.

Professional Literature on Balanced Literacy

Calkins, Lucy McCormick. 2001. *The Art of Teaching Reading*. New York: Addison-Wesley.

Cunningham, Patricia and Richard Allington. 1994. *Classrooms That Work: They Can All Read and Write*. New York: HarperCollins.

Cunningham, Patricia, Dorothy Hall, and C. Sigmon. 1999. *The Teacher's Guide to the Four Blocks: A Multimethod, Multilevel Framework for Grades 1–3*. Greensboro, NC: Carson-Dellosa.

Fountas, Irene, and Gay Su Pinnell. 1996. *Guided Reading: Good First Teaching for All Children*. Portsmouth, NH: Heinemann.

Hindley, Joanne. 1996. *In the Company of Children*. York, ME: Stenhouse.

Mooney, Margaret. 1990. *Reading To, With and By Children*. Katonah, NY: Richard C. Owen.

Routman, Regie. 2000. *Conversations: Strategies for Teaching, Learning, and Evaluating*. Portsmouth, NH: Heinemann.

Taberski, Sharon. 2000. *On Solid Ground: Strategies for Teaching Reading, K–3*. Portsmouth, NH: Heinemann.

4 Interactive Read-Aloud

We read to children for the same reasons we talk to children: to reassure, to entertain, to bond; to inform or explain, to arouse curiosity, to inspire.

—Jim Trelease, *The Read-Aloud Handbook*

What Is Read-Aloud?

Each morning, Mr. Alvarez's class gathers on the rug, eager to hear him read a story. The children love listening to the sound of his voice when he mimics the characters in a story. They love the way he stops the story from time to time, sets the book in his lap, turns his eyes toward the ceiling, and tells them what he is thinking as a reader. They also know that when he says, "Turn to your partner and tell them what you are thinking in this part of the story," he expects them to turn as if they are in swivel seats to sit knee-to-knee with their partner and talk about the story. They know that he will kneel beside them and listen in on their partnership conversations. They also know that they will be able to share their ideas with the rest of the class.

As an English learner in the speech emergent stage, Kelsie would avoid talking during interactive read-aloud, but would say a few ideas to her partner. Knowing that she has ideas but struggles to get her ideas across in front of the class, Mr. Alvarez listens carefully to the comments she makes to her partner. He encourages her to share them with the class, but as a new English speaker, she remains hesitant. He knows that she is not yet comfortable expressing her thoughts, but wants her to be aware that her ideas matter so that when she is ready, she will more readily share. Instead, he asks if he can share her smart thinking with the class. Mr. Alvarez shares Kelsie's ideas with the class thereby making her ideas known to the class. As Kelsie sees her peers admiring her ideas, she comes to feel more comfortable and eventually starts sharing with her classmates. At first, Kelsie simply states an idea, and then she begins to connect them and formulate her own opinions about a text and is able to support her ideas with other students. Mr. Alvarez pairs Kelsie with Rahim, who is also at the speech emergent stage of second language acquisition, so they can support each other. He knows that Rahim's English abilities are slightly more advanced than hers and that the two students work well together, taking turns and sharing ideas.

As the year progresses, the students in Mr. Alvarez's class begin to respond directly to each other rather than wait on him to call on each student in order to have whole-class conversations. They learn to challenge each other's ideas in a confident way.

Foundations of Read-Aloud

Reading aloud to children is a wonderful way to invite them into the world of text. It is a time when teachers can build children's background knowledge by exposing them to a variety of stories, content, and genres. "In reading aloud, we also: condition the child's brain to associate reading with pleasure, build vocabulary, and provide a reading role model" (Trelease 2001, 6). Reading aloud to children sets the foundation for developing lifelong readers. Children learn that reading books and text can provide information and access to the outside world. Because the teacher is doing the difficult task of reading the text, children gain access to information they are not capable of getting on their own. This exposure to ideas, worlds, and experiences begins to inspire children to learn to read. Reading sets no limits on what a child can learn and experience.

Children's exposure to the read-aloud experience can begin before entering school. In fact, this is one of the single most important factors in children's readiness for literacy at school. It is important for parents to share read-aloud experiences with their children regardless of language. Parents who have native language texts at home should be encouraged to share these books with their children, as the focus is on developing literacy experiences, not necessarily English literacy experiences. When meeting with parents who have limited English proficiency, I often share my experiences with reading at home as an English learner. Although I was born in the United States, my parents chose not to teach me English because they figured that I would learn English in school. This way, I could have a firm foundation in Chinese and maintain my native language. What my parents did was read aloud Chinese fairy tales to me as I was growing up. Through these experiences I was able to develop vocabulary in Chinese and construct the meaning of these stories. This helped me better understand stories as I entered kindergarten. For those children who have been read to at home, the read-aloud generates feelings of excitement and comfort, reminding them of the time spent reading with loved ones at home. They are not aware of the instructional power of the read-aloud; they simply enjoy the stories they hear and the time spent with family or classmates. Children benefit from being read to because they begin to understand the purpose of reading and how print works to tell a story or provide information.

Context in Our Book

Reading aloud to English learners must go beyond traditional models of reading and then discussing at the end of the text. While there are multiple methods and purposes of reading aloud, we emphasize the use of *interactive* read-alouds as an effective method for English learners in developing comprehension and language simultaneously. During an interactive read-aloud, the teacher makes predetermined stops to impart her thinking about the text and to discuss the text with the class. These stops are important for ELs because a stop breaks the language and content up into smaller chunks to help them process the information before continuing. Furthermore, modeling think-alouds makes comprehension more visible (Keene and Zimmerman 1997). These frequent "checks for understanding" help ELs keep up with the story. "You can help your students listen and comprehend by stopping at certain places in the book to discuss a picture as it relates to the story or to review the plot" (Peregoy and Boyle 2005, 186). And with the teacher reading the text to the children, English learners hear a model of English. When the teacher reads fluently, English learners can hear the inflections and tone involved in reading different kinds of sentences. For example, if the teacher is reading a story and there are exclamatory sentences, the teacher's voice will vary in tone and pacing. In hearing these models of oral language, the children will continue to acquire English. In essence what we are developing here is the idea of what sounds right in the English language. We are serving as models of the English language for our students.

In addition, to further help build oral and written language skills, the interactive read-aloud should include oral pair-shares and sometimes stop-and-jots for self-extending readers. For a pair-share, the teacher stops and asks the students to turn and talk to a partner sitting next to them about their thinking; for a stop-and-jot, the teacher asks them to write down their thinking. These two experiences offer students an opportunity to monitor their comprehension of the story as well as practice using the English language. Further, "conversations and writing during read-aloud time draw our students deeper into the story and promote thoughtful reflection and response" (Sibberson and Szymusiak 2003, 79).

Language Theory in Practice

Interactive read-aloud is an effective way to develop a second language. Children are read a variety of texts that present different phonological models in how they are read and the vocabulary (semantics) they present. "Read aloud helps students learn vocabulary, grammar, new information, and how stories and written language work" (Routman 2003, 20). These models of language are presented within the context of the story, which helps English learners understand the language. Krashen's *input comprehension hypothesis* and *acquisition hypothesis* support the development of a second language during read-aloud. Because students are able to understand the language being shared through rich stories, they can acquire language naturally.

The read-aloud structure further helps lower ELs' *affective filter* because they experience and enjoy stories in a comfortable, risk-free environment. The teacher does the reading and when asked to talk, the students are not forced to speak out to the entire group; on the contrary, they have a chance to try out language with a partner in a pair-share. Be sure to partner students up for pair-shares with second language acquisition levels in mind (see suggestions for language partnerships in Figure 1–2). These partnerships are important in order to keep the *affective filter* down and provide language and information slightly above what the students can do on their own ($i + 1$, *input comprehension hypothesis*). Students are also developing comprehension by talking to their partner about the text. Brian Cambourne (1988) further supports the use of read-aloud as a language learning tool because the demonstrations emphasize how language functions and is used.

What Does an Interactive Read-Aloud Look Like?

Key Elements (Across All Levels of Readers)

Read-aloud is an important time of day when all children can improve their listening and speaking skills while enjoying a text and sharing ideas with classmates. It is important to take the time to read aloud to children daily (Allington and Cunningham 2003). When possible, teachers should draw students in close together to encourage community building and set the expectation for sharing language and ideas. Figure 4–1 lists the purposes for read-aloud and Figure 4–2 specifies the teacher's role and the students' role during a read-aloud.

- To present information students cannot access on their own as independent readers
- To build community through the enjoyment of stories and informational texts
- To encourage a love of reading
- To promote reading as a learning and thinking tool
- To provide models of the English language through oral reading
- To develop and encourage active listening
- To share information and build background knowledge
- To demonstrate problem-solving strategies readers use to comprehend texts
- To provide exposure to a variety of genres and purposes for reading

FIGURE 4–1: Purposes of an Interactive Read-Aloud

ROLE OF THE TEACHER	ROLE OF THE STUDENTS
<ul><li>Read with the intent of being a model of English.</li><li>Encourage active listening and participation by inviting the students into the story through pair-shares and grand conversations.</li><li>Clarify unfamiliar vocabulary to aid with comprehension.</li><li>Think out loud to model comprehension strategies for students.</li><li>Provide opportunities for students to make connections to the text.</li><li>Establish a comfortable learning environment for risk taking.</li><li>Purposefully match students together as partners to maximize learning and language development.</li><li>Assess students' understanding and language development by listening to their conversations.</li><li>Scaffold language during conversations when needed.</li><li>Listen for opportunities to expand ideas and keep students accountable to their conversation.</li></ul>	<ul><li>Listen carefully.</li><li>Ask questions.</li><li>Share their comprehension of the story or information.</li><li>Make connections between the text and their personal lives.</li><li>Take risks with language.</li><li>Take risks with ideas.</li><li>Be ready to critique and evaluate the text as well as the statements of others.</li><li>Apply what they've learned to independent reading contexts.</li><li>Press fellow students for clarity of their ideas.</li></ul>

FIGURE 4–2: Teacher and Student Roles in an Interactive Read-Aloud

Selecting Texts for Read-Aloud

Normally the text used during a read-aloud is at a level just above what the children can read with the help of others (see "Frustration Level" section in Chapter 2). This provides students access to information and stories they could not read on their own. The teacher does the difficult task of decoding the text with proper pacing and intonation while the children enjoy the demonstration of reading and focus on the story.

Read-aloud texts should vary in type, structure, content, and genre. Do not limit your read-aloud materials to books. To build background knowledge, teachers can also read aloud news articles (from children's magazines) and Internet resources. Other materials can include poems, plays, songs, chants, and language experience charts. Figure 4–3 offers a list of questions to think about when selecting a read-aloud text.

Once you have selected a text, it is important to read it ahead of time to determine any language challenges the text may provide for English learners. If there are challenging vocabulary words that may interfere with the students' overall comprehension of the story, you should take very little time to front-load words prior to reading the story. Front-loading vocabulary is not giving a vocabulary lesson; it is just presenting students with a simple definition of the word to enhance comprehension of the story. This is not a time to ensure that all students learn and internalize the words, but a chance to supply them with the meaning so that the words will not interfere with their comprehension of the story. In fact, by not pre-teaching every possible vocabulary word, you are also setting up the opportunity to demonstrate how to use context clues to figure out unknown words. For example, before reading the story *Amazing Grace*, by Mary Hoffman, a teacher wrote four words on chart paper: *tutu*, *audition*, *exasperated*, and *imagination*. She then asked the class if they were familiar with any of the words. She wrote the student-generated definitions and taped a visual representation next to each word. Because the teacher took the time to front-load these words, when the students heard the teacher read them in the story, they were able to follow along and maintain

- Does the book make connections to the lives of students from different social, cultural, and linguistic backgrounds?
- Does the text "reflect and value the culture of the students so that they can see themselves in the characters and make connections to their own lives" (Routman 2003, 20)?
- Are there language and the vocabulary barriers to comprehension of the text?
- Does the story provide a good model of varied uses of English, including the use of dialogue and exclamatory, interrogative, and declarative sentences?
- Is the book enjoyable?
- Does the book present an appreciation of diversity?
- Does the book support subject matter across the content areas?
- Does the book have strong picture support?
- Does the book offer opportunities to use drama, gestures, and expression?

FIGURE 4–3: Questions to Consider When Selecting Texts for a Read-Aloud Lesson with English Learners

comprehension. Keep in mind that the teacher selected only the words that she felt would interfere with the students' comprehension of the story. And even though the word *tutu* seems like a simple word, knowing that students come from different sociocultural backgrounds, the teacher selected it because she knew not all children are exposed to ballet.

Teachers must also rehearse their oral reading of the story. Because the read-aloud presents a model of English, teachers should practice their expression, pacing, and intonation. Rehearsing also helps teachers think about strategic stopping points. The more familiar the teacher is with the story, the easier and more natural it will be when she stops for discussion (Allen 2000).

Planning for Interactive Read-Aloud

It is important to keep in mind that the goal of interactive read-aloud is to provide a scaffolded experience in which students will talk and further deepen their understanding of the text as well as their English language skills. This begins with reading with fluency and expression, then modeling the thinking a reader does while reading by thinking aloud. Once a teacher has selected the text for interactive read-aloud considering the aforementioned criteria, she must plan for the lesson. Whenever we plan for a lesson, we read through the book and use sticky notes to flag places where our students may encounter difficulty, either in literacy or in language. We take into account what we know about our students from conferences in reading workshop. What kinds of texts are difficult for them? What words will pose difficulty for them? What is the thinking or comprehension work that I want my students to do? These questions determine what types of think-alouds we will need to model and set up for the students to emulate. Then, on each of those sticky notes, we write what we will say to demonstrate thinking aloud as a strategy.

After determining what language and comprehension challenges the text poses for the students, the teacher introduces the book, then reads aloud portions of the book, stopping to think aloud in preplanned places in the text. Then students either turn and talk or stop and jot their ideas down as the reading of the text progresses. Eventually, the students engage in a whole-class conversation where they listen to each other's ideas and press each other to think more deeply about the text. Students are given opportunities to practice these behaviors with assistance during the interactive read-aloud by talking to their partners and by the teacher providing support as she listens to them talk. The goal is for students to transfer their comprehension experiences gained during interactive read-aloud time to their reading partnerships and then do the thinking automatically as they read independently during reading workshop.

Getting Thinking and Talking Started

An essential element for interactive read-aloud is to get students to have conversations about the text. In the midst of conversation, students are not only further comprehending the story but also developing their English. When first trying to get students to talk, our goal is to have the students say anything—yes, anything at all. We all know that young children will say anything whether it is related to the context or not! In any case, this expectation is important because we want to build a community in which children will take risks. This is foundational to the success of interactive read-aloud. My colleagues Gaby Layden and Donna Santman developed an assessment tool that reflects a continuum of talk called the hierarchy of talk, where they identified different levels of talk that build upon each other. As literacy consultants, they use this tool to help teachers identify stages of talk so they can better scaffold students in higher levels of talk. The goal is for students to be able to have conversations with each other that go beyond basic agreements and disagreements; we want them to be able to provoke each other's thoughts or challenge the author's perspective.

For the purposes of this book, we have used their hierarchy of talk to identify typical stages of talk students go through and modified Gaby and Donna's hierarchy of talk a bit to simplify a few steps (see Figure 4–4). First, we want students to get accustomed to *saying* something, *anything* at all. This is particularly pertinent for our new arrivals at the preproduction stage of second language acquisition (stage I). These students are often afraid to say anything. During interactive read-aloud, students often talk in pairs, which allows them to take risks more easily.

In these beginning stages, what children say (especially our youngest) may not be completely relevant to the text. The key is to make them accustomed to the expectation that they will think and talk during these sessions. Keene and Zimmermann (1997) identify different ways in which we as readers connect to text: text to self, text to text, and text to world. *Saying something relevant* means that students are making some type of connection to the text.

During the first few stages of *say anything* and *say something relevant*, the students are often engaged in a dialogue one-on-one with the teacher or their partner. One goal of the interactive read-aloud is to move toward a whole-class conversation where children are listening to each other and responding to each other's comments. The purpose is for them to deepen their understanding of the text as a result of the conversation. *Say something back* places the expectation on children to speak to each other. This is often scaffolded by the teacher. When I hear a student making a follow-up comment to the previous student, I explicitly take notice of the moves of the reader by saying something like, "So you are actually disagreeing with what Victor just said." It is important to take notice of this as well as welcome this type of engagement.

When encouraging students to *say something to clarify*, we are holding students accountable to the comments they make. In addition, we are providing a context in which ELs are pressed to further use their language skills to elaborate on their responses. When we ask students to *say something to revise*, we are expecting that as we read a story, we will come up with some ideas or theories, but we do not have to hold fast to these ideas; rather, further reading of a text paired with conversation could cause us to think differently and revise that thinking. The last step, *saying something to provoke*, captures the idea that through the process of thinking and talking about texts in a variety of ways, we embark on a journey of thinking that might otherwise not have existed had we just listened to the story from start to finish. As a result of listening to one another, we have thought about the text in different ways, and perhaps that will leave us with bigger ideas—ideas that could perhaps be carried over to other texts and experiences. As students move up the stages of the hierarchy of talk, there is also a gradual release of teacher control of the conversation. The role of the teacher changes from being the first source of modeling thinking and initiating ideas, to being the facilitator who looks for opportunities to highlight pivotal moves in talk and to keep the conversation progressing.

The *hierarchy of talk* reflects a similar progression to that found in the stages of *second language acquisition* as well as the *functions of language*. We thought this side-by-side comparison would be helpful in identifying how teachers could support the language needs of their students as they progress through the hierarchy of talk during interactive read-aloud. For instance, when a student is in the *early production* (stage II) of *second language acquisition*, we encourage the student to *say anything* as in the early stages of the *hierarchy of talk*. During this time, the student might be using *functions of language* such as *identifying* or *retelling* in *saying anything*. As this child moves into the *intermediate fluency* (stage IV) of second language acquisition, he is more equipped to say something to revise or provoke through the use of more developed functions of language such as *evaluating* or *criticizing*. The chart in Figure 4–4 shows the parallel progression of the stages of second language, hierarchy of talk, and language functions. Please note that these stages are flexible, occurring throughout the stages.

I remember once reading aloud a book about a boy and his pet dog. Before I knew it, I heard various stories about every child's pet, real or imagined. Once I was able to get students comfortable saying anything, I needed to focus them back on the text. By the time I heard the third pet story, I began to say, "Tell me how your pet story reminds you of this story." Sometimes this helps stop much of the contagious

STAGES OF SECOND LANGUAGE ACQUISITION	HIERARCHY OF TALK	LANGUAGE FUNCTIONS
• Stage I: Preproduction		
• Stage II: Early Production	• Say Anything	• Identifying
	• Say Something Relevant	• Retelling
• Stage III: Speech Emergence	• Say Something Back	• Expressing Likes and Dislikes
	• Say Something to Clarify	• Sequencing
		• Suggesting
		• Agreeing and Disagreeing
		• Explaining
		• Comparing
• Stage IV: Intermediate Fluency	• Say Something to Revise	• Planning and Predicting
		• Inferring
		• Hypothesizing
• Stage V: Native Language Fluency/Proficiency	• Say Something to Provoke	• Obligating
		• Evaluating
		• Expressing Position
		• Criticizing

FIGURE 4–4: Aligning the Hierarchy of Talk, Language Functions, and Stages of Second Language Acquisition

STEP IN HIERARCHY OF TALK	EXAMPLE FROM INTERACTIVE READ-ALOUD
Say Anything	My mommy took me to the aquarium this weekend.
Say Something Relevant	I saw tiny red fish like that at the aquarium this weekend.
	I've seen a big fish eat a little fish just like that on TV.
Say Something Back	[Responding to the previous student's comment] That's not a big fish.
Say Something to Clarify	S1: Now they will not have any trouble because they are a big fish.
	S2: Are you saying that they turned into one big fish?
Say Something to Revise	S1: No, I mean they just look like a big fish; they're really a bunch of small fishes.
Say Something to Provoke	S1: I don't think small fish are smart enough to make the shape of a big fish. Besides, the other fish would know that they were not a big fish.
	S2: Well, the book's not really about that. It's about how they work together to not be afraid.

FIGURE 4–5: The Hierarchy of Talk: Interactive Read-Aloud Using *Swimmy*, by Leo Leonni

chatter that has just swept across the room. Soon after that, I find that children really think about what they are saying to make a connection to the text.

The Structure of Read-Aloud for Emergent and Early Readers at Different Levels of Second Language Acquisition

Read-aloud is a time of day when emergent and early readers sit eagerly awaiting the sound of a great story. At this level, fictional stories are easy for students to connect with. Selecting books with familiar experiences or characters encourages listening and enhances comprehension. Because emergent and early readers are still understanding how text is organized and works, it's important to use books with rich illustrations that support the story. Bring children in close to read to them and point out artwork (Allington and Cunningham 2003).

Before the Read

Prior to reading the text, the teacher should focus on generating background knowledge. Children can better comprehend information when they can attach it to something familiar. Some quick activities include the following:

- *Picture walks*—Go through the story from beginning to end, talking about the meaning of the pictures.
- *Making predictions*—Look at the front cover and ask students what they think the story will be about.
- *Concepts about print*—Review parts of the book, including the title, the name of the author and the illustrator, the front cover, and the back cover.
- *Front-loading vocabulary*—Present pictures or oral definitions of key words from the story.
- *Making connections*—Ask students to think about how the theme of the story relates to experiences in their life.
- *Pair-shares*—Ask students to tell their partner what they know about the topic, characters, theme of the story, or a personal connection.

It is important to select one or two of these activities and keep it brief. The heart of the teaching rests in the teacher and students interacting with the text.

During the Read

While reading the text, it is important for teachers to point out the connections between what they are reading and the illustrations. This models the reading strategy of using picture clues and context to help the reader read the text. This is the time to ask questions and stop and allow students to share their thinking with a partner or with the class. This is also the time for students to hear how the teacher makes sense of the text. This can be done by thinking aloud, or verbalizing your thinking so that the students can hear how you are making sense of the text. The teacher continually supports the students' language and comprehension skills through the use of the hierarchy of talk.

After the Read

After the read-aloud, the teacher can recap the story or ask questions that extend the students' comprehension of the story. This can include asking the students to make personal connections to the story or with the characters. Students can also draw a picture or write in a journal about their favorite part, character, or setting from the story. The after-the-read task does not always have to be an independent activity. A read-aloud sets the stage and offers information as a preparation for other times of the school day, such as subject area study or independent reading time.

Interactive Read-Aloud in Action: An Interactive Read-Aloud with *I See Animals Hiding*, by Jim Arnosky

Read-aloud is a great opportunity to integrate content area studies as well as model and actively teach comprehension. During a nonfiction unit of study in reading workshop, we decided to integrate the read-aloud with some of the work the class had been doing in science. The first graders had been learning about the concept of camouflage with animals. This lesson came after the concept had already been introduced to the students. During reading workshop, the students had been selecting nonfictional texts about animals. They had been sharing with their partners things that they were learning about their animals. We selected *I See Animals Hiding*, by Jim Arnosky (1995), as a way to extend the conversation about camouflage. After reading the book several times to myself, I placed stickies with notes of what I would draw attention to on each page, depending on what my students knew about the concepts and language used in the book. Figure 4–6 provides an outline for my plan for reading aloud *I See Animals Hiding*.

These stops in the text help the students follow along with the comprehension of the text. The students become engaged by sharing their thinking *during* the reading of the story. We want to be sure we don't lose students while reading and that we utilize rich sources of information from the text to support students' thinking. In the example in Figure 4–6, you might also notice I intentionally made stopping points to discuss content area vocabulary to enrich the science unit on camouflage.

PAGE	TEXT AND ILLUSTRATION DESCRIPTION	PLANS FOR SCAFFOLDING EACH PAGE
Title Page	(has picture of deer in the snow, standing amid bare trees)	• Set context for animals hiding by discussing the pictures. • Even if there are children that do not understand everything being read in English, they will be able to understand the concepts from the pictures.
Pages 1–2	*I see animals hiding. I see a <u>porcupine</u> high in a tree.* *Wild animals are shy and always hiding. It is natural for them to be this way. There are many dangers in the wild.* *Even when they are caught unaware out in the open, wild animals try to hide. They stay behind whatever is available—a thick tree trunk or even a single blade of grass. Most of the time they go unnoticed.* (picture of a porcupine on a tree branch, in the shape of a V)	• Students will not be familiar with the word *porcupine*. Before reading the page, have students discuss what they see hiding. • Think aloud what I see on this page, describing how the porcupine is camouflaged.
Page 3	*The colors of wild animals match the colors of the places where the animals live. Because of this <u>protective coloration</u>, called <u>camouflage</u>, wild animals can hide by simply staying still and blending in.* (two-page spread of woodcocks hiding among leaves, branches, and twigs)	• Think aloud *protective coloration*. "Hmm, what does that mean? I know from our studies that camouflage is hiding. Protective coloration. I see *protect* and *color* in those words. Maybe that means that the color of the birds helps hide them and protect them. Let's see if that matches the picture . . . yes it does!"
Page 7	*There are 20 deer on the hill. Can you find them all?* (text embedded among trees in the forest)	• "Look at how this page has smaller print. I wonder what that is? Let me read it." • "Wow! I wonder if we can find all the deer. Let's do it. . . ."

FIGURE 4–6: Read-Aloud Plans for *I See Animals Hiding*, by Jim Arnosky

The Structure of Read-Aloud for Transitional and Self-Extending Readers Across Levels of Second Language Acquisition

Read-aloud further supports transitional and self-extending readers by providing access to new information, genres, and ideas. Richard Allington and Patricia Cunningham (2003) express that transitional and self-extending readers should be read "real things." These include informational texts (including newspapers and magazines), traditional texts, poetry (including songs and chants), and easy books. According to Allington and Cunningham, the use of easy books is helpful for reluctant readers.

All readers should be read to daily. Even self-extending readers, who can read on their own, need to be exposed to new genres to expand their reading repertoire. Further, reading aloud should not be limited to the language arts instructional block but can enhance all content areas. Because read-alouds provide rich background knowledge, they can help students comprehend their content area textbooks. For example, if students are learning about animal classifications in science and the first part of the unit is on mammals, the teacher may choose to present a read-aloud picture book on mammals prior to beginning the unit. This will bring out students' familiarity with mammals they have seen or encountered to support their learning.

Before the Read

Just as with emergent and early readers, transitional and self-extending readers need to build background knowledge before interacting with a read-aloud. In addition, to further focus the reading, teachers can pose a question to students that will guide the class discussion during or after the read.

During the Read

Three main strategies when reading aloud to transitional and self-extending readers include think-aloud, pair-share, and stop-and-jot. Because these students are learning to think deeply about text, the teacher must share how he is making sense of the text. The think-aloud should include the teacher's confusion and clarification of text. Students need to hear how to problem solve their way through the meaning of text.

Pair-shares should vary in focus and intent. At times the teacher can just ask students to share with their partner what they are thinking: "Turn and tell your partner what you're thinking right now." Notice there is no direction as to what to think or what to tell their partner; students are simply asked to share their thoughts about the text thus far. At other times, the teacher should focus the talk around higher-level thinking questions. These are the types of questions that begin with the text but ask the students to think on their own. These kinds of questions normally begin with words like *should*, *could*, *what if*, *why*, and *would* (see Appendix B). In answering these types of questions, students will be forced to think. They cannot solely rely on the text for the answer. Self-extending readers need opportunities to think about text and to share their ideas with others. This will lead to higher levels of comprehension. When you have a chance to hear what others think, it makes you think more deeply about your own thoughts.

A stop-and-jot is similar to a pair-share except that instead of orally sharing their thinking, students write or draw it. This helps students develop their writing fluency and monitor their comprehension.

After the Read

Similar to those for emergent and early readers, the after-the-read activities for transitional and self-extending students can include a simple recap of the story or a final pair-share or stop-and-jot. Because the read-aloud can serve as a preparation activity for other subject areas or times of day (such as the minilesson during reading or writing workshop), it is not necessary to have an in-depth, lengthy after-the-read activity.

Interactive Read-Aloud in Action: Explicit Language Instruction During a Read-Aloud for Transitional and Self-Extending Readers

In the following example of a second-grade interactive read-aloud (see Figure 4–7), the students were paired up by varying levels of second language acquisition so that they could support each other better. In addition, we attempted to match experienced talkers with less experienced talkers. In this particular class there were some students who came from a class that had had strong interactive read-aloud

CLASSROOM TRANSCRIPT	REFLECTION
T: Today we're going to read a book called *Henry and Mudge and the Wild Goose Chase.* Some of you might be familiar with Henry and Mudge. Let's find out what is happening to Henry and his dog, Mudge.	Notice how the teacher not only emphasizes the meaning in the title but carefully studies the picture to help make meaningful predictions. She also reminds students to be careful to make predictions that are closely tied to evidence from the book.
Hmm . . . Mudge is wagging his tail, I wonder what is going on here. . . .	
S: He wants to eat them.	
T: What made you think that?	
S: His tongue is sticking out.	
T: Remember, whenever we are making predictions, we need to make sure what we are thinking matches what we read or see in the pictures.	

FIGURE 4–7: Read-Aloud with Transitional and Self-Extending Readers Using *Henry and Mudge and the Wild Goose Chase,* by Cynthia Rylant (2004).

CLASSROOM TRANSCRIPT	REFLECTION
T: Let's continue with the story. . . . *S:* There's a goose! *T:* Yes, we read the word *goose* on the cover—in the title—and now this is the first time we see the goose. *S:* The dog is not moving his tail and the duck is quacking. . . . *T:* So what you noticed is that Mudge isn't very happy. So what you noticed is that maybe he is not so happy now because he is not wagging his tail.	You will notice that the teacher is continuing with not only the cover but also the title page. Often children in transitional literacy levels do not bother spending much time with the pictures and details of each page to help them make sense of the story. The teacher also responds to the students in full sentences with the characters' names.
S: I think Grandma is going to be upset. *T:* What makes you think that? *S:* The goose is honking. *T:* Why is the goose honking at them? *S:* I think that because maybe they disturbed the goose. *T:* What made you think that? *S:* Because he looks mad. *T:* Who can add on to that idea? *S:* I think that, like, they're making fun of them. *T:* So that's like Fernando's idea that the goose is disturbed. *S:* I think they want them to get out of it. *S:* I think they want them to get out of the farm and he's mad because they're just there to take something without asking.	The teacher continually presses for students to base predictions on text evidence. The teacher encourages others to respond to the comments being made. She also helps in making connections between students.
T: Let's review the good thinking started with Fernando. The idea grew from, he's mad because they want him to leave, and Nubia added that it's because they took something without asking at the farm. *S:* Duck will chase them out. *T:* You are changing the idea. Let's go back [reviews the pictures in the book]. *T:* "Looks like you've been on a wild goose chase." [turns back to the cover] Aha! But they were being chased by the goose. Oh, and I see here that Mudge is wagging his tail again—I wonder if he's happy again. Remember when we grew the idea? Now that this part of the story is over, do we know why the goose is behaving that way? Does the author tell us that?	The teacher draws attention to how through conversation, students are beginning to expand their ideas. The teacher presses the students to remain focused on the point at hand. The teacher points to the picture where there are curved lines around the dog's tail, indicating the "wagging" motion. The teacher demonstrates chunking the text by summarizing after a section of the text has been read.

(continues)

FIGURE 4–7: *Continued*

CLASSROOM TRANSCRIPT	REFLECTION
S: They let us find out. *T:* Smart idea. *S:* We have to figure it out. *T:* She, the author, Cynthia Rylant—actually, a lot of books don't always tell us everything. We don't have all the answers, but it helps us think of different ideas and gives us clues to help us think.	The teacher continues to draw attention to comments from students that provoke thinking.
T: So when you are reading on your own, you want to think and see if what you're thinking is true in the text.	The teacher connects what they have done today as a whole group to an important skill they must utilize when reading independently. They need to keep their ideas grounded in the text.

FIGURE 4–7: *Continued*

conversations and some from another class that had not had those experiences.

Summary of Features from This Lesson That Support English Learners and Language Development

- The selected text had familiar characters that students could relate to.
- Prior to reading the story, the teacher built background knowledge by engaging in an in-depth discussion with the class about the illustrations.
- Attention to the illustrations helped English learners make connections and clarify their thinking.
- The teacher repeated the students' ideas in complete, simple sentences.
- The students heard each other use language. This helped them develop their own language, by being exposed to new vocabulary.
- Asking students to respond to each other's ideas encouraged active listening. With attention to listening, students paid more attention to language.

Conclusion

Interactive read-aloud should occur regularly each day so that the teacher has an opportunity to model thinking strategies. Often during guided reading, word work, and shared reading, we teach students how to use print strategies. It is not a coincidence that students often feel comfortable with those strategies. What poses difficulty for students is having an understanding of what proficient readers do in their heads. Interactive read-aloud is about making those strategies known to the readers so that they can practice them on their own. During interactive read-aloud, children talk both in partnerships as well as to the whole group in the midst of a text. We do this because thinking doesn't begin to occur at the end of the text. At key points throughout any text we read, we think about what is happening and we develop theories and interpretations about what we have read so far. By encouraging students to talk, we are sharpening their comprehension and language skills simultaneously.

Suggested Books to Use for Interactive Read-Aloud

Picture Books for Emergent and Early Readers

Koala Lou, by Mem Fox
Tough Boris, by Mem Fox
Stellaluna, by Janell Cannon
How Do Dinosaurs Say Good Night? by Jane Yolen
How Do Dinosaurs Get Well Soon? by Jane Yolen
Quick as a Cricket, by Audrey Wood
Giraffes Can't Dance, by Giles Andreae
Dear Mr. Blueberry, by Simon James
The Jolly Postman, by Janet and Allan Ahlberg
Julius, the Baby of the World, by Kevin Henkes
Chrysanthemum, by Kevin Henkes
Chester's Way, by Kevin Henkes
The Most Thankful Thing, by Lisa McCourt
Elizabeti's Doll, by Stephanie Stuv-Bodeen
The Dot, by Peter H. Reynolds
Ish, by Peter H. Reynolds
The Art Lesson, by Tomie dePaola
Birthday Presents, by Cynthia Rylant
I'm Gonna Like Me, by Jamie Lee Curtis and Laura Cornell
It's Hard to Be Five, by Jamie Lee Curtis and Laura Cornell
When I Was Five, by Arthur Howard

Series Books for Emergent and Early Readers

Clifford series, by Norman Bridwell
Critters series, by Mercer Mayer

Picture Books for Transitional and Self-Extending Readers

The Pain and the Great One, by Judy Blume
Two Mrs. Gibsons, by Toyomi Igus

Bedhead, by Margie Palatini
Abuela, by Arthur Dorros
The Story of Ruby Bridges, by Robert Coles
A Chair for My Mother, by Vera B. Williams
Hairs/Pelitos, by Sandra Cisneros
The Relatives Came, by Cynthia Rylant
Chato's Kitchen, by Gary Soto
Too Many Tamales, by Gary Soto
Gracias: The Thanksgiving Turkey, by Joy Cowley
Miss Nelson Is Missing, by Harry Allard
Miss Nelson Is Back, by Harry Allard
Amazing Grace, by Mary Hoffman

Series Books for Transitional and Self-Extending Readers

Henry and Mudge series, by Cynthia Rylant
Junie B. Jones series, by Barbara Park
Ready Freddy series, by Abby Klein
Frog and Toad series, by Arnold Lobel
Arthur series, by Marc Brown
Froggy series, by Jonathan London

Teacher Resources for Read-Alouds

Codell, Esme R. 2003. *How to Get Your Child to Love Reading*. New York: Algonquin.

Hahn, Mary Lee. 2002. *Reconsidering Read-Aloud*. Portland, ME: Stenhouse.

Keene, Ellen and Susan Zimmermann. 1997. *Mosaic of Thought: Teaching Comprehension in a Reader's Workshop*. Portsmouth, NH: Heinemann.

Lewis, Valerie V. and Walter M. Mayes. 1998. *Best Books for Children: A Lively Opinionated Guide*. New York: Avon.

Miller, Debbie. 2002. *Reading with Meaning: Teaching Comprehension in the Primary Grades*. Portland, ME: Stenhouse.

Trelease, Jim. 1992. *Hey Listen to This: Stories to Read Aloud*. New York: Penguin.

———. 2001. *The Read-Aloud Handbook*. 5th ed. New York: Penguin.

5 Emergent Storybook Read-Aloud

Children emergently acquire all of the aspects of conventional literacy and . . . they reorganize these aspects into a coordinated, flexible, integrated system which enables them to figure out print independently.

—Elizabeth Sulzby, 2001

What Is Emergent Storybook Read-Aloud?

It is late October and the students in Ms. Lee's kindergarten class are scattered around the room, sitting side by side with partners, sharing a book between them, laughing and pointing to pictures on the page. As you approach a pair more closely, you notice that they are "reading" the old favorite *Caps for Sale*, rhythmically pointing and chiming, "You monkeys you, you give me back my caps!" almost verbatim. You wonder, "Are these five-year-olds actually reading this text?" You listen further. As the pair proceed to the next page, they start to skip some of the words and you realize that they have magically memorized the text. They turn one page after the next, seemingly reading the story to the best of their ability—sometimes pausing to laugh and point to particular parts and other times hurriedly proceeding to the next page. As you wander around the room, you find that the other pairs are doing similar work, at varying degrees, with other texts such as *Corduroy* and *The Three Billy Goats Gruff*. Vy chimes in with her partner from time to time even though you don't hear her speaking much during class. How captivating and endearing to witness these little ones so engrossed in stories, but why are they doing this? And how are they able to tell the stories with such ease?

Foundations of Emergent Storybook Read-Aloud

When working for Teachers College Reading and Writing Project, I had the privilege of learning from Elizabeth Sulzby (1991) about emergent reading of favorite storybooks. Elizabeth and her colleagues have done extensive work with prekindergarten and kindergarten emergent literacy. Children become literate not at the point of reading print, but well before—such as during the earliest bedtime experiences of sharing a favorite storybook. Imagine at bedtime when a child slips under the covers and says, "Daddy, read me a story." As she curls up next to her father, he reads her all-time favorite story, *The Three Billy Goats Gruff*. He holds the book in the middle between them; first he reads the title, then he turns the first few pages and reads the beginning of the story, "Once upon a time, there were three Billy Goats. . . ." As he reads each page, she listens and looks at the pictures on the page. Because she knows the story so well, she sometimes even helps him turn the pages when he is finished reading. At times, he might even point to some of the words he is reading. And when they get to some of her favorite pages, she chimes in with him, saying, "TRIP, TRAP, TRIP, TRAP! . . . WHO'S THAT TRIPPING OVER MY BRIDGE?" with the same robust voice he has used time and again when reading the part of the troll. Even though she has heard the story a hundred times over, she still cheers at the page when the big Billy Goat Gruff tosses the troll into the river below. As her father turns to the last page, the little girl reads the last line with him, "So snip, snap, snout, this tale's told out." They close the book, hands on top of each other, she wriggles farther under her blanket and rests her head on the pillow, and he tucks her in, kisses her on the forehead, turns out the light, and says good night.

This might seem like such a common experience; however, it is full of literary experiences that lay the foundation for conventional literacy that emerges later during school. Through the familiarity and comfort of this nightly social and intimate interaction with her parent, the child is making simultaneous connections between the oral and written literacy on the page. She is learning concepts about print, the connection of meaning to words read from the page, and that pages go together to make a story. Looking back on the essential elements of literacy (described in Chapter 2), we see that the child in this scenario is developing all but the ability to decode print and manipulate sounds.

Sulzby's practice of emergent storybook reading is based upon the following four assumptions: (1) children are literate long before they are able to read from print; (2) early literacy is developed through social interactions with those who are important to the child; (3) children acquire oral and written literacy simultaneously; and (4) children acquire all aspects of conventional literacy emergently and are able to coordinate the experiences in a flexible and integrated system that allows them to figure out print independently.

Through repeated exposure to these familiar storybooks, children generally follow a developmental continuum Sulzby (1991) identifies as a storybook reading classification scheme. Depending on the book, a child does not always discretely follow each stage. Broadly, these are identified in the categories described in Figure 5–1.

STAGE DESCRIPTION	CHILD'S BEHAVIOR	EXAMPLE
Stage 1: Attending to Pictures, Not Forming Stories	• Labels and comments on pictures across pages. • Follows the action of the story.	"Caps." "Man." "Monkeys." "Monkeys throw caps."
Stage 2: Attending to Pictures, Forming Oral Stories	• "Reads" the story by looking at the pictures, but speech consists of storytelling intonation, not that of a reader.	"Here's a peddler, he has all these caps." (sounds as if the child is telling or describing a part, often in present tense)
Stage 3: Attending to Pictures, Mixing Reading and Storytelling	• Speech consists of both the intonation of a storyteller and that of a reader.	"Once there was a peddler. He has lots of caps." (often a mixture of present and past tense)
Stage 4: Attending to Pictures, Forming Written Stories	• "Reads" similar to the original story or reads the story as if verbatim.	"Once there was a peddler who sold caps. He was not a regular peddler."
Stage 5: Attending to Print	• Uses some aspects of print to read conventionally. At times the child might refuse to read print, recognizing that she cannot read all the words.	"Once there was a peddler who sold caps. But he was not like an ordinary peddler." (hesitates at the word *ordinary*, then looks at the *or*, says "or," and then makes letter-sound connection with what she knows about the story)

FIGURE 5–1: Sulzby's Classification Scheme

Context in Our Book

Children who enter kindergarten do not typically read conventionally; however, we set the stage for their development in literacy through emergent storybook reading. The classroom teacher reads an old favorite storybook repeatedly over the course of several days, allowing all children to become familiar with the story. The purpose is for the children to be familiar with the meaning and language of the story. Once they have heard the story several times, the teacher gives individual copies to the children to then "read" on their own with a partner. This is particularly effective with students who are hearing and learning in English for the first time. To a certain extent the children memorize the story, but in the midst of these repeated readings, they are also building comprehension of the story. English learners hear the syntax of the English language through these stories, then repeat it in context when they read the story on their own. As they look at the pictures from page to page, they are reminded of the story as they read.

This practice is used specifically in our kindergarten classrooms on a regular basis; however, similar versions of this strategy can be carried over to first and second grade as well. Children progress across these stages over a short period of time because they hear the stories being read and are given opportunities to read their old favorite storybooks on a daily basis. Particularly, English learners are using English syntax that they may not normally use in social conversations. Over time, this syntax and vocabulary also transfers to their writing.

Language Theory in Practice

As a staff developer working in different schools, I noticed how quickly English learners developed English through experiences with emergent storybook reading in kindergarten classes, and I thought to myself, "How can the same aspects be transferred to older children, particularly new arrivals?" Many of the first-grade classes have extended the same practice, but use it more with small groups rather than the whole group. In second grade, teachers have used some read-aloud books that hold the same criteria as the emergent storybooks. Reading these texts repeatedly to children in early stages of second language acquisition helped them develop English syntax.

In this setting, children thrive in learning language because they are able to take risks in a supportive environment. Everyone is exposed to the stories and given opportunities to practice reading them on a consistent basis. English learners feel just as successful as readers and speakers of English.

What Does Emergent Storybook Reading Look Like?

Key Elements

Emergent and beginning readers are not yet fully reading texts conventionally. They need multiple opportunities to practice the connection between print and meaning. In the absence of solid conventional reading skills, students strengthen their syntax and meaning-making skills by taking a familiar old favorite and reading it from page to page over and over again. This repeated exposure and practice helps students become more familiar not only with the meaning of the story but also with the structure of language used in the story. Figure 5–2 describes the purposes for emergent storybook reading.

You may remember that in Figure 3–1, we allotted fifteen minutes a day to emergent storybook reading in kindergarten. At the beginning of the year, this entails the teacher reading aloud the text to the entire class. Because these stories are often fairly long, it may take up to fifteen minutes. It is important to make a distinction between reading aloud emergent literacy texts and interactive read-aloud. Emergent literacy texts are read aloud straight through from start to finish without stopping for discussion. It is important that the children get a sense of the entire story without interruption so that they can read the text continuously on their own or with a partner later on.

You might ask, "When are the students reading the emergent literacy texts?" In the beginning of kindergarten, the students have these emergent storybooks in their reading bags during independent reading workshop and read these books both independently and with partners. When they are reading these books with partners, they take turns reading entire books. For example, Jose and Lydia are sharing *Caps for Sale*, but Lydia is the one reading the entire text while Jose listens and supports Lydia when she needs help. Then it is Jose's turn, and he reads *Corduroy* while Lydia listens and supports him as needed. Again, it is important that one student reads the entire story instead of having partners take turns from one page to the next.

While the children are reading emergent storybooks, it is the teacher's job to listen carefully in order to: (1) identify at what Sulzby

---

- To build community through the enjoyment of stories
- To encourage a love of reading
- To provide models of the English language through oral reading
- To provide foundational experiences and set the stage for conventional reading
- To develop meaning and syntax in the act of learning to read

FIGURE 5–2: Purposes of Emergent Storybook Reading

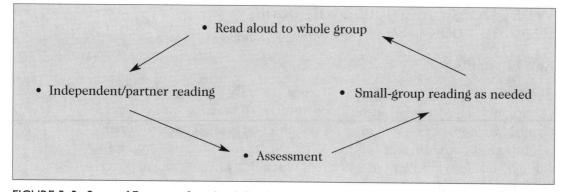

FIGURE 5–3: Steps of Emergent Storybook Reading

classification stage the child is currently reading and (2) provide support to the child that will scaffold his progression to the next level. For example, if a child is in the first stage as described in Figure 5–1 and points to the peddler and the caps while saying "man" and "caps," I might respond, "Yes, once there was a peddler who sold caps." You will notice in this scenario that I have replied only with the essential parts of the text to help the child make connections between objects seen on the page. A child that is simply labeling is not ready to hear all the text that is actually on the page. Over time, he will be ready for the additional details. Figure 5–4 lists the teacher's and students' roles during emergent storybook reading.

As you go around listening to students reading to their partners, you will find that some students encounter some difficulty. When you listen to the students, it is important to identify what stage they might be in so that you can group the students together in small groups. For instance, in one class, about six students were new arrivals to the class and had difficulty understanding the current story. During read-aloud time, the teacher did not hear them chiming in on certain parts of the story; they didn't seem engaged. Instead, the children often looked around at what other children were doing. Once I noticed this was happening, I worked directly with just these students so that they would understand the story better. The reason students are able to "read" the story is because they know it makes sense. I selected *The Little Mouse, the Red Ripe Strawberry, and the Big Hungry Bear*. Before rereading the book, I said to the students that we would try something new today—we would act out the story. I located a big book version of this text and placed it on an easel. As I turned to each page, I stood in front of the students and acted out parts of the page. As I continued to turn each page, the children started to initiate their own movements instead of looking at me and mimicking my actions. The children loved re-creating the expressions of the timid little mouse as he conceded to the demands of the narrator. By acting the story out in a small group, these students were better able to comprehend the text and were subsequently supported in their reading of the text.

ROLE OF THE TEACHER	ROLE OF THE STUDENTS
Part I: Whole-Group Read-Aloud	
• Read with the intent of being a model of English. • Read with expression. • Establish a comfortable learning environment for risk taking. • Read the text several times so that the story becomes very familiar to students.	• Listen carefully. • Look at pictures as the teacher reads the text. • Chime in during familiar lines.
Part II: Partner Reading	
• Purposefully match students together as partners to maximize learning and language development. • Assess student understanding and language development by listening to "reading." • Listen to students as they are emergently reading each book. Take notes as to what stage they seem to represent. • Scaffold the child's reading toward the next stage. • Jot down possible ways to support the child in different aspects of literacy.	• Take risks with language. • Apply what is learned to independent reading contexts. • Read the story continually from one page to the next.

FIGURE 5–4: Teacher and Student Roles in Emergent Storybook Reading

Selecting Texts for Read-Aloud

The texts for emergent storybook read-aloud need to connect with children in order for them to want to revisit them time and again. As the teacher, you will be reading these texts repeatedly as well, so your affinity for the text is also an important consideration. We all know that if we read a story that we do not truly love ourselves, this will come across. Figure 5–5 summarizes some of the characteristics of emergent storybooks. There is also a list of suggested books to use at the end of the chapter.

- Strong, clear story line with rich language and vocabulary
- Clear picture support
- Content that children can relate to and understand
- Emotional appeal to children
- High interest
- Can be revisited often

FIGURE 5–5: Characteristics of Emergent Storybooks

Structure of Emergent Storybook Reading for Emergent Readers at Different Levels of Second Language Acquisition

There are two parts to emergent storybook reading. The first part consists of the teacher reading a story several times over the period of several days in order to familiarize the students with the story. Unlike interactive read-aloud, the teacher does not interrupt the reading of the story with think-alouds or with student conversation. The purpose of this read-aloud time is for the children to hear the story from start to finish so they can get a sense of the fluency of the whole story.

Read-Aloud Schedule

Day 1 *Caps for Sale*	Day 2 *Caps for Sale*	Day 3 *Caps for Sale*[*]	Day 4 *Caps for Sale*	Day 5 *Corduroy*
Day 6 *Corduroy*	Day 7 *Corduroy*[*]	Day 8 *Corduroy*	Day 9 *The Little Mouse*	Day 10 *The Little Mouse*
Day 11 *The Little Mouse*[*]	Day 12 *The Little Mouse*	Day 13 *The Three Bears*	Day 14 *The Three Bears*	Day 15 *The Three Bears*[*]
Day 16 *The Three Bears*	Day 17 *The Three Billy Goats Gruff*	Day 18 *The Three Billy Goats Gruff*	Day 19 *The Three Billy Goats Gruff*[*]	Day 20 *The Three Billy Goats Gruff*
[*]Denotes days in which individual copies of the book are distributed to the students so they can practice reading independently.				

As students hear the story being read aloud, they become familiar with the story and become ready to read it aloud to a partner. You will notice there is an asterisk on the third day for each book in the read-aloud schedule above. On these days, you can make the book available to students during independent reading so the students can practice reading it to each other. The teacher continues to read aloud the text even after children receive the books in order to increase familiarity. Typically, each book has a star on the cover, indicating that it is an emergent storybook. The students often know them as "star books." They know that when they have a star book, they should hold the book between them and one child should read the entire book from beginning to end. Then the other child should select another star book and read it to his partner. They do not take turns reading from the same book. The following section contains excerpts of a child reading a portion of *Caps for Sale* from beginning to end.

Emergent Storybook Reading in Action

Let's take a look at the emergent storybook reading of a kindergarten student named Jae who is an English learner between the speech emergence and intermediate fluency levels of second language acquisition. Just taking a peek at a few pages of his reading in various parts of the text will give you an indication of his language development, which I have described in the "Reflection" column.

PAGE	JAE'S READING	REFLECTION
1–2	Once there was a peddler who sells his caps. He's not a regular peddler. He got a gray cap and the brown cap, and the blue cap, and the red cap on the very, very top.	• Starts story off verbatim. • Uses present tense, which reflects more storytelling rather than reading speech. • Does not yet expand on the details of the peddler. • Understands that the peddler has different caps, but does not yet use the story language; uses *got* (instead of "had on") which matches child's own verbal syntax. • Does not yet use collective noun, *bunch* but instead uses singular *the*, to refer to a "bunch of brown caps."
5–6	But peddler was really hungry. Don't have any money for lunch. He walk down to town to eat.	• Doesn't yet capture the entire text on this page, perhaps because there is quite a bit. This is one of the longest passages in the book where the narrator explains in detail how the peddler was not able to sell any caps. • Does understand that the peddler was taking a break for lunch. The child only seems to capture the middle part of the text when the peddler takes a break for lunch.

(continues)

FIGURE 5–6: Emergent Storybook Reading with Reflections

PAGE	JAE'S READING	REFLECTION
5–6 (*cont.*)		• Child omits the part where the peddler walks "slowly, slowly, so as not to upset his caps."
11–12	When he woke up he.	• Doesn't yet include the descriptive vocabulary (omits last part of the sentence, "was feeling refreshed and relaxed").
13–14	When he, when he start to go stand up. He put his hand up on his ear and touch his head and fill his own cap with in right place but all it was was his check cap.	• He understands this page but struggles a bit to "read" it fluently, resulting in adding more words to describe the scene.
15–16	He look in back of him and the other side of him and the front of him and the other side and, and the back of the tree, but there was no caps.	• Doesn't yet pick up on the repetitive text structure the line, "No caps" is repeated in the text after the peddler looks at each side around him) but does understand that the peddler looks all around him, picking up on some of the descriptive phrases.
17–18	He looked at up and what is he saw?	• On the cusp of capturing this syntax that is very different from his own spoken language ("What do you think he saw?)"
19–20 (two-page spread)	Monkeys! Who what monkeys gray caps and brown caps and blue caps and the red caps at the very, very top!	• He captures the excitement in the illustration of this two-page spread with his own improvisation of language—"Monkeys!"—and also adds "at the very, very top!" (whereas the actual text is not as embellished) • He describes the caps in the correct sequence.

FIGURE 5–6: *Continued*

PAGE	JAE'S READING	ACTUAL BOOK TEXT	REFLECTION
29–30	Peddler was really angry both shake his hand and shake his both feet, and say, "You monkeys you, you give me back my cap." But monkey both shake his feet and both shake his hand and say, "Tsz, tsz, tsz, tsz, tsz, tsz."	*By that time the peddler was really very, very angry. He stamped both his feet and shouted, "You monkeys, you! You must give me back my caps!"* *But the monkeys only stamped their feet back at him and said, "Tsz, tsz, tsz."*	• He recognizes the building tension in this scene by adding "really angry." • He embellishes the gestures by adding the part about the peddler shaking his hands (whereas the original text only mentions the stamping of the feet).
31–32	But he, peddler was really angry he throw his own check cap, but . . .		• He is able to capture the action and sentiment on this page, but he doesn't yet articulate the story language used— "At last, he became so angry that he began to walk away."

FIGURE 5–6: *Continued*

Summary of Features from This Lesson That Support English Learners and Language Development

You might notice from the transcript that Jae seems to be at level 3 in the Sulzby scale; he mixes storytelling and reading of the story. At times, Jae captures the story almost verbatim, but other times he abbreviates the text with his own words. You will notice that when he abbreviates, he still understands the text and substitutes with words that carry the same meaning. In the passage below, however, he ends up adding more words because the syntax and vocabulary poses a challenge for him.

| 13–14 | When he, when he start to go stand up.

He put his hand up on his ear and touch his head and fill his own cap with in right place but all it was was his check cap. | *But before standing up he felt with his hand to make sure his caps were in the right place.*

All he felt was his own checked cap! | • He understands this page, but struggles a bit to "read" it fluently, resulting in adding more words to describe the scene. |

It is also interesting that he embellishes on language that is not present in the text ("and the red caps at the very, very top").

| 19–20 (two-page spread) | Monkeys! Who what monkeys gray caps and brown caps and blue caps and the red caps at the very, very top! | • He captures the excitement in the illustration of this two-page spread with his own improvisation of language—"Monkeys!"—and also adds "at the very, very top!" (Wheras the actual text is not embellished)
 • He describes the caps in the correct sequence. |

Often when children first begin to enter stage 3 of reading this story, they repeat the dialogue between the peddler and the monkeys. It is also typical that children in this stage move between past and present tense as they connect the pages of the text to form story. English learners in particular also vary between their own language or syntax, and story language.

Conclusion

This chapter represents an adaptation of Sulzby's work on emergent literacy. Of particular focus is reading stories aloud repeatedly in order for students to understand the meaning of the stories and become familiar with the English syntax of stories. As children hear the sound of stories, they transfer it into their own language use and written composition over time. As with other methods, it is the consistency and regularity of practice that allows the children to truly benefit. Although this practice pertains primarily to students in the emergent stages of literacy, it can also benefit early readers as well. Many of our first-grade classes begin the year with bins of emergent literacy, or "star," books to immediately provide familiar literacy practices.

Suggested Books to Use for Emergent Storybook Read-Aloud

The Three Bears, by Byron Barton
Big Al, by Andrew Clements
Will I Have a Friend? by Miriam Cohen
Are You My Mother? by Patricia Eastman
The Three Billy Goats Gruff, by Paul Galdone
The Ginger Bread Boy, by Paul Galdone
A Pocket for Corduroy, by Don Freeman
Corduroy, by Don Freeman

Little Red Riding Hood, by Jacob Grimm
Jamaica's Find, by Juanita Havill
Peter's Chair, by Ezra Jack Keats
The Snowy Day, by Ezra Jack Keats
Leo the Late Bloomer, by Robert Kraus
Carrot Seed, by Ruth Krauss
Red Riding Hood, by James Marshall
Caps for Sale, by Esphyr Slobodkina
The Little Engine That Could, by Piper Watty
Bunny Cakes, by Rosemary Wells
The Little Red Mouse, the Red Ripe Strawberry, and the Big Hungry Bear, by Audrey and Don Wood
Little Red Hen, by Harriet Ziefert
Harry the Dirty Dog, by Gene Zion

Professional Reading

Calkins, Lucy McCormick. 2001. *The Art of Teaching Reading*. New York: Addison-Wesley.

Sulzby, Elizabeth. 1985. "Children's Emergent Reading of Favorite Storybooks: A Developmental Study." *Reading Research Quarterly* 20: 458–481.

———. 1991. "Assessment of Emergent Literacy: Storybook Reading." *The Reading Teacher* 44 (7), 498–500.

6

Shared Reading

Shared reading is the driving force underlying a balanced literacy program and contributes to all aspects of it.

—Brenda Parkes, *Read It Again!*

What Is Shared Reading?

"Catch me, catch me, if you can!" The children in Ms. Mamdou's first-grade class chant along rhythmically as she points below each word on the last page of *Dan the Flying Man*. As Carlos reads the last lines, his body also sways in time with the words while he shouts them with a sense of confidence. Sitting beside him is May, who smiles as she moves rhythmically with the rest of the class but is not yet vocalizing her words. Carlos is an English learner who came to the United States during March of kindergarten and is in the speech emergence stage of second language acquisition (see "Stages of Second Language Acquisition" in Chapter 1). Along with the rest of the class, he has been exposed to this shared reading text repeatedly since mid-September. Now, in October of first grade, he is comfortable chiming in with the repetitive lines in the text. May arrived in the United States with her family a month ago from China. She is positively and actively engaged in the shared reading experience but has not yet internalized the repetitive lines. Soon, she will also be chiming along with her classmates as she engages regularly alongside them each day during this fifteen- to twenty-minute time period called shared reading.

When you watch a well-orchestrated shared reading session, it not only seems effortless but also draws you in. The learning seems to be incidental, but when planned deliberately and strategically, the lesson meets the needs of all learners. Shared reading directly addresses Margaret Mooney's (1990) notion of *with*. It is a collaborative learning experience in which students read with the teacher as she navigates them through the text. Students become engaged in the reading of the text as well as in the thinking work of shared reading. Here all sources of information (semantics, syntax, graphophonics, and pragmatics) are explicitly modeled and practiced in an integrated fashion. Knowing that proficient readers use all four sources of information simultaneously to process text, teachers use shared reading to demonstrate strategies that children will use when reading independently.

Foundations of Shared Reading

Shared reading was developed from the work of Donald Holdaway (1979) when working with English learners in Australia. It is a classroom practice that emulates the experience that some students have when engaging in bedtime stories with their parents (lap reading). This experience was found to better prepare children for the challenge of learning to read once they entered school. Because the child is in such close proximity to the text while being read to, he sees how his parents read the markings that are on the page and the connections those markings have with the illustrations. Children with these experiences quickly learn concepts about print (good readers read from left to right and top to bottom, turn the pages from left to right, and read the words on the page; words make sentences; etc.) and that sometimes the special features of the text make Mom or Dad read more quickly or slowly, with excitement or with sadness. These intimate and enjoyable experiences with text help students prepare for more complex understandings of print and books once they enter school. You will notice that these home experiences are the same as the emergent storybook reading experiences we describe in Chapter 5.

Context in Our Book

Shared reading is the time of day when children learn how to read text and make meaning when being read to while *seeing* the text. Teachers model effective reading behaviors while the students see how the text is organized to support the reading. Teachers model their thinking and where it comes from as students see the text during a teacher think-aloud. The visibility of the text with modeling truly makes shared reading an effective method for teaching reading. Students can actually see what the teacher is reading and how she is working through the text to decode and make sense of it. For English learners, this visible access to text makes the connections between oral and written language explicit. They see the symbols, words, and pictures when trying to understand the teacher's oral language. These visual clues help English learners follow along and remain engaged in the story. The difference between shared reading and emergent story-book reading is that in shared reading, the text is enlarged and there is attention paid to print in order to transition students into conventional reading.

The classroom transcript of a shared reading lesson that appears later in this chapter (Figure 6–6) is reflected upon with attention to students' second language acquisition levels and how language is developed through teacher modeling, text selection, and opportunities to talk with classmates.

Language Theory in Practice

Shared reading provides opportunities to build a safe and comfortable learning environment. The intimate setting around an enjoyable book helps lower students' affective filter in order to develop language (see "Affective Filter Hypothesis" in Chapter 1). Whether in the whole-group setting or during a pair-share, English learners can feel safe trying out language. In order to help maintain a low affective filter, it is important to plan partnerships carefully across levels of second language acquisition (see Figure 1–2).

During shared reading, the teacher reads books that are slightly above the children's literacy levels with attention to the language of the text. Also, the text used during shared reading is large enough for the students to see the pictures and the text as the teacher reads. This visual, along with the gestures and expressions the teacher uses when reading, help make the content and language comprehensible for the students. All of these intentional strategies, strategic partnerships, opportunities for purposeful talk, dramatic readings, and enlarged text (visuals) at a level slightly above the students' literacy and language abilities help students develop language during shared reading.

What Does Shared Reading Look Like?

Key Elements (Across All Levels of Readers)

Shared reading provides opportunities for reinforcing and developing oral language. Students become familiar with various forms of written language and the many purposes for using language. A key element of shared reading is repeated readings, which help students develop a sense of automaticity in reading. While initial readings allow children to make predictions, repeated readings familiarize them with the text and lead them to make self-corrections (Holdaway 1979). The repeated exposure to text provides opportunities to widen and deepen their experiences with new vocabulary and syntax. English learners also have opportunities to practice their oral language in a supportive environment when invited to chime in during shared reading. Figure 6–1 describes the purposes for shared reading and Figure 6–2 lists the teacher's and students' roles during shared reading.

- To re-create rich *bedtime*-type reading experiences
- To provide opportunities for everyone to participate and feel successful as a reader
- To make accessible a text that may be too difficult for students to read alone (input comprehension hypothesis)
- To lay the foundation for reading and writing skills, strategies, and behaviors
- To teach the structure and organization of different genres of text to help with comprehension
- To serve as a bridge between read-aloud and independent reading
- To serve as the foundation for preparing students for conventional reading
- To help children come to make sense of the way they read when they can decode text for themselves with fluency

FIGURE 6–1: Purposes of Shared Reading

ROLE OF THE TEACHER

- Plan lessons and select texts that address the students' language and literacy needs.
- Select texts that will excite children about reading (nonfiction or fiction).
- Make his or her thinking transparent as he or she asks: Does this make sense? (semantics), Does this sound right? (syntax), Does this look right? (graphophonics), and What does this mean in this context? (pragmatics).
- Demonstrate and develop specific reading behaviors and strategies.
- Provide many opportunities for students to explore and identify letter-sound relationships in meaningful contexts.
- Practice reading selected texts and strategically plan for stops and discussion.
- Observe students' participation in the reading of the text and during whole-group and partnership discussions.

ROLE OF THE STUDENTS

- Engage in the collaborative construction of meaning.
- Follow along in the text and match spoken words with written ones.
- Read aloud with the teacher when prompted or invited.
- Understand concepts of print such as directionality, book orientation, and word and sentence concepts.
- Become familiar with phonemic awareness, such as matching sounds, rhyming words, identifying sounds, and counting syllables.
- Think about what is going on in the story while noticing how letters and words work to build the story.
- Make predictions about the reading.
- Self-regulate predictions based upon evidence from the text.
- Make connections to their personal experiences and across the text.

FIGURE 6–2: Teacher and Student Roles in Shared Reading

Selecting Texts for Shared Reading

Text selected for shared reading should be interesting and highly enjoyable. You want children to become excited about reading and eager to pick up a book on their own and try out the strategies taught during shared reading. Children should see the value and beauty of literature that they independently do not have access to just quite yet. Those hilarious, scary, quirky, sad, mysterious, or informational books completely draw children into the world of books so that they never want to leave. It is an instructional way of motivating children to want to learn how to read, or to keep reading for many purposes.

Finding and using the appropriate text is the key. "When intriguing texts are chosen, high levels of engagement and personal connection should move our students to accountable talk" (Fountas and Pinnell 2001, 68). In order to get students talking about books, you need to give them texts with interesting content or an engaging story to get them thinking and talking. They need to be able to connect with the text.

Texts for shared reading can include books, short stories, excerpts from books, articles, poems, stories from student anthologies, interactive writing pieces, fairy tales, folktales, myths, fables, and fictional and nonfictional sources of information. It is important to expose children to a wide variety of texts and genres of literature to provide variations in language use and structure (Cummins 2003). Exploration into the different features of a variety of texts will expand and deepen students' level of comprehension. Further, it will expose them to models of language in a variety of contexts. Figure 6–3 provides a list of questions to consider when selecting texts for shared reading experiences.

Once you have selected a text, it is important to provide visible access to the text and illustrations through an enlarged text during the shared reading. Even if individual copies are available for each student,

* Is it an enjoyable book/text?
* Is the plot familiar to the students' lives?
* Is there a strong story line?
* Are there memorable or interesting characters to discuss and relate to?
* Does the book provide illustrations that support the text?
* Does the text have repetitive or predictable sentences, words, or ideas that can invite students to join in the reading?
* Is the text challenging enough to teach students something new or refine their reading skills and strategies?
* What are the text's different supports and challenges for vocabulary and oral language development?
* Is there room for developing the story or taking the plot in different directions?
* Nonfiction: Is the structure of the text helpful in teaching elements of nonfiction (e.g., table of contents, headings, captions, text boxes, index, charts)?

FIGURE 6–3: Questions to Consider When Selecting Texts for a Shared Reading Lesson

the enlarged text is necessary for the students to see how you are making sense of the text when you point to places in the text that support your language or thinking. For example, if you are talking about a book with lots of animals, you will point to the illustration of an animal as you speak its name. This helps the students better understand your oral language. Enlarged texts also help students

- actively engage with the text
- notice patterns in words (letter-sound relationships)
- see how words work and are put together to form meaningful sentences
- attend to the structural patterns of sentences and paragraphs
- see how structural features affect how the text is read by the teacher
- notice punctuation (quotation marks, commas, periods, exclamation marks, question marks) and how it works
- see the interaction between the text and the pictures
- clearly see the layout or organization of the text, which helps with comprehension (e.g., chunking text into smaller meaningful units to aid with comprehension)
- see where the teacher's thinking comes from

Enlarged text can take on many forms. Figure 6–4 shows different sources of enlarged text to use with emergent and early readers versus transitional and self-extending readers.

EMERGENT AND EARLY READERS	TRANSITIONAL AND SELF-EXTENDING READERS

Big books
  • Narratives
  • Informational text
  • Poems
  • Songs
  • Nursery rhymes
	All sources of text below can be copied, transferred onto overhead transparencies, or copied onto chart paper.

Charts (original, bought, or copied)
  • Poems
  • Chants
  • Nursery rhymes
  • Songs
	Typed text
	  • Picture books
	  • Early chapter books

Time for Kids (teacher poster) Interactive writing pieces	Magazine articles Poetry Newspaper articles Short texts (e.g., *The Stories Julian Tells*, by Ann Cameron, 1989) Excerpts from texts (various genres) Comprehension passages from standardized tests *Time for Kids* (teacher poster and student copies)

FIGURE 6–4: Sources of Enlarged Text

Structure of Shared Reading for Emergent and Early Readers at Different Levels of Second Language Acquisition

Shared reading for emergent and early readers should be planned daily for fifteen to twenty minutes. The books you select must be very predictable. The repetition of these predictable texts develops confidence and fosters nonconventional reading (pretend reading). Repetition of sentence structure is also very important in text selection. The repetitive models of language will help develop oral language. The goals for emergent and early readers are that students enjoy reading, have opportunities to revisit text (reread), and become active readers by thinking, talking, and acting out the stories.

Typically, emergent and early readers gather together on the rug to share in the reading of a text. This brings the students in close to the text so they can follow along as the teacher reads. Students get excited to hear a story while looking at the illustrations. The excitement grows when there is a repetitive sentence structure and they are asked to chime in with the teacher. Sometimes they won't even wait to be invited; they just catch on and the excitement of being able to read the text has them calling out the repetitive sentence. During a shared reading experience, emergent and early readers feel successful.

The reading of the text is also a model for children of what fluent reading and language sound like. Children hear the rhythm of the text as the teacher reads with expression and intonation. These models of fluency support children as they learn how language is used to read books. It brings to life the interrelationship of the four cueing systems. (See Figure 3–1.)

Before the Read

The initial reading of a text during shared reading provides opportunities for students to practice making predictions. By discussing the front cover, including the title and illustrations, students can use their prior knowledge to anticipate what the story will be about. These predictions will be revisited during the read and extended as students hear the story. When revisiting a text, the teacher can begin the shared reading lesson by reminding students what the text was about.

During the Read

The key to a shared reading lesson is what happens during the read. When introducing a new text, the teacher should read the story from beginning to end so that students can get a sense of the story. To make the initial read more effective, the teacher should point out what she is reading and how the text is supported by the illustrations. This will help English learners follow along in their comprehension of the text.

Now that the students have a basic understanding of the text, there are a number of strategies a teacher can focus on to guide students through reading the text. These include

- allowing or inviting students to join in the reading when there are repetitive sentence structures or familiar words; this will help students practice automaticity when reading and speaking
- pausing where the text supports rhyme and phonemic awareness
- highlighting a repetitive phonics pattern or pointing out sight words for the word wall
- stopping to allow students to make personal connections with the text and share their thinking with a partner
- practicing a language function, such as character descriptions, to continue to build English oral language

For readers in the emergent and early stages of reading, the power of shared reading lies in the process of reading the text together. The experience of integrating the four cueing systems in the act of reading serves as a model for what students can do with their independent texts. Student engagement during the reading of the text is key to their ability to word solve while reading and to comprehend the text.

After the Read

In some respects, the measure of success at the end of a reading is students' desire to hear the text again. The more they want to read the text, the more they will learn through repeated readings. This, however, does not mean there aren't opportunities to talk about the comprehension of the text in pairs after the reading of the text. As with interactive read-aloud (see Chapter 4), students can discuss ideas ranging from character motivation to content area information, depending upon the text selection. The difference is that with shared reading, the purpose is to balance meaning, syntax, and visual sources of information, rather than just focusing on meaning or comprehension as in interactive read-aloud.

Shared Reading in Action

Now that we know what is involved in a shared reading lesson for emergent and early readers, let's take a look inside a real classroom with English learners at various levels of second language acquisition. Figure 6–5 shows the lesson plan that was developed, and Figure 6–6 contains a transcript of the implementation of the lesson.

Purpose/Objective/Focus for Literacy and Language

- During independent reading, it was observed that the students had difficulty connecting pages of the text. This particular text forces students to carry their predictions from one page to another.
- During read-aloud, students are making predictions regularly but not supporting them with evidence from the book (pictures or text). This text gives inferential evidence to determine the next animal through the sounds each animal makes and the manner in which the character encounters them.

Outcomes/Standards

- Make predictions based on the cover and illustrations (emergent level—semantic).
- Confirm predictions by referring back to the text for support (early level—semantic).

Selection of Text

Walking Through the Jungle, by Debbie Harter with illustrations by Julie Lacome

Synopsis of book: A young boy goes on an imaginary walk through the jungle (this must be inferred through the pictures). Before he encounters different animals, he hears noises that give him clues as to which animal he will see. The way in which the boy walks through the jungle also gives the reader a hint about which animal will be next. There are many opportunities to use prediction-confirmation skills.

Resources Needed

- Big book stand or easel
- Pointer
- Concrete examples of jungle animals—have picture cards for animals to compare what students predict with what is in the text
- Whiteboard for placing student predictions (either write or draw predictions or place pictures of animals)
- In later lessons:
  - Frames for words that match up with first letter of names of students
  - Nonfictional book with pictures of animals in jungles

Potential Text Challenges for English Learners

- Three pattern changes, with the last one being a surprise at the end.
- Students may not understand the ending. The text does not set the readers up for the ending.
- Students may get locked into making predictions and not understand that the story is imaginary.
- Vocabulary challenges on every other page for walking (*creeping, stomping, wading*).
- Background knowledge of what kinds of animals are in a jungle.

FIGURE 6–5: Planning Shared Reading for Emergent and Early Readers: *Walking Through the Jungle*, by Debbie Harter with illustrations by Julie Lacome (1993)

Introduction (Activating Prior Knowledge)

- "Today, we are going to read a book together called *Walking Through the Jungle*, by Debbie Harter and Julie Lacome. Let's look at the cover. Do you see how the little boy is standing in the middle of this jungle? Look how the jungle has so many trees and flowers. Turn to your partner and tell him or her what you see in the jungle."
- "Oh, I also see eyes! I wonder whose eyes they are?! Let's read the title again together; *Walking Through the Jungle*. Hmmm, so this little boy is walking through the jungle. He doesn't look like he is dressed to go into the jungle. Hmmm, I wonder what he is going to see while he walks through the jungle?"
- Have students make predictions.
- "Shall we find out?"

Reading the Text

- Remember to keep thinking about what the little boy will find while he walks through the jungle.
- Read the text through once with the students while confirming or disconfirming predictions.
- Read the text a second time, getting students to chime in, particularly in the following parts:
  - Sounds animals make, in special font
  - Name of animal (now that they know which animals are in the text)

Discussion Prompts to Use During and After the Reading

- As each animal is revealed, in addition to confirming and disconfirming predictions, also discuss the evidence that tells them whether or not they were correct (e.g., check sound animal makes, the little boy's actions).
- Have students turn and talk to each other before giving ideas to the full group to allow students to have opportunities to talk.
- Tell students that when they read their own books, they can also check the pictures to see if their predictions matched what happened in the book.

Follow-up Lessons/Readings

- Background knowledge of jungle animals
- Fantasy versus reality
- Vocabulary: walking: *creeping*, *wading*, and so on, and how they connect to the overall comprehension of text; act out the words
- Word work with key words and beginning letter of students' names
- Sight words
- Patterns, same words
- Punctuation: ? !

FIGURE 6–5: *Continued*

CLASSROOM TRANSCRIPT	REFLECTION
Ms. Johnson: Today we are going to read this book together called *Walking Through the Jungle,* by Debbie Harter and Julie Lacome.	The teacher points underneath each word of the title. She reminds the students to look at the words as she points and says them aloud.
Let's see what's on the cover. Oh, here's a little boy who is standing here. It looks like he is standing in a jungle. Let's look at other parts of the cover page.	As the teacher thinks aloud while she looks over the cover, she points to each item as she talks to facilitate meaning.
Ms. Johnson: Tell your partner what you see in the jungle on the front page.	The teacher asks them to turn and talk so that they all have an opportunity to talk and to rehearse what they want to say. Oftentimes, she pairs up students with differing language abilities in order to scaffold their language development.
[Students take a moment to think and then turn and talk with a partner.]	
Ms. Johnson: So what did you share with your partner? What do you see in the jungle?	Two students immediately start to speak in Spanish about the front cover. This helps them continue to develop their cognitive abilities. They will get to hear their classmates' ideas in English during share out.
Samantha: I see eyes.	
Ms. Johnson: Can you come up and point to the eyes?	
Henry: I see a flower.	
Ms. Johnson: What else do you see?	
Gustavo: I see eyes.	
Ms. Johnson: Do you see different eyes? [Student points to two different sets of eyes.]	
Ms. Johnson: Whom do those eyes belong to?	Having children point to what they are seeing allows them to be more motivated and active, and it helps them convey meaning without being fully reliant on the English language.
Henry: To the flower.	
Ms. Johnson: Do flowers have eyes?	
Class: No.	
Ms. Johnson: What kind of thing?	
Gustavo: The person.	
Ms. Johnson: People—you think that people have eyes.	You will notice the teacher repeats back the correct syntax: *people have eyes.*
Gustavo: [Nods yes]	The goal here is to draw all the students into the world of this story.
Ms. Johnson: Do you think he is going to see people in the jungle?	The teacher is setting the students up to predict what will happen in the text based upon what they see on the front cover and in the title.
Alex: No, he's going to see animals.	
Caroline: A giraffe.	

FIGURE 6–6: Shared Reading in Action: Transcript of *Walking Through the Jungle*

CLASSROOM TRANSCRIPT	REFLECTION
Alex: A bird.	
Ms. Johnson: He might see a bird.	
Samantha: A lion.	
Ms. Johnson: What's your prediction? What do you think will happen?	Notice that the teacher uses the word *prediction* but scaffolds the term with *What do you think will happen?*
Henry: A monkey.	
Ms. Johnson: What do you think?	
Abraham: Dogs.	
Ms. Johnson: Do you think you would find dogs in the jungle?	When children are giving their ideas, the teacher asks them to think about the context of the jungle—would they likely find a dog in the jungle? She knows that some of the students do not have the schema for a jungle, but she wants them to confirm some of their predictions against some evidence from the title— *Jungle*, another source of information.
Abraham: No.	
Ms. Johnson: You don't think so? Let's find out. Should we find out? Let's find out. I want you to look at the words when I point to them.	
[Ms. Johnson reads the text: "Sssssss."]	For the first few pages, the teacher simply asks the students to predict and confirm on the following page when the answer is given. She pauses slightly in the text prior to when the answer is given to enable the students to chime in with her. You will notice after two or three animals, the students chime in together on *elephant.*
Ms. Johnson: What do you think it will be? Ssss . . .	
Class: Snake!	
[Continues reading, "Grrrrrrr."]	
Steven: A bear.	
Jennifer: A bumblebee.	
Jose: A lion.	
[Turns the page]	
Caroline: Tiger.	
Ms. Johnson: "Trump, trump, trump."	
Lilian: Elephant.	
[Students chime in on *elephant.*]	
Ms. Johnson: "Roarrr."	Now that the students are accustomed to the basic structure of the text, the teacher attempts to draw the students' attention to the central plot line where the boy is the main character. So far, they are very aware of the various animals; however, the teacher wants them to think about the relationship of the boy to the animals, so she reemphasizes the repeated line *Is he following me?* (continues)
Caroline: Lion.	
Steven: Bear.	
Henry: Monkey.	
Ms. Johnson: Do you think you would find a bear?	

FIGURE 6–6: *Continued*

CLASSROOM TRANSCRIPT	REFLECTION
Steven: No, lion. Lion.	
Ms. Johnson: Do you think all the animals are following him?	
Class: Yeah.	
Ms. Johnson: "Chitter chatter."	
Gustavo: A monkey.	
Ms. Johnson: Why do you think that? Is it a monkey?	Now that the students are predicting the animals and at least a few students at a time are predicting correctly, the teacher wants them to be accountable to their predictions with text or picture evidence. What clues does the author give to cause the reader to predict the next animal to come?
Gustavo: The sound. It's a monkey because he's [student makes the motion of swinging arms raised overhead and sways back and forth].	The students are starting to notice that the sound that the animal makes gives a clue. Also the motion the little boy makes mimics each subsequent animal.
[Teacher rereads the clue on the page of swinging.]	
Ms. Johnson: [Continues to read] He was swinging in the other one, what about now?	Now, the teacher wants to focus their attention on the boy's actions as a way to help them confirm predictions.
Samantha: Piecing, piecing [Looking a bit anxious, she restates in Spanish, *pisando*].	It is interesting here that Samantha makes the walking motion with her hands and legs but tries to say *pisando*, which is *walking* in Spanish. You will notice that she approximates her pronunciation of *pisar* combined with the English present-tense inflectional ending *-ing*.
Ms. Johnson: Snap, snap.	
Henry: A bear, a monkey.	
Ms. Johnson: Why?	
Henry: Because I say it.	
Ms. Johnson: Do you see any more clues in the picture?	
Julie: A crocodile.	
[Student comes up and points to the clues in the illustration that look like a crocodile.]	
[Teacher reads on.]	

FIGURE 6–6: *Continued*

CLASSROOM TRANSCRIPT	REFLECTION
Ms. Johnson: "Hope he isn't hungry." Why is he saying that? *Julie:* He's hungry. *Ms. Johnson:* You think he is afraid the crocodile would eat him? *Class:* Yeah.	Knowing that the ending of the story may pose a challenge for the students, the teacher draws attention to this last line, which is a change from the predictable pattern set before. She asks them why the author might make this statement.

FIGURE 6–6: *Continued*

Summary of Features from This Lesson That Support English Learners and Language Development

- The text selection contains a repetitive and highly predictable pattern so that English learners can join in the oral language of reading the text.

- The illustrations correlate with the text, making it easy for ELs to make meaning from the text and the English language.

- Though the students will need additional instruction on the jungle, their familiarity with animals can help connect the text to their personal experiences and prior knowledge.

- There were some unfamiliar vocabulary words, such as *creeping* and *wading*, so as a follow-up lesson the teacher can have the students act out the actions (verbs) for each animal from the book.

- There were opportunities to teach beginning sounds and letters (e.g., /s/ is the beginning sound in *snake*, which is the same beginning sound and spelling for the names of some students in the class—Steven, Samantha).

- Subsequent lessons can involve a greater level of overall comprehension of the text (e.g., this is an imaginary story about a boy who thinks he might encounter these animals in a jungle, but he is just playing at home).

Possible Literacy Goals for Emergent and Early Readers During Shared Reading

Teachers often ask, "So what do I teach during shared reading? What kind of lessons can I cover during shared reading?" Figure 6–7 lists a variety of possible literacy objectives for emergent and early readers. They have been separated by cueing systems to highlight how we continue to develop our cueing systems through shared reading. These

CUEING SYSTEM	RELATED GOALS
Semantic	Identify the parts of a book (front and back covers, title page, name of the author, name of the illustrator). Make predictions based on the cover and illustrations. Read the illustrations to tell the story (pretend read). Make connections from the text to life experiences and across texts. Identify and describe story elements (characters, setting, plot in sequence). Identify important events from the text. Make and confirm predictions throughout the text. Retell familiar or shared reading stories. Identify and retell favorite parts, characters, or scenes in the story. Respond to who, what, when, where, and how questions.
Syntactic	Follow words from left to right as the teacher reads. Identify letters, words, and sentences. Identify and correctly use singular and plural nouns. Identify and correctly use contractions. Identify and explain the purpose of different end punctuation marks (declarative, exclamatory, interrogative). Recognize how text is read when different end punctuation is used.
Graphophonic	Recognize and name all upper- and lower-case letters of the alphabet. Identify individual letter sounds. Identify, produce, and match rhyming words. Identify and match initial, medial, and ending sounds. Segment individual sounds in a word. Add, delete, or change target sounds in order to change a word. Orally identify the number of syllables in a word. Begin to match all consonant and short and long vowel sounds to letters. Distinguish and name initial, medial, and ending sounds and their corresponding letter(s). Read simple one-syllable words. Read simple high-frequency words. Identify, read, and create new words from the study of word families (onsets and rimes). Use knowledge of consonant blends, long and short vowels, digraphs, and *r*-controlled letter-sound relationships to read words. Understand and read compound words and contractions. Read and understand inflectional morphemes (-*s*, -*ed*, -*ing*) and root words. Read aloud in a way that models natural speech.
Pragmatics	Describe characteristics of fictional and nonfictional texts. Identify environmental print, visual literacy, and everyday print (signs, labels, billboards, logos, storybooks, poems, etc.).

FIGURE 6–7: Literacy Goals for Emergent and Early Readers

objectives were adapted from the California and New York State language arts standards because we believe in the importance of meeting and even exceeding state standards.

The Structure of Shared Reading for Transitional and Self-Extending Readers Across Levels of Second Language Acquisition

Shared reading further supports transitional and self-extending readers to more deeply comprehend text when they read independently. They are taught and encouraged to use strategies effectively when reading both narrative and content area texts. Through the use of narrative texts, teachers can support readers in activating or building background knowledge, establishing purposes for reading, using knowledge of text structure and genre to comprehend text, using appropriate resources to meet their purpose for reading, establishing word knowledge connections, and learning to problem solve when confronted with challenging texts. In the content areas, shared reading can help students learn science concepts, comprehend social studies themes, and strategically work through math word problems. Further, shared reading is a great context for teaching students how to work through comprehension passages they will encounter on standardized reading tests. It is a great opportunity for teachers to model test-taking strategies. Even though shared reading was originally used as a strategy for helping young children who were just beginning to learn to read, many teachers have found the value of shared reading in deepening students' levels of comprehension across subject areas and texts. It provides a comfortable, enjoyable arena for sharing ideas about text and coming to new understandings through interaction with others to create and re-create schemata. "Students have the right to *experience* reading—not just the skill of reading but the experience of words making us see the world in a different way. . . . Shared reading is the heart of the reading curriculum" (Allen 2000, 79).

Before the Read

Just as with emergent and early readers, the selection of text is key when planning shared reading for English learners at the transitional and self-extending levels of reading. Teachers must access multiple copies of text, make copies of short texts, and/or create overheads of a text to make it visible so students can follow along. In addition, a number of lessons will require students to go back into the text to identify and note text support for their ideas or practice other note-taking skills. Students will then need writing utensils, sticky notes, highlighters, or any other note-taking materials necessary to fully participate in the lesson. These preparations are important to keep the shared reading lesson focused on the skill or strategy at hand. You do not want the novelty of these items to interfere with learning.

Unlike with emergent and early readers, a teacher might not do a full read of the text with transitional and self-extending readers prior to focusing on a particular strategy or skill. Prereading activities might include generating background knowledge by asking students to make personal connections with the content or theme of the text, making predictions, and exploring text challenges such as vocabulary, sentence structure, and text organization. For nonfictional texts, this might be an exploration into the features of expository text, such as the table of contents, headings, subheadings, captions and pictures, and key vocabulary to aid in comprehension.

During the Read

Depending on the classroom setup, students can remain at their seats or gather together on the rug for shared reading. The important thing is that they have visible access to the text. The job of the teacher is to provide explicit strategy lessons for the students to try out while he reads the text aloud to them. As the teacher reads, the students must be following the meaning of the text to prepare for talk and discussion. The teacher should plan pauses in the reading to allow for students to stop and talk, stop and jot, or simply stop and think. What the students talk about will depend on the literacy goal for the lesson.

After the Read

The use of graphic organizers helps English learners demonstrate their comprehension of text in simplified language. Without the pressure of having to write out complex sentences, English learners at early stages of second language acquisition can use their simple sentences or one- or two-word utterances to record key ideas on an organizer. Further, designing organizers that can support language development along with literacy development is helpful for students at all levels of second language acquisition (see Appendix D). Though graphic organizers are a great tool to support English learners, it is not necessary to have students fill one out after every shared reading lesson. It is just one of many possible application or extension activities that can follow a shared reading lesson. Others include having an oral pair-share, writing a response in a reading journal, or having a whole-group discussion.

Shared Reading in Action

Figure 6–8 demonstrates a shared reading lesson for transitional and self-extending readers with literacy and language objectives in mind.

Purpose/Objective/Focus for Literacy and Language

- During independent reading, many ELs were having difficulty comprehending texts beyond the literal level, particularly when there were multiple meanings for words.
- This book, *The Stories Julian Tells*, by Ann Cameron, was read aloud to students previously. The teacher is taking the opportunity to teach a close reading of text with a familiar text.

Outcomes/Standards

- Make predictions based on the plot and confirm with information from the text.
- Use context to determine the meaning of words.
- Understand homographs, or multiple meanings of words.
- Make theories about characters based on their actions, thoughts, and words.
- Read, understand, and use declarative, interrogative, imperative, and exclamatory sentences.

Selection of Text

The Stories Julian Tells, by Ann Cameron

Excerpt from "The Pudding Like a Night on the Sea" (pp. 12–16)

Synopsis of book: In the short story, Julian and Huey watch their father make pudding. After making the pudding, their father asks them to make sure nothing happens to the pudding so that it is ready for their mother when she returns. As their father naps, the two boys decide they want to try a bit of the pudding to see if it indeed tastes like "a raft of lemons" and "like a night on the sea." Tasting a bit turns into tasting most of the pudding. The boys realize they are in trouble for almost finishing the pudding they were to keep safe for their mother.

Resources Needed

- Overhead projector
- Transparencies of pages 12–16
- Overhead markers to highlight and underline key words and phrases
- Student copies of the text (optional)

Potential Text Challenges for English Learners

- Children may not understand that the father is not really upset at the boys; rather, he is using the words *beating* and *whipping* in reference to them making the pudding and not what he was going to do to the boys. Students may be too focused on the words used.

Introduction (Activating Prior Knowledge)

- "Today, we are going to be looking closely at a part of the story The Pudding Like a Night on the Sea in the book *The Stories Julian Tells*. Remember how we got a little confused in this part yesterday? Today we will look at how words can have different meanings depending upon the context in which they are used."

(Continues)

FIGURE 6–8: Planning Shared Reading for Transitional and Self-Extending Readers: *The Stories Julian Tells*, by Ann Cameron (1989).

- "Remember in this story when Julian and Huey get carried away and eat most of the pudding their father made for their mother? Then they realized that they might get in trouble so they tried to hide from their father. Let's take a close look at the part of the story when their father discovers that the pudding is gone."
- "Sometimes the same words carry different meanings. Read the following lines: 'There is going to be some beating here now! There is going to be some whipping!' What do you think is happening here? They think they are being punished because they finished the pudding."
- "Let's find out where these words are used in other parts of this text. In order for us to see it better, let's underline all the places where we see these words being used, *beating* and *whipping*." (Underline all the parts where the words are used.)
- Work with the students to highlight the places that imply how the boys are feeling.
- Discuss why the words in the text make the children think that the boys are scared or relieved.

Follow-Up Lessons/Readings

- When the same word is being used, students could ask themselves, "What does the author mean by this?"
- How did the author choose these words purposefully to make the reader (as well as the characters) wonder what was happening?

FIGURE 6–8: *Continued*

Summary of Features from This Lesson That Support English Learners and Language Development

- In this lesson, the teacher has planned according to needs that developed during the read-aloud of this text. English learners often comprehend specific words in a very literal way. Sometimes in texts, the author uses a play on words as a literary device. Instead of avoiding this type of text because it may confuse ELs, the teacher takes the opportunity to use it to teach toward language.

- The teacher breaks down the task of understanding the play-on-words concept by having the students first clearly identify the part of the text in which the words are first used (and the point of confusion). Students then continue to underline other places in the text where the words are repeated.

- Once the words or phrases are located, the teacher pushes the students to find the evidence in the text that helps the reader infer how the characters feel. After students highlight these ideas, the teacher then links this highlighted information to the underlined words. This way the students can see a direct correlation between the words used by the father in the story and how the sons respond.

- Lastly, the teacher pushes the students to see how the characters change in the end when they realize what the father really meant with the words he used.

Possible Literacy Goals for Transitional and Self-Extending Readers During Shared Reading

Once again, to guide teachers' planning of shared reading lessons, we prepared Figure 6–9 to provide teachers with a variety of possible literacy objectives for transitional and self-extending readers. They have been separated by cueing systems to highlight how we continue to develop our cueing systems through shared reading. These objectives were also adapted from the California and New York State language arts standards.

CUEING SYSTEM	RELATED GOALS
Semantic	Use sentences and context to determine the meaning of unknown words.
	Know the meaning of simple prefixes and suffixes.
	Understand antonyms, synonyms, homophones, and homographs.
	Set a purpose when reading.
	Determine the author's purpose.
	Identify the point of view.
	Summarize a story.
	Identify the main idea of a text.
	Ask questions to determine the meaning of a text.
	Restate facts and details in the text to support ideas.
	Recognize cause-and-effect relationships.
	Interpret information from diagrams, charts, and graphs.
	Make comparisons between characters in a story.
	Make comparisons between themselves and a character in a story.
	Make theories about characters based on their actions, thoughts, and words.
	Make theories about characters and how they change throughout the text.
	Question the actions of the characters and how they affected the outcome of the story.
	Make connections between the characters and their setting.
	Make comparisons between characters across texts.
	Compare and contrast plots, settings, and characters across texts.
	Determine how a change in setting could affect the characters, plot, and ending.

(Continues)

FIGURE 6–9: Literacy Goals for Transitional and Self-Extending Readers

CUEING SYSTEM	RELATED GOALS
	Determine the underlying theme or author's message in fictional and nonfictional text.
	Generate alternative endings.
	Generate alternative events in the story and how they may affect the ending.
	Make predictions throughout the text and confirm predictions with text support.
	Use knowledge of table of contents, index, chapter headings, and glossaries to find information in expository text.
	Extract key information for expository text.
	Identify the use of rhythm, rhyme, and alliteration in poetry.
Syntactic	Distinguish between complete and incomplete sentences.
	Identify subject-verb agreement.
	Identify parts of speech such as nouns, verbs, adjectives, and adverbs.
	Identify verb tenses.
	Recognize and read common abbreviations.
	Identify commas and their different roles in text.
	Identify and understand the use of quotation marks.
	Read, understand, and use declarative, interrogative, imperative, and exclamatory sentences.
Graphophonic	Use knowledge of diphthongs and complex vowel letter-sound patterns to read words (e.g., *-eigh, -igh, -ough*).
	Understand and apply basic syllabification rules when reading (open and closed syllables).
	Decode two-syllable nonsense words and regular multisyllabic words.
	Identify and correctly use regular and irregular plurals.
	Read aloud fluently and accurately with appropriate expression, intonation, and prosody.
Pragmatics	Identify and describe the characteristics of a variety of genres (e.g., fairy tales, fables, myths).
	Identify and describe the elements of nonfictional text (table of contents, index, headings, captions, graphs).
	Identify elements of poetry.
	Understand the structure of a paragraph in narrative and nonnarrative text.
	Use genre as a structure and tool for reading and writing.

FIGURE 6–9: *Continued*

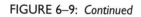

Conclusion

Shared reading is often overlooked as a method of instruction; however, we believe that it is important for developing language for ELs. It is for this reason that we have written this chapter in greater detail perhaps than some of the other chapters. Shared reading is a great opportunity for teachers and students to enjoy stories together that are at a reading and language level slightly above the students' independent level. Essential aspects of shared reading, such as selecting slightly more difficult text and the use of visually stimulating enlarged text, provide *comprehensible input* for learning to occur. Teachers select interesting books to provide lessons in phonology, syntax, semantics, and pragmatics and demonstrate how good readers integrate all these sources of information to comprehend what they read. These lessons will vary depending upon students' levels of literacy development; however, the purpose of shared reading across all literacy levels is to guide students through text and model strategic, thoughtful reading.

Suggested Books to Use for Shared Reading

Big Books

Brown Bear, Brown Bear, What Do You See? by Bill Martin Jr.
Hattie and the Fox, by Mem Fox
Mrs. Wishy-Washy, by Joy Cowley
The Carrot Seed, by Ruth Krauss
Zoo Looking, by Mem Fox
Greedy Cat, by Joy Cowley
Joshua James Likes Trucks, by Catherine Petrie
The Biggest Cake in the World, by Joy Cowley
Ready to Read series, published by Richard C. Owen

For Emergent and Early Readers

Bella Lost Her Moo, by Judith Zorfass
My House Is Your House
The Runaway Pizza
The Wolf's Story

(RIGBY: PO Box 797, Crystal Lake, IL 60039-0797)

From Peanuts to Peanut Butter
Pasta Please
Where Does All the Garbage Go?
Spinning a Web

(Newbridge: PO Box 1270, Littleton, MA 01460)

For Early and Transitional Readers

Adventure Sports on the Edge
Greetings from Route 66

Out in Space
Make Mine Ice Cream

How to Make Masks
Foiled Again
Fossils
The Great Chase

Popcorn Science
Pasta Please
Investigating Your Backyard

(RIGBY: PO Box 797,
Crystal Lake, IL 60039-0797)

(Newbridge: PO Box 1270,
Littleton, MA 01460)

For Transitional and Self-Extending Readers

Can Kids Save the Earth?
The Mighty Ocean
The Tour of the Planets
A World of Change

(RIGBY: PO Box 797, Crystal Lake, IL 60039-0797)

Short Texts for Transitional and Self-Extending Readers

The Stories Julian Tells, by Ann Cameron
Five True Dog Stories, by Margaret Davidson
Childtimes: A Three-Generation Memoir, by Eloise Greenfield

Magazines with Narrative and Informational Articles for Transitional and Self-Extending Readers

Cricket
Highlights
Time for Kids
Click

Spider
Scholastic News
Ranger Rick

Professional Literature on Shared Reading

Allen, Janet. 2000. *Yellow Brick Roads: Shared and Guided Paths to Independent Reading 4–12*. Portland, ME: Stenhouse.

Fisher, Bobbi, and Emily Fisher Medvic. 2000. *Perspectives on Shared Reading: Planning and Practice*. Portsmouth, NH: Heinemann.

Hoyt, Linda, Margaret Mooney, and Brenda Parkes (eds.). 2003. *Exploring Informational Texts: Theory to Practice*. Portsmouth, NH: Heinemann.

Mooney, Margaret E. 1990. *Reading to, with, and by Children*. Katonah, NY: Richard C. Owen.

Parkes, Brenda. 2000. *Read It Again! Revisiting Shared Reading*. Portland, ME: Stenhouse.

Pinnell, Gay Su, and Patricia L. Scharer. 2003. *Teaching for Comprehension in Reading Grades K–2*. New York: Scholastic.

Taberski, Sharon. 2000. *On Solid Ground: Strategies for Teaching Reading K–3*. Portsmouth, NH: Heinemann.

7 Independent Reading Workshop

The more that you read, the more things you will know. The more that you learn, the more places you'll go.

—Dr. Seuss

What Is Independent Reading Workshop?

As you open the door to Ms. Mamdou's first-grade class, she has just finished her minilesson and students are just breaking from their rug spots and taking their "little libraries" to cozy spots in the room. As pairs sit back-to-back in chairs beside their tables, on the rug, and in the corner on cushions, they each seem to have a sense of mission and deliberateness to their actions. After they settle into their spots, they peruse their little libraries and choose a book to read. In each reader's large zip-close plastic bag (her little library) are five books she has chosen as her just-right books. Generally these are books that children can read on their own.

While the children are reading independently, Ms. Mamdou moves around the room strategically to confer with individual readers. She sits beside Marisol, who is reading *The Way I Go to School*, and notices that Marisol has trouble with some of the words she doesn't know because she looks only at the beginning letters and then gives up. Ms. Mamdou reminds Marisol of a previous minilesson where the students were taught to look across the word and check the picture to make sure the word made sense. Next Ms. Mamdou sits alongside José, who is quickly reading *Danny the Dinosaur* page by page, without stopping to look at the pictures. She asks him what he thinks about the story he is reading. José simply responds, "It's good," and gives basic retellings without revealing higher levels of thinking about the book, indicating that he may not be fully comprehending because he is not taking the time to take in all the information in front of him. She asks him to turn a few pages back, and she models how to tell the full story on each page back to herself, including what she sees in both the text and the pictures. Then she has José repeat the same process across a few pages before leaving him. Ms. Mamdou reminds him to do more of this work when he reads so that he can get the most out of each story.

After the children read for about twenty minutes independently, Ms. Mamdou gently reminds the class that it is now partner reading time. Now the pairs move from sitting back-to-back to sitting side by side. One partner selects a book and the two hold the book between them. Ms. Mamdou looks over her record-keeping notes from the week and decides to confer with May and Dennis because she hasn't conferred with them this week. As she reviews her notes quickly, she is reminded that last time she met with them, she had to teach them how to take turns talking. Dennis tends to talk more, and May is perfectly happy with listening. May is an EL who is currently at the intermediate fluency stage of second language acquisition, and Dennis is a native English speaker. Both May and Dennis are reading at similar reading levels and reading the same types of books. Because they are matched by level, they are able to discuss similar books instead of one tutoring the other. Dennis is a strong talker and easily dominates the conversation. He is also a creative thinker who wants to quickly tell May everything that is on his mind. May is a strong reader and tells Ms. Mamdou what she is thinking about while she is reading, but she doesn't do this so readily with her partner. Sometimes May needs a few seconds longer to process what you say to her in order to articulate a response. Dennis is often impulsive and unintentionally takes over the conversation. As Ms. Mamdou comes by, she hears a mostly one-sided conversation and supports them in listening to each other as they continue with their talk time. She whispers in Dennis' ear to remember to wait by counting to three in his head to give May a turn. She also tells May that it is important to share her ideas because she and Dennis both can learn more together if she does.

After the children read with partners and share their ideas, the students methodically return their little libraries in the same fashion as they retrieved them. In no time, the students are now back in their rug spots, ready for the share session.

Each day during independent reading workshop, the class follows the same routine. Ms. Mamdou gathers the class together on the rug to share a minilesson. Then the students go off to read independently so each reader can practice the orchestration of multiple reading strategies alone. Students then read with a partner, and they discuss their book and read together side by side. Each workshop always ends with a whole-class share time so that Ms. Mamdou can draw attention to successful independent and partner work that the entire class can learn from and emulate.

Foundations of Independent Reading Workshop

Independent reading workshop is the time of day when all of your hard work during shared and guided reading, interactive read-aloud, and word work comes together. It is the time when students get a chance to apply everything you have modeled and they have practiced, in whole-group or small-group settings, on their own. Students need these opportunities *during* the school day to read on their own. With a diverse student population with various home-literacy experiences, we cannot assume that they go home and read. We need to make sure we provide those cherished moments with books in school. The more time they have with books, the more they will learn about the world and build background knowledge. Books give students opportunities to learn beyond their here and now.

Independent reading workshop gives all children a chance to be readers. It gives them a chance to select a book they want to read and have some quiet time to themselves and their thinking. "What's more, it's fun, it's easy to implement and manage, and kids love it. They get to choose books they are interested in, to talk about those books with their friends, and to have uninterrupted time in school—to read!" (Routman 2003, 87). It also gives teachers a chance to learn about their students as readers. While children read, the teacher will have opportunities to talk one-on-one with them and provide individualized instruction. Figure 7–1 lists the purposes for reading workshop. Figure 7–2 describes the teacher's and students' roles in reading workshop.

Context in Our Book

Independent reading workshop provides English learners exposure to various models of language. When they read books they are learning new vocabulary words and seeing how the English language is

- To develop a love of reading
- To provide students opportunities to process and apply reading skills and strategies taught during shared and guided reading
- To provide students opportunities to build fluency by reading books at their independent level
- To help students develop their independent reading skills
- To develop academic language

FIGURE 7–1: Purposes of Independent Reading Workshop

ROLE OF THE TEACHER

- Help students select books at their independent reading level.
- Guide students through the application of skills and strategies during minilessons.
- Develop individual readers when conferring with students.
- Provide a library full of books that represent different reading levels, genres, and cultures.

ROLE OF THE STUDENTS

- Read, read, read!
- Choose books at their independent level.
- Read and share their thinking with a partner and with the class.
- Take responsibility for their reading.

FIGURE 7–2: Teacher and Student Roles in Independent Reading Workshop

structured (syntax) and organized (discourse). The opportunity to read widely and often helps ELs develop language naturally. In this chapter these opportunities for vicarious language development are emphasized along with more intentional, explicit language instruction. During minilessons, talk time, and sharing out, teachers will see how they can make language explicit so that children can develop both cognition and oral language.

Language Theory in Practice

Daily opportunities to see, read, and talk about texts help English learners develop language. However, "recreational reading is not enough to guarantee full competence and the acquisition of 'academic language.' It is, rather, the bridge, the missing link that makes harder reading and more demanding input more comprehensible" (Krashen 2004, 3). Independent reading workshop will also involve explicit instruction on how to talk about text. Teachers will provide minilessons on expectations for talk and models of language functions and forms (see "Language Functions and Forms" in Chapter 1). Further, when students talk with their partner they will have opportunities to try out academic language in a comfortable setting. They select an enjoyable book that they are able to read and comprehend, making their talk time less stressful. This lowers their affective filter, allowing for comprehensible input (see "Second Language Acquisition" in Chapter 1). They are motivated and able to learn language.

What Does Independent Reading Workshop Look Like?

Key Elements (Across All Levels of Readers)

During independent reading workshop all readers need "a predictable structure because it is the work children do that will be changing and complex" (Calkins 2001, 66). Though the structure may look different from one classroom to the next, it typically includes a minilesson, time for independent reading by students, individual conferring sessions with the teacher and students, a time for partnership talk, and a whole-group share. Figure 7–3 summarizes the structure of the independent reading workshop.

Minilessons

Minilessons are intended to teach children how to become thoughtful independent readers. They are the bridge between what you are doing during guided practice and independence. They will include reading skills, comprehension strategies, models of fluent reading, models of language, think-alouds, and celebrations of reading. (For more information regarding the structure of minilessons, please refer to the minilesson section in Chapter 8.)

At the beginning of the school year a teacher can begin to plan minilessons by thinking about the following questions: *What can independent readers think and do? What are my expectations for my students as readers by the end of the school year?* When I was working with second-grade teachers in Los Angeles, they generated a list of goals that included helping children to

- enjoy reading
- be able to just sit and read for long periods of time
- be able to understand what they are reading
- make connections with the text from their lives and other books
- read fluently, with expression and a natural speed
- stop and think when they are reading
- be able to talk about what they read

- Minilesson
- Independent Reading Time with Conferring
- Partner Talk Time with Conferring
- Whole-Group Share

FIGURE 7–3: Structure of the Independent Reading Workshop

- be able to read longer books and make connections from one chapter to the next
- read chapter books and remember what they read from beginning to end

This list helped the teachers better understand the purpose of minilessons.

Independent Reading Time

The independent reading time is one of the most important times during the reading workshop because it is the time children put all that they have learned into practice on their own. It is also the time when teachers have the opportunity to assess readers through one-on-one conferences. Teachers often feel nervous that young children are not able to sustain themselves for long periods of time reading; however, with proper training we can expect children to accomplish this. Teachers and students should generate a list of behavioral expectations for independent reading time. These expectations will address the following issues:

- book selection: the number of books to select and when to switch books
- how to care for books
- how to read with a partner
- how to respect other partnerships
- how to find a good reading spot
- how to choose just-right books
- ways readers can talk about books
- what a reader can do when he gets stuck on a word (print strategies)

Conferring

Teachers meet with students as they are reading independently. It is important to remember that this should sound like a conversation rather than an interrogation. This might seem like an odd statement to make; however, as teachers we often revert back to the way we were taught reading. We can remember reading a passage and then having to answer questions at the end. When the teacher assessed our reading, it was more of a test of whether or not we understood, not necessarily how we understood. It might have gone something like this: "Who were the characters in the story? What were they doing? Where did the story take place? What changed in the story?" These predetermined questions confirm whether the readers know the answers to the questions we ask but do not give us a window into what the students understand about the text or how they came to those understandings. An open-ended conversation gives us more information about a reader.

When assessing children, we must listen to how they read and comprehend the text. It is important to remember that just being able to read all the words and sound fluent does not mean that a child understands the text. If a reader does not understand what he is reading, we will either need to help him find a better match for a just-right book or teach him strategies to become a stronger reader. When we sit down beside a student during a conference, we often begin by listening to the child read to make some preliminary determinations about the child's reading abilities. At this point we ask ourselves a number of questions to better understand the child as a reader. Figure 7–4 lists those questions and describes what we are looking for from the reader. To a certain extent, these questions are roughly listed in a hierarchical order. If a child cannot read most of the words, he will not be able to easily formulate ideas about the text.

CAN THE READER...	WHAT TO LOOK FOR
Read almost all of the words using various strategies? (For early, transitional, and self-extending readers only.)	• When the child gets stuck on a *few* (not many or most) words, can he utilize what he knows about word-solving strategies—semantic, syntactic, and graphophonic—to figure out the words without assistance? • When the reader stops at a word, does he ask, "Does it make sense?" (semantic cueing system)? Sometimes a student might read a word, stop, and consider or even verbalize this question. • When the reader stops at a word, does he ask, "Does it sound right?" (syntactic cueing system)? This is a particularly difficult way for ELs to monitor their comprehension because they are still acquiring the structure of the English language. During read-aloud and shared reading, ELs are constantly exposed to English language syntax. This is also modeled by the teacher and other English speakers during conversations. • When the reader stops at a word, does he ask, "Does it look right?" (graphophonic cueing system)? ELs often rely heavily on this cueing system by sounding out words, looking for letter-sound patterns and sight words. It is quite astonishing sometimes that an EL can read so much text relying on this source of information. Sometimes the student even sounds fairly fluent. The key is that the reader needs to be able not just to decode but to really understand what he just read. *(Continues)*

FIGURE 7–4: Does the Reader Understand the Text?

CAN THE READER . . .	WHAT TO LOOK FOR
	• Does the reader use these cueing systems fairly flexibly depending on need? This is often the sign of a stronger reader. Every time a child gets stuck on a word, the context may differ. A stronger reader will be able to discriminate and match the context to the type of strategy needed to problem solve.
	• Does the reader try multiple strategies and not simply continue to repeat a strategy that is not successful? Sometimes it pains us to observe a child try to read the beginning sounds of a word over and over, then look at his teacher, searching her face, anticipating that his teacher will provide the word. We need to encourage and teach children the importance and effectiveness of utilizing a variety of strategies.
	• If a reader cannot read almost every word *independently*, the book is too difficult.
Look at pictures and diagrams available on the page to help construct meaning?	• Emergent readers should be relying heavily on this strategy to help them understand what they are reading. When they are reading emergent storybooks, they look at the pictures to remind them of the part of the story they are to tell next. When they are reading high-interest books, they often study the pictures carefully by comparing and contrasting images within or between books of similar concepts.
	• Early readers often need to be taught this strategy explicitly, which will help them use their word-solving strategies more effectively. As recent emergent readers, they were quite accustomed to paying attention to the pictures; however, when they realize that meaning is carried in the text, they tend to focus more on that than the pictures. They need to be encouraged to continue to use the pictures to help them comprehend.
	• Often transitional and self-extending readers get to a point where they are fairly strong decoders. They tend to equate the idea of being able to read all the words with being a successful reader. It is important to consider all pieces of information on the page, including pictures and diagrams. There are many early chapter books, such as Cynthia Rylant's Henry and Mudge series, that contain elaborate pictures. Many nonfictional texts also have diagrams that give quite a bit of information that a reader would otherwise not have if focusing only on the text.
Easily retell and summarize what has been read?	• After listening to and watching a child read, we begin to ask him some questions. Usually we begin by saying, "Tell me about what you just read."
	• Does the child retell almost word for word without an indication of understanding?

FIGURE 7–4: *Continued*

CAN THE READER...	WHAT TO LOOK FOR
	• Does the child turn back to each page to tell minor details of each page? This often is an indication that a reader has not connected ideas but pays attention to details in a disconnected manner. • When a child retells, the teacher can also ask him to show her where he found the information to further confirm.
Easily give ideas, opinions, and evaluations that are connected to the text?	• It is not sufficient that a reader merely understand the text at a fairly literal level. It is important that a reader can analyze, synthesize, and evaluate what he has read and be able to connect it to his experiences and to other texts. • During partner conferences, we can hear to what extent readers are able to talk about the books they have read. We listen for their level of understanding and also to their use of the English language. ELs may not be able to fully articulate what they are thinking. It is important to listen carefully for what they are on the verge of saying and grasping toward. We then extend what they are saying in a basic way and add more specific and sophisticated vocabulary. To scaffold appropriately, we should extend their language only a bit beyond what they are able to do independently. Otherwise, they will not be able to apply the use of the language we are modeling independently because it is beyond their zone of proximal development.

FIGURE 7–4: *Continued*

It is important to watch what a reader does while he reads in addition to listening. Watch his eyes to see where on the page he is looking as well as to ascertain his level of engagement. Watch the child's mouth to determine whether or not he is forming it in anticipation of reading beginning sounds. Watch how the child holds the book and what he does with his fingers while he reads. Does he point word by word, slide his fingers below sentences, or cover some of the words with his finger as he reads? We often write down notes on what we notice the reader doing. We also pay particular attention to the miscues the reader makes and how he problem solves in the midst of reading. We find that we determine the teaching point in the conference through the consideration of these observations.

Teachers must keep records of the conferences they have each day because this is the source of future minilessons and conferences. Keep notes on all the things you notice about the reader as well as the one teaching point that you teach during the conference. All of the information you gain will help determine future instruction. For instance, if you notice that most of the children are now more comfortable with the print and are not looking at the pictures to help them generate understanding of the text, it is important to draw attention to this important skill during a minilesson. If only a few students demonstrate this need, then you can gather a small group together and remind those students to look at the pictures.

Talk Time

Students will always be provided a chance to talk about what they are reading with a partner. We recommend that this step not be overlooked, especially for English learners, because it is a chance to develop academic oral language. Students will be talking about their thinking and sharing their joys with text. The talk in reading workshop can vary in structure. Teachers might ask students to try out new language forms, talk about how they used a particular strategy, or just openly share their thinking. The groundwork for talking with partners about texts is laid during interactive read-aloud. With the teacher's assistance, students learn to listen to each other and share their thinking about the text read aloud. During reading workshop, the children are given opportunities to transfer what they have learned. It might be helpful to guide children with their talk time with conversation prompts or language frames. These language frames are first modeled by the teacher and used to scaffold student talk. It is not expected that children be limited to talk only in these ways; rather, it simply helps them get started. Figure 7–5 is an example of a chart used in a first-grade class as they begin to use language frames to support their partner talk time.

Whole-Group Share

Though reading workshop seems like a very independent time of the day, it is a place for building community. Students are responsible for helping their classmates enjoy their time with books as well as understanding that their thinking and talk can further help the entire class improve their reading. Students or partnerships will share out the strategies they used as readers. This helps the class develop a sense of a learning community. They all respect each other's reading time, listen to each other's ideas, and offer suggestions for becoming better

DIFFERENT WAYS TO HELP US TALK ABOUT BOOKS WITH OUR PARTNERS

- My favorite part was . . .
- This part of the story reminds me of . . .
- I agree with you because . . .
- I disagree with you because . . .
- I think the character is . . . because . . .
- I think . . . because . . .

FIGURE 7–5: Language Frames to Support Partner Talk

readers. Although the whole-group share is a short period of time, it poses another important opportunity to teach. While the teacher is conferring, she is constantly searching for students who might share. When teachers are conferring with students or listening to students during talk time, they should select those students who are models of the goal of the minilesson for the day or students who have tried out something new as readers. The whole-group share should not take more than five minutes.

Selecting Texts for Independent Reading Workshop

During independent reading workshop, students self-select books at their independent reading level. These are books they can decode and comprehend on their own. "Reading has to feel effortless for it to result in language development; studies indicate that a text needs to be about 98% comprehensible in order for it to help the reader acquire new vocabulary" (Krashen 2004, 6). This also helps students build reading fluency. Because they are not struggling with decoding the text, they can practice reading with proper intonation and expression. Further, because they can understand what they are reading, they can talk about what they are reading and will enjoy the book more.

Our classrooms have partially leveled libraries, which helps children choose their just-right books. What you will typically see in the classroom library are bookshelves filled with baskets of books labeled by genre, concept, author, and level. We use the Fountas and Pinnell (1996) guided reading levels to organize the leveled books. We find that their criteria for different levels are fairly consistent and used widely, which makes their system a practical choice. But instead of using the letters they use to identify levels, we tend to use colored dots as suggested by Lucy Calkins (2001) so that the children can quickly identify a just-right level but we are not emphasizing the levels. Teachers assess readers, determine what level they are in, and then guide them in their selection.

When meeting with a student regarding her just-right level, we usually say something like this: "I have noticed that these books with the green dot seem just right for you. When you read these books, you sound like you are telling a story [emphasizing fluency], you can read almost every word [accuracy rate], and you can easily tell what is going on and have good conversations with your partner [basic and higher-level comprehension]." Then we send the child off to the classroom library to choose books from the appropriate baskets. A partially leveled library creates a greater chance that a reader will pick a just-right text. Instead of choosing from five hundred books, the reader chooses from one or two baskets of fifty to sixty books. It is important to note that even books within a level have some range within them.

Teachers are often concerned about what will happen if a student constantly picks books that are not just right for her. Some students want to select books in bins that are too easy for them. We usually talk with them about how they have grown as a reader and help them understand that they have to choose books that match their growth. Just as they continue to grow out of their clothes, they grow out of some books also. The challenge that occurs more, however, is when children constantly want to reach for books that are too difficult. Working with hundreds of teachers, we have noticed that teachers sometimes tend to move children to books that are more difficult particularly because they are able to decode the text easily. It is essential to confer with students regularly to make sure that they are appropriately matched to books. Children beginning at the transitional reading level tend to assume that the ability to decode words equals the ability to comprehend the texts. During conferences, the teacher needs to listen to the child read not only for accuracy, but also for the child's sense of fluency. In addition, we need to ask students questions and engage them in a conversation about the text in order to determine if they fully understand what they are reading. It is always better to err on the side of putting a child in a text that is too easy rather than too hard. When a child feels that he can read harder books, it is harder to take those books out of his hands. When this happens, we usually have a conversation with the child regarding the importance of reading just-right books, just like they wear clothes that are just right—not too big and not too small because that would be uncomfortable. Figure 7–6 lists some questions we might discuss with children when nudging them toward just-right books. In having conversations such as these, we are able to emphasize that the ability to independently comprehend, problem solve words, and read fluently are important elements of reading just-right books.

Assessing Readers

In order to better match readers to texts, it is important to assess students' current reading levels. In our classrooms, teachers listen to students read texts and take simple running records. This is a practice used in Reading Recovery where a child reads a passage of text while the teacher takes notations that indicate how the child is reading the text. When children make miscues, sources of these miscues are identified as semantic, syntactic, or graphophonic. Teachers an-

- Does this book interest me?
- After reading the first page, do I understand what I am reading?
- Do I know almost all the words?
- Can I picture the story in my head?
- When I read the words aloud, does it sound like I am telling a story? Am I reading the words smoothly?
- Have I been successful with this reading series? Do I enjoy it?

FIGURE 7–6: Questions for Students to Consider When Selecting Texts for Independent Reading Workshop

alyze these miscues to gain insight into how the reader goes about problem solving. This is valuable information that helps us teach the child to become a more balanced reader. The running record also generates an accuracy percentage that, paired with the ability to comprehend, helps teachers ascertain a just-right level for a student. This can often feel like a daunting and time-consuming task, but it is worth the effort. We recommend that each teacher routinely conduct running record conferences with students every other month, and more frequently with struggling students.

What Do We Teach Across the Year in Independent Reading Workshop?

At the beginning of the year, we tend to focus on setting up the structures and routines for independent reading workshop. Once that important step is accomplished, we need to focus our attention on the teaching of the skills and strategies of proficient readers. Figure 7–7 summarizes some possible units of study we might teach across the

We Are All Readers

- Structures and routines of reading workshop
- How to select just-right texts
- Expectations during minilessons, independent and partner reading times, and the share session
- How to talk about books with a partner

Print Strategies

- Looking at beginning sounds, word patterns
- Looking across the word to stretch out the sounds
- Checking the picture to consider what makes sense

Character

- Who is a character?
- Character attributes, actions, and intentions
- How characters change

Nonfiction

- How is reading for information different than reading stories?
- How to read captions, diagrams, and charts
- Comparing and contrasting information between books about the same topic

Retelling

- Page-by-page retelling
- Retelling the whole story from start to finish
- Retelling by summarizing the story

FIGURE 7–7: Possible Units of Study in the Independent Reading Workshop

year. For more information on year-long plans for reading workshop, we suggest that you refer to Calkins (2001) and Collins (2004).

Structure of Independent Reading Workshop for Emergent and Early Readers at Different Levels of Second Language Acquisition

Emergent and early readers are learning to make meaning from text while learning how to read text on their own for the first time. Their knowledge of sounds and how to read letters will be practiced in the context of reading books. These beginning readers look forward to the time of day when they get to pick up books and spend time making sense of them. Reading workshop also provides time for them to practice fluent reading. They will have opportunities for repeated readings, revisiting books shared during shared and guided reading and interactive read-aloud. Sometimes you might see an emergent reader pretend reading, or creating her own story from the pictures she sees in her book, and that is a wonderful sign that she is beginning to enter the world of books. You might see early readers trying to sound out words, using their word-reading skills, picture clues, and background knowledge. All in all, the time emergent and early readers will spend independently with text will motivate them to want to learn to read as well as help them practice reading strategies and skills. The goal at this stage is making meaning on a surface level (see Appendix B) while reading independently.

In Chapter 3, we outlined how the day might look across different grades. As readers change, their needs change as well. Readers in the emergent stages of reading will need more time with partners, sharing their high-interest books and reading their emergent storybooks and shared reading texts. As students become early readers, they will need to spend more time reading independently as they are now reading conventionally. It is important that they have time by themselves to problem solve how to balance decoding and comprehending the text simultaneously. Figure 7–8 shows the structure of the workshop for emergent readers and for early readers.

STRUCTURE	EMERGENT READERS	EARLY READERS
Minilesson	5–12 minutes	5–12 minutes
Independent Reading and Conferring	10 minutes	15 minutes
Partnership Reading and Talking with Conferring	15 minutes	15 minutes
Whole-Group Share	5 minutes	5 minutes

FIGURE 7–8: Structure of the Reading Workshop for Emergent and Early Readers

Also, because early readers are such new conventional readers, they will need time during their partnerships to read the text together as well as talk and share. During partnerships with early readers, partners can help each other read the text. Since reading partners are matched by ability, they are both engaged in similar texts. While reading together, the students can help each other figure words out. You might want to create and post a chart like the one in Figure 7–9 to help partners remember what they should be doing.

Minilessons

The minilesson will last approximately five to twelve minutes. The teacher will remind students of a strategy readers use when they read to help the students see the connections between guided reading, shared reading, interactive read-aloud, and word work and independent reading. Students will also have opportunities to develop their oral and academic language through exposure to a variety of books and when they talk with a partner. They will build background knowledge when they see pictures or read stories of items and concepts. For example, when looking at a book about animals, they might see each animal in its habitat, eating. They learn not only what the animal looks like and its name but also what the animal eats and what its home looks like. The exposure to books also helps ELs build their English semantics (word and meaning bank). Think about the animal book again. An EL may already possess the cognitive proficiencies in his first language (how the animal looks, eats, and lives), but he may not know the English words to describe those ideas. The increased exposure to books will continue to increase the students' cognitive and oral vocabularies.

English learners also learn oral discourse during talk time. The teacher might model how to talk with a partner, offering examples of turn taking. Language lessons might also include specific examples of how to construct sentences around a particular purpose or function of language. For example, if students are asked to express likes and dislikes, the teacher might say, "Today when you are talking with your partner, I want you to share with him or her what you liked about the story. So you might say, 'I liked the part where . . . ,' or 'My favorite part was . . . ,' or 'A funny part was . . .'" Notice the teacher is modeling the forms of language used to express likes. Sometimes these forms will already be available if a chart was created during shared

When we read together as partners, we . . .

- Sit side by side
- Decide which book to read and who will read it
- Hold the book between us
- Let one partner read while the other one listens

FIGURE 7–9: Partner Reading Chart

reading when the class talked in a whole group about likes and dislikes. In this case the teacher might say, "Yesterday when we read *The Little Red Hen*, we talked about our favorite part and I wrote down what you said about the story," pointing to the shared writing chart titled "Our Favorite Part in *The Little Red Hen*." "Well today when you are talking with your partner, I want you to talk about your favorite part of the story you're reading."

Additional language minilessons are presented in Figure 7–10. You can refer to the language functions chart in Appendix A for sample language forms and cue words for the listed functions of language. Keep in mind that the minilessons suggested in Figure 7–10 are a start; your minilessons will come from what you are seeing your students doing as readers. You will assess their needs as readers while conferring with them.

Independent Reading and Conferring

For emergent and early readers, since many of the books they are selecting are short, they will need to select a few books to place in their book bag for the week. Each pair is given a plastic bag to store the books they are reading during reading workshop. We like to use the large zip-close freezer bags because they are sturdy and large enough to hold most picture books. Partnerships will be given their book bag after the minilesson and will find a comfortable place in the room to read. Some students like to lie or sit on the rug, sit on the floor, or sit at a desk. This is their time as readers, and we want them to take control of what makes them successful as readers, including selecting their own books and knowing their comfort zone when reading.

Students will begin the year reading independently for as little as ten minutes and increase the time throughout the year as they build endurance as readers. By the end of first grade students should be able to sit and read quietly for at least thirty minutes. You might also hear students reading out loud, in a whisper or hum, and that is common for students who are just learning to decode. They like to hear themselves in order to process what they are reading.

The number of books partnerships should select at this stage will vary. We suggest having a partnership select between three and four books. This will give them plenty of reading material to take them through the week, and they will not be constantly getting up to pick new books when others are reading. We suggest having a book day when pairs are allowed to change books.

Conferences for emergent and early readers often start with the child reading or talking about what she's read. This is your chance to question the child about the strategies she is using to read unfamiliar words and to ask her what she is understanding about the story. After listening to the child you will make your decisions about what to ask next or teach her at that moment.

READING STRATEGIES	EXPLORING NARRATIVE TEXT	EXPLORING EXPOSITORY TEXT	LANGUAGE DEVELOPMENT
Concepts about print, including identifying the front cover, back cover, title, author, and illustrator	What is fiction?	What is nonfiction?	Taking turns
	Using pictures and context to make predictions	The features of nonfiction, including title and table of contents	Listening to your partner
Understanding the role of authors and illustrators	Identifying characters	Identifying simple facts and ideas	Expressing likes and dislikes
Picture walks	Identifying setting	Relating prior knowledge to new information	Labeling
Sounding out unfamiliar words	Identifying important events		Identifying
	Retelling	Asking questions to seek more information	Describing
Chunking word parts to read unfamiliar words	Sequencing (beginning, middle, end)		
Using context, including picture clues, to read unfamiliar words	Describing elements of plot, setting, characters		
Identifying question marks and exclamation points	Answering who, what, when, where, and how questions about the story (literal recall)		
What does fluent reading sound like?	Asking questions when something doesn't make sense		
Making connections to life experiences			
Visualizing	Asking questions to seek more information		

FIGURE 7–10: Possible Minilessons for Emergent and Early Readers

Talk Time

After students have a chance to read independently, stop them and ask them to share with their partner what they read about. You can refer them back to the minilesson and say, "Remember to share with your partner your favorite part." You do not need to limit students to talking about the focus of the minilesson, but sometimes the younger students are not quite ready to just talk about their thinking, so giving them direction helps them be successful during talk time.

Group Share

The little ones love to talk and share. We are sure that on a number of occasions you have found yourself spending hours hearing stories about pets, family members, vacations, trips to the park and McDonald's, favorite video games, and so on and so forth. They just love to talk! What you want to be careful of during group share is that the talk stays focused on reading. Otherwise your five minutes of group share can go on and on and on. Remind your students that they all had an opportunity to talk with their partner and that not everyone will get a chance to share with the group. Believe us, you'll hear the moans and groans when they are not selected to share, so always value their talk time in partnerships.

Types and Uses of Books

Profile of Felix as a Reader
The books in Felix's book bag consist of *Corduroy, Dan the Flying Man*, an alphabet book, a book on the letter *f*, and an Eye Witness book on snakes. Felix just came to California from Mexico at the beginning of the school year. He is an emergent reader at the preproduction stage of second language acquisition (stage I). Because he is not yet reading conventionally, he has books that support his reading. *Corduroy* is an emergent storybook (see Chapter 5) that has been read to him many times by a student teacher in a small group with other emergent readers. His work in that book is to tell the story on each page to practice using story language and reinforce his comprehension of the text. *Dan the Flying Man* is a text that Ms. Mamdou uses during shared reading. In this book, he is able to point to each word as he reads it because he has experienced this with Ms. Mamdou time and again. He is connecting words to what is happening in the picture on each page. He has selected a reptile alphabet book because he loves snakes, but this book also familiarizes him with letters. He also has a little *f* book in which each page contains a picture of an object that begins with the letter *f*. Ms. Mamdou has helped him select this book because it's about the first letter of his name. When students are learning sounds, we connect them to familiar words, such as their names, that have the same beginning letter and sound. During one-to-one conferences, Ms. Mamdou has gone through the pages in this book with Felix because he doesn't know all the English words for the objects represented in the book. As he turns from page to page, he remembers *fan, flower, frog*, and *fish*. With these five books, Felix has a lot of work ahead of him. You might ask how he knows the differences between the books. How does he know what to do in each book? The chart in Figure 7–11 summarizes possible ways of using different types of books. Because children have been immersed in the various books in different contexts, their reading behaviors will reflect their experiences.

TYPE OF BOOK	EXPECTED READING BEHAVIORS
Emergent Storybook See Chapter 5 for details regarding criteria of these books. Example: *Corduroy*	• Pretend read by telling the story on each page. • Orally practice storybook language. • Build comprehension with each rereading of the text.
Shared Reading Small versions of familiar big books used during shared reading sessions Example: *Mrs. Wishy-Washy*	• Point to each word while reading. • Practice sight-word recognition and beginning knowledge of letters and sounds to assist in reading familiar text. • Practice fluency and phrasing with expression as modeled in whole-group shared reading sessions.
Alphabet Book Range from simple books with one letter or one word per page to elaborate content-related books Example: *Eating the Alphabet*	• Recognize letters while perusing the book. • Attempt to match objects to the letter represented on each page. • Practice sequence of letters in the alphabet.
Letter Book Simple, small books that contain one clear picture on each page, perhaps accompanied by a word that begins with the same letter	• Practice one letter at a time. • Say object name on each page and check it with the letter title of the book.
High-Interest Book Difficult books that cannot be read independently but have enough information in the pictures in order for students to connect ideas; often nonfictional or reflect an interest of the student with support in background knowledge	• Select books that are more intellectually challenging and match reader interests. • Make connections between similar texts. • Make connections with prior knowledge about the subject. • Connect information on the page to help make meaning.
Just-Right Book Books with high picture support and one word per page or one to two lines of text per page that can be read independently (for early readers who are reading conventionally)	• Use word-solving skills simultaneously with comprehension strategies to create meaning from the text. • Read with 95 percent accuracy while still comprehending the text. • Reread to clear up confusion. • Retell book with no hesitation. • Read with fluency and expression. • Discuss higher-level ideas from the book with a partner.

FIGURE 7–11: Types and Uses of Books in Emergent and Early Readers' Independent Book Bags

Independent Reading Workshop in Action

Profile of Marisol as a Reader

Different from Felix, Marisol is an EL who is on the cusp of transitioning from the speech emergence stage to the intermediate fluency stage. She is reading books that have clear picture support and one to two lines of text per page, such as *Mom*. When she is familiar with English words to describe what is happening in the picture, she is able to read the pages; however, when she is not familiar with the vocabulary represented on the page, she begins to rely primarily on her graphophonic cueing system, trying to decode the letters and sounds. When she gets stuck on these words, she alternates between trying to make the beginning sound of the word and looking at the picture.

Ms. Mamdou listened to Marisol read *The Way I Go to School*. While Marisol read the text, Ms. Mamdou supported her only after she had made some attempts to problem solve on her own. Marisol tended to get stuck on words that reflect vocabulary that she has not yet acquired in English such as *wheelchair* and *taxi*. After the reading of this book, Ms. Mamdou and Marisol had a conversation transcribed in Figure 7–12.

CONFERENCE TRANSCRIPT	REFLECTION
T: Marisol, you did a great job working hard at reading all those words! Tell me what this book was about.	Ms. Mamdou wants to make sure that Marisol understands what she has just read.
S: The book about go to school.	
T: What about going to school?	She pushes for Marisol to tell more about the book.
S: [Marisol hesitates for a moment while Ms. Mamdou looks at her with expectation. Then Marisol points to the cover.] This boy is walk to school.	
T: Yes, I see that. The boy on the cover of the book is walking to school. What about everyone else? What are they doing? [Ms. Mamdou opens the book to the first page that has the same picture as on the cover.] Oh, here it is again, he is walking to school. Let's keep going . . . [gently pushes book toward Marisol and looks at her expectantly]. This was a tricky page, wasn't it? Have you seen a wheelchair before [pointing to it]? Yes, she can't walk so her mother is pushing the wheelchair so she can get to school. There sure are many ways to get to school. Let's keep going [turns to the next page].	Ms. Mamdou knows that Marisol was stuck on this page because she does not know the word *wheelchair* in English. She takes a moment to elaborate a bit more on this than she did during the reading of the text in the hopes of teaching her a bit of vocabulary. You will notice how the teacher also adds inferring to the retelling of that particular page by saying the mother is pushing the wheelchair.

FIGURE 7–12: Marisol's Conference

CONFERENCE TRANSCRIPT	REFLECTION
S: Bike.	Ms. Mamdou knows that Marisol had some difficulty with the preposition *on*. Most of the book uses *in*. Marisol's miscue could have been either a visual error or a semantic error for an English learner.
T: This boy is going to school *on* a bike. He is riding *on* a bike. See how he is sitting on the bike?	
S: [Nods affirmatively]	
[They continue this way from one page to the next.]	
[Now they are on the last page with the boat.]	
T: Marisol, can you tell me what happened on this page?	
S: She ride in a boat.	
T: Yes, she is riding *on* a boat [points index finger directly below the word *on*]. Is this word *in* or *on*?	Ms. Mamdou wants to make sure that Marisol understands that sometimes in English it can be *on* or *in*.
S: [looks carefully at it] On.	
T: Yes, the girl is riding on the boat. She is standing on the boat. She is not inside the boat. [Flips to the page before] This girl is *in* a bus. She is going *in*side the bus. [Turns back to the boat page] This word is different— *on*. [Writes the word *on* on a whiteboard and then writes *in* directly below it] In English sometimes we use *in* and sometimes we use *on* depending on our location. Where are we, *in* or *on* something?	
T: Can you read that sentence again? Be sure to look carefully at each word as you point underneath it. [She demonstrates.]	
S: [Reads while pointing with index finger] I go to school on a boat.	
T: Good. When you go back to reread this book, make sure you pay special attention to the words *in* and *on* because this changes sometimes in the book.	Ms. Mamdou wants to leave Marisol with the expectation that she will reread this book and continue working.

FIGURE 7–12: *Continued*

The Structure of Independent Reading Workshop for Transitional and Self-Extending Readers Across Levels of Second Language Acquisition

Transitional and self-extending readers can already decode and read with fluency. Reading workshop is a great place for them to learn how to think more deeply about texts they read independently and learn from one another in partnerships. Different from emergent and early readers, transitional and self-extending readers spend more time reading independently since they are now more efficient decoders. They still need time to discuss their reading with their partners because this deepens their comprehension of the text. Figure 7–13 outlines suggestions for allocating time during the reading workshop for transitional and self-extending readers.

Minilessons

Though transitional and self-extending readers will still need word-reading strategies for multisyllabic words, minilessons will guide students to think more as readers. Again, the work you are doing in shared reading, interactive read-aloud, and word work will be revisited and connected to their work as independent readers.

Figure 7–14 offers suggestions for minilessons to use with transitional and self-extending readers. But your minilessons will come from what you see your students doing as readers. As you confer with students you will make plans for upcoming minilessons. You can also refer to Appendix E for further explanations of literary genres.

Independent Reading and Conferences

To help readers develop more complex comprehension skills, have partnerships read the same book. When students talk to each other about the same book, they will challenge one another's thinking and offer different points of view. This will take students beyond literal recall and into application, analysis, synthesis, and evaluation (see Appendix B). Further, you will want to help students build endurance as readers and practice maintaining comprehension with longer pieces of text. Many transitional and self-extending readers will be reading chapter books. They will need new strategies about how to connect ideas across chapters from start to finish. They need opportunities to reflect on their reading to improve retention. The goal is not to finish the book quickly, as some of them may think, but to understand and enjoy what they are reading.

STRUCTURE	TRANSITIONAL READERS	SELF-EXTENDING READERS
Minilesson	5–12 minutes	5–12 minutes
Independent Reading and Conferring	20–25 minutes	25–30 minutes
Partnership Reading and Talking with Conferring	10 minutes	10 minutes
Whole-Group Share	5 minutes	5 minutes

FIGURE 7–13: Structure of the Reading Workshop for Transitional and Self-Extending Readers

READING STRATEGIES	EXPLORING NARRATIVE TEXT	EXPLORING EXPOSITORY TEXT	EXPLORING POETRY	LANGUAGE DEVELOPMENT
Staying connected: fix-up strategies (what to do when you get lost in the meaning: reread, summarize smaller chunks of text, make connections, etc.)	Comparing and contrasting plots, setting, and characters from different stories by the same author	Elements of exposition	Types of poetry	Comparing and contrasting
		Where we see nonfiction in our lives: newspapers, books, Internet, advertisements, magazines	Identifying rhythm, rhyme, and alliteration in poetry	Synthesizing
				Agreeing and disagreeing
Setting a purpose when reading	Comparing and contrasting plots, setting, and characters from different stories by different authors	Using text features (table of contents, titles, headings, indexes) to locate information	Recognizing and understanding figurative language: similes and metaphors	Sequencing
				Wishing and hoping
Sensory visualization	Comparing and contrasting different versions of the same story that reflect different cultures	Using text features to build background knowledge: title, headings, subheadings, pictures	Identifying mood	Comparing
Making connections	Identifying story elements	Restating facts to clarify and organize ideas		Classifying
Drawing inferences	Creating alternate endings	Interpreting information from diagrams, charts, and graphs		Explaining
Determining author's purpose	Determining the theme	Asking questions to seek further information		Reporting
Making and modifying predictions	Identifying the mood	Skimming		Evaluating
Identifying problem and solution	Identifying elements of fairy tales, folktales, and fables	Note taking		Hypothesizing
Identifying the main idea and supporting details	Features of chapter books and how they aid in comprehension (e.g., chapter titles)			Predicting
Identifying cause and effect				Inferring
Identifying facts and opinions				Suggesting
Identifying point of view				Criticizing

FIGURE 7–14: Possible Minilessons for Transitional and Self-Extending Readers

Together partnerships will select the same chapter book to read. Unlike emergent and early readers, who switch books on book day, transitional and self-extending readers can change their books as needed. Different pairs will finish their chapter books at different times because the length of the books as well as students' reading fluency will vary. The partnership will still have only one book bag for storing their books and any additional materials they may need to support their discussion. Additional materials may include the following:

- *Literary response journal*—Students can record their thinking, reflect on their reading, try out comprehension skills, answer questions posed by the teacher or their partner, and write down questions to discuss with their partner or for note taking. These journals can be guided in terms of what the teacher wants students to write in them but should also serve as a running journal for students to use as needed when reading.

- *Sticky notes*—Since students cannot write in their books, stickies can serve as margins for note taking and marking talking points. Students can mark points in the text they want to talk to their partner about or have questions about. Just as with literary response journals, stickies use can be guided by the teacher but should be open for students to use as needed.

Independent reading time should now be increased to twenty to thirty minutes in one sitting. Students are practicing building their endurance as readers with longer texts and need more time.

When conferring with transitional and self-extending readers, you'll want to focus on why questions. The more you challenge partnerships to answer why things are happening in the story, the more you'll get them thinking. When we were working with self-extending readers at a school in Los Angeles, teachers were concerned that they weren't going to be able to talk to their students about their books because the teachers had not read the books themselves. We modeled for teachers how to ask why questions, and they were able to see their students going deeper with text. For example, when we were conferring with two students who were reading *Ready, Freddy! Help! A Vampire's Coming!* by Abby Klein, we began the conference by asking the partnership what their story was about. The students shared that they were reading about dream catchers and how the Native Americans used to make dream catchers. At that point we asked them why questions. "Why do you think the Native Americans made dream catchers?"

The students replied, "To keep the bad dreams away."

We continued probing. "Why do you think the author chose to talk about dream catchers in this story? What do dream catchers have to do with Freddy?"

The students stopped to think for a minute and then one began, "Well, Freddy has been having trouble going to sleep and so the dream catchers help keep the bad dreams away. But he could also use a night-light or a teddy bear."

The partner interrupted, "That's true, uh-huh, sometimes when you have bad dreams you can use something special to make you feel safe. So maybe the dream catchers are just something that made them feel safe and so Freddy thought it would be a good idea to try it."

Asking students to explain why things are happening in the story, why authors choose certain objects to present to the main character, and why the characters make certain decisions makes students go outside of the text and into their minds for the answers. This leads to inference, analysis, and critique. Other helpful words to start your questions with when talking to students are *should, would, could,* and *what if*.

In addition to cognitive development, transitional and self-extending readers will further practice developing their academic oral language. In the same manner that was explained with emergent and early readers, teachers will model frames of language to meet a purpose when talking. Further, when students are talking with one another, they will learn language through talk and interaction.

When we were working with a second-grade teacher on reading workshop, she noticed that her students were not talking the way she had expected when focusing on cause and effect. The minilesson for the week asked students to identify different events in their story and explain what the cause was for each. They were looking for relationships and connections across ideas and events. When it was time to talk, the teacher noticed the students saying the same thing from one partnership to the next: "The event was . . . and the cause was . . ." She was concerned that the students were not talking naturally. We asked the teacher to think about her expectations for talk when discussing causes and effects with her students. She said she wanted students to be able to say things like, "There was a part in my story where . . . The reason it happened was because . . . ," or more specifically, "When Junie B. Jones was screaming in the bus, it made other students mad, and that's why the other students started calling her names." We stopped to analyze the sentence frames with the teacher and came up with the understanding that using words like *because* and *that's why* leads to the kind of talk she was looking for. As a result, the next mini-lesson focused on how to talk about causes and effects. It sounded something like this. "We have been working on cause and effect this week in our story of *Whale's Song* during shared reading. When I was thinking about that story, I thought about how the little girl would take flowers to the whales because she thought they were singing to her." The teacher reminded them that when they talked about causes and effects, they were expressing *why* something happened, and they could use the word *because* to explain a cause and effect. This provided students with a new model of how to use oral language to express a cause and effect. See Appendix A for additional cue words and sentence frames to share with students when meeting certain cognitive functions.

Talk Time

After the students read for an extended period of time, ask them to share their thinking with their partner. This talk time can come from notes or ideas they recorded in their journals or on stickies, or it may be directed by the teacher, based on the minilesson.

Group Share

The group share will take only about five minutes. The teacher should select a partnership that has demonstrated the goal of the minilesson, modeled ways of talking, or used a reading strategy during workshop.

Conclusion

All readers need opportunities to read. Throughout the school day they receive scaffolded instruction as teachers read *to* them and *with* them during shared and guided experiences. The purpose of these scaffolds is to help children become thoughtful independent readers. Independent reading workshop provides students the opportunity to try out what they have learned while enjoying a book they chose and sharing their thinking with a friend. Opportunities to talk with a partner help them practice their oral language in a comfortable, risk-free environment. Independent reading workshop gives English learners time to practice reading and time to explore text. This time with text exposes ELs to new vocabulary, proper syntax, different discourse structures (genres), and practice with the phonological and graphophonic systems of the English language. Giving students time to read is key to any language arts program because the more children read, the better readers they will become while developing language.

Professional Literature on Independent Reading Workshop

Calkins, Lucy McCormick. 2001. *The Art of Teaching Reading*. New York: Addison-Wesley.

Calkins, Lucy, et al. 2002. *A Field Guide to the Classroom Library A–G*. Teachers College Reading and Writing Project. Portsmouth, NH: Heinemann.

Collins, Kathy. 2004. *Growing Readers: Units of Study in the Primary Classroom*. Portland, ME: Stenhouse.

Cunningham, Andie, and Ruth Shagoury. 2005. *Starting with Comprehension: Reading Strategies for the Youngest Learners*. Portland, ME: Stenhouse.

Dorn, Linda, and Carla Soffos. 2005. *Teaching for Deep Comprehension*. Portland, ME: Stenhouse.

Fountas, Irene, and Gay Su Pinnell. 1996. *Guided Reading: Good First Teaching for All Children*. Portsmouth, NH: Heinemann.

———. 1999. *Matching Books to Readers: Using Leveled Books in Guided Reading, K–3*. Portsmouth, NH: Heinemann.

Graves, Donald H. 1991. *Build a Literate Classroom*. Portsmouth, NH: Heinemann.

Hindley, Joanne. 1996. *In the Company of Children*. Portland, ME: Stenhouse.

Keene, Ellin O., and Susan Zimmermann. 1997. *Mosaic of Thought: Teaching Comprehension in a Reader's Workshop*. Portsmouth, NH: Heinemann.

Orehove, Barbara, and Marybeth Alley. 2003. *Revisiting the Reading Workshop: Management, Mini-Lessons, and Strategies*. New York: Scholastic.

Serafini, Frank. 2001. *The Reading Workshop: Creating Space for Readers*. Portsmouth, NH: Heinemann.

Taberski, Sharon. 2000. *On Solid Ground: Strategies for Teaching Reading, K–3*. Portsmouth, NH: Heinemann.

8

Writing Workshop

We all know we have stories to tell, ideas to share, and opinions to voice. To express oneself is a fundamental characteristic of being human.

—Donald Graves

What Is Writing Workshop?

Ms. Lee's room was abuzz with activity. Some students were busily making cards and letters for their friends while others were writing stories. One group of students in the corner had decided that they wanted to make signs for the lunchroom to remind everyone to clean up after they ate. Two children decided that they wanted to write a letter to the school custodian to ask how they could help with recycling. One little boy loves rocket ships. He draws them, reads about them, dreams about them. Harris wants to write about rocket ships every day! Today, he decided that he wanted to write a piece about how to draw a rocket ship. Vy, a little girl who has just come to the United

States, looked around her as all her classmates were engrossed in their various writing projects. She went to the writing center and took the postcard paper and started to fill in the lines with writing that resembled the Vietnamese language.

The children in Ms. Lee's room have discovered that they are writers. And as writers in this unit of study, they have come to understand that there are many different reasons to write. If you asked the children in this class why they write, they would tell you that they write signs for the lunchroom because people need reminders and instructions. They have also seen that as a result of their efforts, the lunchroom staff now point to their signs and remind students to clean up. And the lunchroom is now cleaner. They will tell you that when they write letters to their friends, the friends write back. They will tell you that Al, their custodian, writes them back and teaches them about recycling as a result of their letters. You will find that Harris can write about rocket ships in nearly every genre and never seems to run out of ideas. Vy may not understand everything that is being said in the room, but she has a sense of what she is expected to do at this time. On her postcard, she drew a picture of a beach with a sun. She also added her name to the bottom of the postcard, where we usually sign our names. Vy is approximating the work that writers do, and once she is able to communicate in English, we will quickly have more evidence that she has internalized the reasons to write.

When children make this magical connection that they can communicate their ideas through words on a page and there are real reasons to write, they can't seem to stop. While this feels absolutely magical, it happens by design. During the writing workshop, we create an environment where children are immersed in beautiful literature and varied genres that help them envision what they themselves could do as writers. We provide tools, time, and expectations for the children to practice their writing. We demonstrate how we come up with ideas to write, how we get them on paper, and how we continually make our writing better through a process of several steps. We give strategic guidance during critical times at the beginning of the workshop in a minilesson for all children, followed by individualized instruction during conferences. We also assure them that everything doesn't always have to look perfect and that we need to do the very best that we can. Children who do not yet understand English can communicate the best way that they can, through either pictures or their native language.

Foundations of Writing Workshop

Writing is communicating through written forms. These forms of writing can vary from scribbles to standard symbols such as the use of letters to create words and sentences. Writing development is similar to reading development in that children will learn that writing is a way of expressing meaning. When developing concepts about print, they are exposed to illustrations that tell stories and see how they too can tell a story through images. As they continue their development as readers and learn about the English orthography (written system), they start to connect writing to their pictures to tell their story.

Writing instruction happens throughout the entire day. When children are read to during read-aloud and shared reading and when they read alone during independent reading workshop, they see how the English language works. They are exposed to all levels of language, phonology, orthography, syntax, semantics, pragmatics, morphology, and discourse (see Chapter 1) through books. More explicitly, we teach children the symbols of our written language system and how they are organized during word work, shared writing, and interactive writing. All of this exposure, guidance, and direct instruction on writing will be applicable during writing workshop. Writing workshop is the place for children to have time for writing. We want them to have time to think through their ideas and transfer them onto paper. Figure 8–1 lists the purposes for writing workshop. Figure 8–2 describes the teacher's and students' roles in writing workshop.

- To develop a love of writing
- To provide time for students to develop their writing fluency
- To learn how to communicate effectively through writing
- To develop students' knowledge of the English written language system, with an emphasis on syntax and discourse
- To understand the connections between reading and writing to develop writers
- To understand and be able to write across various genres

FIGURE 8–1: Purposes of Writing Workshop

ROLE OF THE TEACHER	ROLE OF THE STUDENTS
• Share your ideas through writing. • Share your thought process as a writer. • Provide models of writing—both original and published pieces. • Guide students through the writing process. • Provide opportunities for students to learn from one another as writers. • Provide time for writing!	• Write, write, write. • Share their ideas. • Respect other writers' ideas. • Help their partners improve their writing, including ideas, structure, and organization.

FIGURE 8–2: Teacher and Student Roles in a Writing Workshop

Context in Our Book

Process Writing

English learners learn to write best through a process model (Peregoy and Boyle 2005; Farrell 2006). A process model of writing instruction places greater emphasis on the teaching and learning involved as children create a piece of writing, including the development of ideas, drafting, revising, editing, and publishing them into the product (see Figure 8–3). Process writing demonstrates the importance of developing an idea and understanding that writing is not a linear process. Ideas and drafts are constantly revisited and edited. Even when a piece of writing has been published, there is still work that can be done to make it better. A piece of writing is never perfected; a writer makes a decision as to when he thinks the piece has communicated his ideas to a point where he is ready to go public with it.

A huge misconception about English learners and writing is that if they have not developed enough oral language they cannot write. When I was working as a staff developer, teachers would often tell me that their English learners were still working on their listening and speaking skills, so they should save writing for later. But this is not true. All children, whether they speak English fluently or not, are filled with ideas and experiences. Writing is a way children can transfer these ideas onto paper through a visual representation. This can mean writing through pictures, images, symbols, or letters and words. Our job is to help ELs understand that writing takes on many forms and as they learn more English, they will have other ways of expressing themselves. In fact, we often find that children in the silent period use writing as a vehicle to communicate their ideas. Once I was working with a little girl who had just moved from Guatemala and had been in school for just a few days. Although she did not yet speak English, she did carefully watch what all her classmates were doing during writing workshop. She also noticed that the teacher was talking to each child about his or her stories. The little girl ended up drawing a picture of herself and her family. From the picture she drew, we knew that she had a mother, a father, a sister, and a grandmother. She was not yet ready to tell us in words, but she was able to communicate this through pictures, a symbolic representation of writing.

Choice

These experiences and connections can be made only if students are allowed to have choice in what they write. A child can craft writing about anything and within any genre. Limiting students' choice in topics does not lead to the development of writers because students may not possess the background knowledge or language to create full pieces around a limited topic. Giving students writing prompts can stifle their ability and desire to write. Although it seems as if it is more

STEPS OF THE PROCESS	WHAT STUDENTS ARE DOING
Prewriting/Drafting: Collecting and Developing Ideas in Drafts	Students create one or more new pieces each day. Using pencils or pens, writers use pictures and/or words to convey their ideas. Colors are not necessarily encouraged at this stage because using a pencil results in adding more detail to the pictures. When coloring, students often spend more time coloring than drawing details. The more details, the more content they are conveying. At the end of the workshop, they decide whether or not they are done with the piece for now (note that this does not mean publishing). They then place it in either the finished or the unfinished side of their writing folder.
Choosing	After collecting several drafts in his folder, each writer selects *one* piece that he would like to take through the process to publication.
Revising	At this step he will make sure that his piece makes sense, includes all necessary information, and is organized well. Students might look at elements of craft in other pieces of literature in order to emulate other authors.
Editing	Students attempt to make their piece as conventional as possible with correct use of capitals and punctuation marks. At this point, students are told that they must write and spell things in a way that others can read their piece without their help or explanation. Minilessons during this stage explicitly connect to previous class work in word study and interactive writing.
Publishing	Students make their writing piece look beautiful and presentable. In a *few* instances, first and second graders may need to recopy their writing if it is difficult to read. Generally, children are coloring their pictures and possibly decorating their piece with a cover.
Celebrating	It is important to have a celebration at the end of the process. Students always look forward to this event, and it validates their hard work as writers. Concretely, our youngest writers have something to look forward to, prompting them to want to repeat the process again and again.

FIGURE 8–3: Steps of the Writing Process for Grades K–2

supportive to give students prompts, it does not build the independence that we seek to establish in the writing workshop. If children become accustomed to being given topics, they will not initiate their own ideas. In order for us to teach students qualities of writing such as elaboration, we need to instill in the young writers the ability to come up with their own ideas. They will be able to elaborate more on their own ideas than on ours. If we ask our students to write about taking care of a pet, those students who have pets will write about their experiences. The children who do not have pets will try to write what they think, but they will not have enough firsthand knowledge to elaborate on this topic.

For all students, exposure to and time with text will improve their writing. As children read, they see how written language is organized and crafted. During read-aloud, shared reading, guided reading, and independent reading workshop, students are vicariously learning to become better writers. During minilessons in writing workshop, some of those texts can be revisited to focus students on particular structures or crafting styles. For instance, Ms. Mamdou used *Dan the Flying Man* during shared reading, which has a repeating refrain, "Catch me, catch me if you can!" In writing workshop, the children are working on using repeated dialogue to add emphasis. She refers to this repeated phrase as an example of how children can also use the same technique in their own writing.

Writing Genres

During writing workshop it is essential for students to have opportunities to write for a variety of purposes and audiences. This variety will help English learners expand their knowledge of the English language. They will learn how to write within a variety of genres and see how the purpose for writing can affect the syntax and discourse of the writing. For example, they learn that a "how-to" or procedural piece follows a different format than a descriptive piece about dolphins or that the syntax of a poem or friendly letter looks different than that of a personal narrative. Students will learn these variations during writing workshop and when reading widely and often.

Whenever you ask students to write in a particular genre of writing, you should begin by providing models of what the genre looks like. For example, if you ask students to write a how-to descriptive piece, you need to show them how it should be organized. Lessons might start with students reading how-to books and building their background knowledge on procedures. Then, as students move through the writing process, you should provide them with explicit models of how to organize their ideas and what the discourse of the piece should look like. Conversations around discourse at the drafting stage can include "What goes into an introductory paragraph when writing a how-to piece?" "What follows the introduction?" and "What kind of transition words might we use when connecting ideas in a how-to piece?" These conversations around models of writing and attention to English discourse (organization) and semantics (transition words) will help English learners draft more purposefully. Figure 8–4 lists the genres that young students typically write in.

Narrative Genres	Expository Genres
• Personal narratives • Personal letter writing/writing a friendly letter • Fiction (narratives, fairy tales, fables, fantasy stories) • Poetry • Autobiographies	• Descriptions of objects, people, places, or events • Book reviews • Articles • Informational reports • Feature articles • Directions • Procedural writing (how-to) • Poetry

FIGURE 8–4: Writing Genres for K–2 Students

Language Theory in Practice

English learners should have lots of opportunities to share their ideas with one another during writing workshop. Opportunities to give and receive peer feedback throughout the writing process will help them continue to practice and develop their conversational and academic oral language. "As students develop control over their language, their writing gradually begins to approximate standard English" (Peregoy and Boyle 2005, 208).

When working with a partner, students' affective filter will be lowered, allowing for more comprehensible input and in turn language development (see "Second Language Acquisition" in Chapter 1). Further, English learners benefit from working with peers to improve their writing through peer revision and editing, to give and receive support, and to develop positive relationships (Peregoy and Boyle 2005; Farrell 2006). Peregoy and Boyle (2005) recommend reading the book *Peer Response in Second Language Writing Classrooms*, by Liu and Hansen (2002), to get specific suggestions on how to structure and engage students in peer response.

English learners will utilize their primary language skills to foster English writing development (see "Second Language Acquisition" in Chapter 1). They often make connections to letters and sounds in their first language when writing, and in ways to organize their ideas. Their cognitive development and experiences throughout their lives in their primary language will be the foundation of their writing.

What Does Writing Workshop Look Like?

Key Elements (Across All Levels of Readers)

The structure of writing workshop is similar to that of independent reading workshop. As with all the other components of a balanced literacy program, the success of writing workshop builds upon the regularity of daily practice and set routines. It typically includes a mini-lesson, time for independent writing with individual conferring sessions with the teacher, a time for partnership talk, and a whole-group share. Every workshop begins with a minilesson to focus the students on a particular aspect of writing; however, children are expected to use the accumulation of all that they know about writing during the workshop. When we write, we employ many strategies that range from formulating our ideas, to expressing them in words, to making sure that our audience can understand and read our ideas. We have a body of knowledge, or a bag of tricks, to help us in our writing. Minilessons are like little bits of advice and tips that we can add to our bag of tricks so that when we get stuck, we can employ what we have learned to help us improve our own writing. The focus of writing workshop is always on independence. That is why the largest portion of time in the workshop is devoted to independent writing. Everything we do as teachers—from teaching minilessons, to conducting conferences, to facilitating share sessions—is designed to enable students to work independently. As we make each teaching move, we need to ask ourselves, "How am I teaching the students to be independent"? Figure 8–5 shows the suggested structure for writing workshop.

What Do We Need to Do to Get Writing Workshop Started?

Young children make something each time they write in the writing workshop. They make cards, letters, stories, recipes, and informational books. The *folder* is the central tool in writing workshop because it is the place where they keep their ideas and stuff for writing. When we introduce the folders to the students, we show them our own personalized writer's folder with pictures of our family and collections of words and pictures that remind us of things that we love. All of these things represent ideas that we could write about. The folder is also a place where we organize our work—writing is serious work! One side of the two-pocket folder is labeled "Finished" and the other, "Unfinished." We tell the children that when we finish working on a piece of writing during a session, we have to make a decision as a writer whether that piece is finished for now or if we will continue

Minilesson	5–12 minutes
Independent Writing and Conferring	20–30 minutes
Partnership Talk	5–10 minutes
Whole-Group Share	5 minutes

FIGURE 8–5: Structure of the Writing Workshop

to work on it the following day in writing workshop. If we are not finished, we place it on the "Unfinished" side so that we can return to it the next day. This way of using the folder is very concrete and easy for our earliest writers to understand.

Students should have access to the materials they will need to be successful writers. This can include writing folders, paper (various sizes and formats), sharpened pencils, pens, crayons, markers, and staplers. Placing these items in a centralized place such as a writing center will help with management. They won't have to keep asking you if they can sharpen their pencil or get another piece of paper. Those items will already be available for them to get as needed. It will also be necessary for you to provide instructions on how to care for their writing materials at the beginning of the school year. For example, it is helpful to show students how to put their writing away properly in their writing folder to avoid folding or tearing their paper. The use of all materials should focus on the need for independence. The more you have to give permission for students, the less independent they will be and the less time you'll have to confer with students one-on-one. Writing workshop is not a chaotic time; it is a structured time in which students have daily opportunities to convey their ideas through writing and employ strategies they have learned in order to make their writing better. Being able to make deliberate decisions as a writer includes being able to determine which tools and material to use. Figure 8–6 lists some of the common tools used in writing workshop.

Minilessons

Minilessons during writing workshop can vary from five to twelve minutes. They might include a variety of formats such as a writing demonstration by the teacher, reference to a read-aloud, or a revisitation of a piece of writing for a process, strategy, or grammar lesson. "Minilessons are teacher demonstrations and interactive lessons in procedures, craft, and conventions that make the writing workshop run smoothly and help move students' writing forward" (Routman 2000, 298).

- Two-pocket folder for each student
- Various paper choices (story, article, letter, postcard, greeting card, list)
- Pencils or pens for writing
- Date stamp for kindergarten
- Staplers and tape for revision, editing, and publishing
- Construction paper, markers, crayons, scissors, hole punchers, and so on for publishing

FIGURE 8–6: Tools for the Writing Workshop

Lucy Calkins and the Reading and Writing Project have devised a wonderful structure for minilessons that helps teachers concisely and clearly teach writers one teaching point at a time:

- connection
- teaching
- active involvement
- link

In each lesson, the teacher is *connecting* the day's lesson to previous learning. This is followed by a clear *teaching* point and then an opportunity for each child to to *actively engage* in some guided practice before being given a *link* to ongoing independent work. With some practice, this becomes a very effective structure.

Possible Methods of Teaching During the Minilesson

Demonstration—Students need to see teachers write. When a teacher models her thinking process as a writer, it helps students better understand what it means to write. A teacher will create an original piece of writing, sharing her ideas and experiences with the class, as well as model how to put those ideas on paper. Demonstrations are extremely helpful when drafting to show students how to take their ideas and expand them into full pieces of writing. "Children learn to write when they see us writing for real purposes. By watching us, children can learn that writing is not only doable, it is also worth doing" (Calkins 1994, 60).

Referring to read-aloud experiences—At any stage of the writing process, the use of published texts can help students see various models of writing. You will want to select books or texts that demonstrate what it is you are expecting of your students as writers. These discussions around published books supply students with a plethora of writing strategies they can use in their own writing.

Process, strategy, or grammar lesson—You can use the texts created during shared writing, interactive writing, and demonstrations to show students particular revision and editing strategies. This can also include process lessons on how to talk with a partner about your writing. Modeling how to help a friend revise and edit his writing will help build community and respect. Teach students how to provide positive feedback and offer advice for improving their classmates' writing.

Your minilessons will come from close observations of students as they write and consideration of what the students need to know about qualities of good writing, the writing process, and writing genres. When you confer with students and observe their involvement in minilessons, you will get a sense of their needs as thinkers and writers (see Figure 8–7).

What habits of writers do my students need to acquire?

• Write easily about self-selected topics; write with quantity across pages; stretch out words to the best of one's abilities

What do my students need to know about using language and conventions?

• Focus; elaboration; organizational style and syntax; vocabulary and word choice; spelling; punctuation, capitalization, and other conventions

What genres and structures do my students need to know how to write?

• Narrative; functional and procedural; report or informational

What steps of the process require more independence from my students?

• Prewriting/drafting; choosing; revising; editing; publishing

FIGURE 8–7: Things to Consider When Planning Writing Minilessons

Independent Writing Time

The time allotted for writing will vary by grade level. What is important is that "you provide the time for writing, the first fundamental condition" (Graves 1994, 113). Students need opportunities to write daily! If this is not possible, Donald Graves (1994) recommends that students should get at least four days for writing each week. With at least four days you will have more opportunities for conferring, and students will be able to move a piece forward through the writing process.

Students also need to know that when it is time to write, the room should be quiet and they should be thinking and writing. This will always hold true during independent writing time unless the students have been directed to engage in peer work, such as revision or editing. It is important to set a tone of writers busily working at their craft. Children are expected to write. In the beginning stages of launching writing workshop, you will often hear children say, "I don't know what to write!" or "I'm done." My response always carries the expectation that there are so many stories to tell that they couldn't possibly be done!

Conferring

Teachers meet with students as they write independently. They listen to a child read her own writing and offer suggestions for how to take the writing further. Teachers keep ongoing records of their students' writing behaviors. Lucy McCormick Calkins (1994) explains three components of an effective conference: research, decide, and teach. During the *research* phase, teachers ask the student questions about her writing to better understand the student's writing process, choices, strategies, and behaviors. This dialogue with the student will inform the teacher about what to teach in the conference. The *decision* on what to teach the student "must be guided by 'what might help this writer' rather than 'what might help this writing'" (Calkins 1994, 228). The teaching point should help students become better writers for future writing. *Teach* them something to make them better decision makers when they develop, create, and revisit writing throughout their writing lives. It is important to teach only one thing to the writer. As teachers, we easily find many things to teach and might feel tempted to bombard a child with all of our ideas; however, if we do that, the student will be left confused, not knowing what to do.

Long before working for Lucy Calkins at Teachers College Reading and Writing Project, I often heard her say, "Teach the writer, not the writing," during one of her summer institutes. Her words resonate within me each time I confer with a writer. We must always ask ourselves what we have taught this writer that will support him through his experiences as a writer. It is easy to sit alongside a child, read his writing, and come up with a million things to fix up in his writing. We often find glaring grammatical and spelling mistakes that distract us from really looking at this child as a writer. We are quick to want to edit the piece. This might help the piece, but what have we taught the writer to do independently? Our youngest writers and our ELs are fully capable of editing their own work. Figure 8–8 offers some advice on how to choose a teaching point for a conference.

Once you have decided on what to teach the writer, you must consider how you will do that. You can refer to the methods of teaching in the minilesson to teach students in a conference. It is also helpful for other students at the table to hear the conference and benefit from the teaching. Initially you might think that this is distracting to other students, but the students become accustomed to it. There are times when nearby students can serve as models for what you are trying to teach. At other times, other students might need exactly the same lesson. By hearing the exchange between you and another student, a child in the early stages of second language acquisition can experience the tone and expectation of this exchange, which will prepare her for her turn.

Talk Time

Though providing ongoing opportunities to talk about academic tasks is not always the standard during writing workshop, we find that English learners need those opportunities. We suggest giving students about five minutes to talk to a partner about their work as writers daily. This is not a structured time, but a time when students are told, "OK, go ahead and talk to your neighbor about what you did today as a writer." Some students like to read their piece to their partner; others just tell what they wrote about. This talk time is not the same as the peer revision and peer editing time described during minilessons

IN ORDER TO DECIDE *WHAT* TO TEACH THE WRITER, THE TEACHER MUST CONSIDER:	REFLECTIONS ON THESE CONSIDERATIONS
What do I already know about this writer? What are the writer's strengths?	It is important to first consider what the writer does well. Building upon strengths is critical. Does the writer seem to write easily about topics of his choice? Does the writer convey his ideas clearly and with detail? What improvements do you notice in both qualities of good writing as well as English language development and syntax?
What have I already taught him through minilessons and conferences?	Drawing connections to previous learning helps the writer become more independent and effective in applying several skills simultaneously. Furthermore, it is essential to keep students accountable to what has already been taught in order to foster independence.
What part of the process is this writer in?	If a child is struggling to come up with initial ideas of his own choosing, the first thing to teach may not be correct spelling. This is often a difficult point for many to understand. The premise of workshop teaching is independence. This begins with topic choice. Once students are able to grasp this concept, they are expected to be more and more independent with the remaining steps of the process. Alternatively, if a student has revised to the best of his abilities and is currently editing in time for the publishing party, I probably won't be focusing the writer on adding more experiences to the piece. We must be able to find out from the writer what he is doing. What are his intentions?
What type of piece is this? What must this writer know about writing this type of piece?	What is characteristic of this genre? Does the child understand the purpose of the genre? Knowing this will help him understand why it is structured in particular ways. How should this type of writing be organized?

FIGURE 8–8: Questions to Consider When Deciding What to Teach Our Youngest Writers in a Conference

and independent writing time. This is just an opportunity to share ideas in an unstructured way. While the content of these talk sessions is unstructured, this is an opportune time to listen in on partners and support them in their language needs.

Whole-Group Share

After students have had an opportunity to talk with a partner about their writing, the teacher will select a student or two to share with the whole class. The teacher will select these students as she observes them during independent writing and talk time. Teachers can choose those who have exemplified the goal of that day's minilesson or have tried out a new writing strategy.

Writing Workshop for Emergent and Early Readers at Different Levels of Second Language Acquisition

For students at the emergent and early stages of literacy development, we would expect to see drawings, one- to two-word labeling, or simple sentences. These students will need an emphasis on the connection between concepts about print, word work, and developing their oral language to continue their development as writers in English. They will need to constantly revisit their pieces and share their stories with one another while referring to what they have created on their papers. It is this reinforcement that enables these young students to make the connection between what is on the page and an idea in their head. In this way, they will come to understand that writing is about communicating their ideas on paper. Early on in kindergarten, many students might mistake writing workshop for drawing time if this point is not emphasized.

Emergent and early readers will need a lot of shared and interactive writing experiences to see how writing works and how their ideas can be transferred to paper. This can be done in small groups and whole-group times outside of writing workshop. Because the emphasis of the writing workshop is to provide opportunities for students to write independently, the experiences in writing *to* and *with* should be done separately. Although we do not include these methods separately in this book, both shared writing and interactive writing can be included in balanced literacy and can be added as short, ten- to fifteen-minute segments of the day. Alternatively, they might also be used as methods in a writing workshop minilesson. In order to transfer learning from whole-class lessons such as shared writing and interactive writing, it is important to connect these experiences explicitly to students' independent work during minilessons and conferences. For instance, during a conference with a first-grade writer who was struggling to structure her friendly letter, I referred to a letter we had written together as a class during interactive writing.

In shared writing, the teacher models the composition of a text by first formulating the idea with the class. The students participate orally by sharing the ideas while the teacher writes down the text in the conventional format. This is a risk-free time for English learners to practice their academic oral language because the teacher has the difficult task of writing the ideas down on the paper. In interactive writing, similar work is done, except the teacher shares the pen with the students and children have an opportunity to write some of the letters or words.

This allows them to have guided practice in forming letters, inserting spaces, sounding out letters, and punctuating sentences. Because children may have different needs in terms of word work, this can be done in smaller groups for children with similar needs.

Writers at this stage may not use standard spelling or grammatical conventions, but they understand that symbols communicate meaning and there are plenty of stories they are eager to share through writing (Avery 2002). In kindergarten, some students will not be writing any letters but they might draw their story. For instance, in the kindergarten sample in Figure 8–9, Carlos is at the early production stage of second language acquisition (stage II). He writes about how he wants to be a red Power Ranger for Halloween. He communicates this first through his picture. You'll notice that there is one person who is colored differently. He also knows that in writing, there are letters that people write to go with their picture. He then adds letters but is not yet matching letters to sounds. A few letters aren't clear because he is also working on letter formation. During partner time in writing workshop, his teacher asks each partnership to read back their own writing. She has modeled this many times and the children have practiced this often. Carlos tells his partner, "I want to be a red Power Ranger," while he points to the figure on the left. He doesn't yet point to the words as he reads, as his teacher has taught. Carlos does know that he has a story to communicate and is able to read back his piece. In the early stages of writing workshop, a huge goal in kindergarten is being able to make this association. This is how writing workshop is different from drawing. There is an expectation of communicating, eventually through written words, but initially through pictures and symbols.

FIGURE 8–9: Power Ranger Piece

Minilessons

Your minilessons for emergent and early readers will begin with helping them understand that they can put their ideas and experiences on paper. You will see many of your students drawing their stories, so you will want to model how to tell a story through pictures. Students can learn how to revise a drawing by adding more information or more details to it. Eventually, they will start to label their drawings with letters, words, and sentences. Giving a lot of opportunities to share ideas for writing is important at this stage. Students need to see that ideas for writing can come from everywhere. With careful and frequent attention to the development of ideas, you can avoid hearing the famous line "I don't know what to write about. I can't think of anything." Before sending your students back to their desks to begin independent writing, give them a chance to turn and talk with a neighbor about what they can write about. Give them time to think before sending them to their seats to begin writing. It might sound something like this: "I want you all to close your eyes for a minute and think about what you will do today as writers. Will you write about your family, something you want everyone to know, one special time with a friend? What story do you want to share? Just think for a minute [pause]. OK, now that everybody has a plan for his or her writing, turn and tell your neighbor your ideas for writing today."

We mentioned earlier that minilessons will come from a variety of sources as well as things to consider when planning minilessons (see Figure 8–7). However, teachers always ask us for specific ideas for minilessons. Figure 8–10 lists several suggestions that incorporate content standards for writing and developing writers. Keep in mind that these suggestions are only a beginning. Minilessons will come from your students' needs as writers. And although you can plan out *possible* units of study you will teach during the year and even have a sense of the types of minilessons you might teach, it is not possible to know exactly what you will teach. You will continue to work with your students and see their development and needs as writers.

Let's take a look at a minilesson in a classroom with English learners at various stages of second language acquisition. In the transcript in Figure 8–11, you will find that there is very little dialogue with students because it is primarily a direct instruction time. As a staff developer, I gave this lesson in a first-grade class near the beginning of the year, shortly after the students had published their initial one-page stories.

Independent Writing and Conferring

Emergent and early readers will need to slowly build their endurance as writers. You might start by giving them ten minutes to write independently and ultimately get them to write for a half hour. Also,

WRITING STRATEGIES	CONVENTION, GRAMMAR, USAGE, AND MECHANICS
Writing about experiences, stories, people, objects, and events	Writing from left to right, top to bottom
Writers try the best they can to write (risk taking); they stretch out words as best as they can	Using spaces between words (finger spacing) and sentences
How to use drawing and writing tools (cross a word out and keep going instead of erasing, etc.)	Proper letter formation: writing legibly
	Spelling words using knowledge of sounds and letters
Rereading your writing	Spelling grade-level sight words correctly
Creating writing through scribbles, shapes, letterlike symbols, pictures	Writing in complete sentences (overuse of *and*)
Drawing a picture and telling a story	Correctly using singular and plural nouns (*-s, -es, -ies*)
Writing a story across many pages	Correctly using pronouns
Writing letters and words to label drawings	Correctly using periods and exclamation and question marks
Writing words and brief sentences to tell a story or share an idea	Using capital letters correctly to begin a sentence and for proper nouns
Selecting a focus when writing: staying on topic	
Using descriptive words (adjectives, adverbs) when writing	

FIGURE 8–10: Possible Minilessons for Emergent and Early Writers

CLASSROOM TRANSCRIPT	REFLECTION
Connection	
Writers, I have noticed that you are all writing a lot! We have so many great stories to tell! Did you know that we have so much to write that we now need more pages to get our whole story down? Just like a book! You have grown so much as writers. Today, I'm going to show you how you can stretch your story across three pages.	I am building on their strengths and connecting to their previous work to set the context of today's lesson. I want for them to also understand that we stretch ourselves as writers.

FIGURE 8–11: Writing Workshop in Action: A First-Grade Minilesson

CLASSROOM TRANSCRIPT	REFLECTION

CLASSROOM TRANSCRIPT

Teaching

Remember how I often tell you different stories about my cat Hopper? He was so special to me and I still think of him often.

Remember how I told you the story of how he followed me to school one day? Oh that was a great story! I have a special booklet—like the ones I have for you guys today—with three pages. Hmmm, I'm going to need to plan out the three pages. Let me tell the story back to myself again.

First [holds up index finger], I was running out of the house because I was late. When I ran down the street, I noticed that Hopper was behind me. I kept saying, "Go back, go back home," but he kept coming. Then [holds up two fingers], when I got to school he tried to hide in the bushes by the school, but I still saw him. I told my principal that I was worried about Hopper and that I didn't want to go inside the school and leave him outside. Then [holds up three fingers] Mr. Rogers let me keep Hopper in the gym until the end of the day. I was so happy that I didn't have to worry about Hopper running away.

OK, I think I'll start with a quick picture here [points to top of paper] so I can remember what I will write on this page.

First [holds up index finger] Hopper was following me to school [begins to draw girl with a cat following behind]. Hmmm, I'm not sure how to draw him following me, so I'll just draw Hopper's face quickly and finish it later.

Now I'm ready to plan for the next page [turns to next page]. Let's see, what happened next? [Holds two fingers up] Yes, Hopper was hiding in the bushes and Mr. Rogers came. I'll draw a quick picture of me, the bush, Hopper, and Mr. Rogers.

Now I'm ready to plan my last page [turns page and holds up three fingers] with the last part of my story. Mr. Rogers let Hopper stay in the gym [draws picture of cat in a gym].

REFLECTION

I often refer to stories in my own life. Students are often curious and pay attention to our stories. Also, because there is much I want to demonstrate in this lesson, I do not want to introduce a new idea that will distract them from focusing on the work I want to teach them today.

I demonstrate with an enlarged version of what they will get. It is three stapled pages of chart paper with the bottom half lined.

I tell each part of the story and symbolize each page with my finger. You will notice that I repeat the story in a more abridged version later. Now I want my ELs to hear a story with detail to better understand it as well as see a model of elaborated language.

Here, I emphasize *quick* when drawing the picture because I want to model how I would like the students to do it. The key is for them to plan across pages. A quick, concrete picture will help them remember what to put on each page. I repeat the story again because I want the students to do the same.

You'll notice that I also make reference to having some difficulty when drawing my picture, but I move along quickly. This was taught in previous lessons, so the children are accustomed to me modeling this aspect of risk taking and maintaining fluency when writing ideas down. I also exaggerate the turning of the pages so that it is very obvious that they will be doing the same. Until now, they have been writing only one-page stories.

(Continues)

FIGURE 8–11: *Continued*

CLASSROOM TRANSCRIPT	REFLECTION

Do you see how I just stretched my story across three pages?! I just quickly did the best that I could to draw quick pictures to remind me. Now I can go back to each page, add more details to the pictures on each page, and then add some words.

Let's go back and review the story I have planned across these three pages. Can you help me by putting up your fingers as I go to each page?

So, on the first page, Hopper followed me to school [all students hold up one finger], then he hid in the bushes and I was telling my principal I was worried about him [all students hold up two fingers]. At the end, Mr. Rogers let Hopper stay in the gym while I was in school [all students hold up three fingers].

I go back and read the story a third time, this time asking the students to join me by holding up their fingers. I am trying to make this experience one step closer to what they will be doing. I also want them to see the habit of telling the story back to themselves over and over again. Not only does this allow students to practice their language skills, but it also reminds them of what to place on the pages.

Active Involvement

Now, I want you guys to think about what story you will stretch across three pages. Do you think you could do that too? [All the faces across the rug nod with enthusiasm.]

OK, close your eyes and think of a story. What happens first? [Waits a few seconds] Do you have the first part? Hold up one finger. Now, what happens next? Hold up two fingers when you have it. OK, now how does the story end? Hold up three fingers once you have it.

Wow! We have so many three-page stories! Now turn and tell your partner your story. Use your fingers to remind you of all three parts.

[Students turn to each other and tell their stories.]

Now I am expecting them to come up with their own stories using the same method. If this might be too difficult for the students from a language perspective, I might have the students tell my story back to each other since they have heard me say it three times. This allows them to practice the language that I modeled. The drawback to this method is that the children will try to emulate my piece. In that case, I would need to emphasize the use of their own stories.

Link

When you go off to write today, I am hoping that many of you will try to stretch a story across three pages. If you think you will try this today, will you hold up three fingers? [Teacher then dismisses students by table.]

Of course young children will want to try this. I ask students to hold up the three fingers so they'll leave the rug with a connection to their story.

FIGURE 8–11: *Continued*

materials should include paper with large spaces for drawing and lined paper with limited spaces for drawing.

During independent writing, you will often hear "Teacher, I'm done," after about five minutes of writing. Make sure your students understand that they are never finished as writers. If they finish a draft and are not ready to revise it, they can look at their list of possible topics or ideas and begin a new draft. Knowing that there is no end will slow the students down. You might want to generate a list with your students titled "What Can I Do When I Think I Am Finished?" Also, be sure you review with your students the expectations for writing time. These can include

- Stay in your seat unless you are getting materials for writing.
- Don't talk to your neighbors when you are finished; give them a chance to concentrate on their writing.
- When you think you are finished, look at your writing and decide if you want to add anything. If not, put the piece you were working on in your writing folder and take out your "Ideas for Writing" page to start a new piece.

The last rule is critical to give you the time you need to confer with students. If this practice is not established, you will be bombarded with students asking you what they should be doing.

A First-Grade Conference

Juan has just come to the United States from Mexico and has been in school for a week. He is able to read and write in Spanish. He has participated in writing workshop since his first day at school. He first looked around carefully at what the other students were doing. He noticed that they would draw a picture and then write below the picture. He also heard students telling each other stories that they would then write. He has also been exposed to interactive writing, when the teacher has composed pieces with students, so he has seen how they have sounded out words and used the word wall to assist them with sight words. During the writing workshop today, the boys at his table have been talking about cars. One of the boys' uncle just bought a new car, and they have been swapping stories about cars. Some of the students at the table have begun to write; however, Juan is listening and watching what the others are writing. When Ms. Mamdou comes to confer with him, his paper is blank. Figure 8–12 contains a transcript of their conference. Figure 8–13 shows Juan's resulting piece.

Talk Time

Just let the students talk. Hearing what their friends are writing about will give them ideas for future writing. Also in talking with their friends about their own writing, they can practice their oral language with

CLASSROOM TRANSCRIPT	REFLECTION
T: Juan, what are you working on today? [Juan looks at her and doesn't speak, then he looks at what the other students are doing.]	Even though Juan does not yet speak English, Ms. Mamdou still confers with him and she begins the conference with the same beginning line that she uses with all the students. Juan has heard her ask students all around him the same thing. Ms. Mamdou wants him to understand that she has the same expectations for him.
T: Tell me the story you want to write today.	In previous workshops, Juan has drawn different pictures of his family. This drawing helps Juan feel successful as a writer. He too can communicate his stories on paper even though he is new to the country and is at the preproduction stage of second language acquisition (stage I).
S: *Mi padre maneja a la playa.*	Juan tells Ms. Mamdou his story in Spanish.
T: Oh, your father uses the car to go to the beach.	She is able to understand what he was saying and repeats it back to him in English.
T: That's great! Now, write your story down on the paper [gesturing toward the paper]. I'll come back to check on you.	She leaves him so that he can write on his own. Notice that she doesn't linger; this could make him be dependent upon her. She leaves with the expectation that he will work.
[After a few more conferences, Ms. Mamdou returns to find what Juan has written. During the time he was working on his piece, he was sounding each word out with a strong accent.]	Juan's strong literacy experience in his native language coupled with the rich literacy experiences he has been immersed in have enabled him to easily transfer skills from one language to another (see "Second Language Acquisition" in Chapter 1).
T: Wow! That is great. That is your story. Let's read it together. [She points to each word and reads it slowly as he joins in with her.]	

FIGURE 8–12: Writing Workshop in Action: A First-Grade Conference

confidence around familiar themes: themselves and their experiences. This intimate and comfortable setting for practicing talk helps you listen to your students' language development because many students may not have the confidence to try out their oral language in a whole-group share.

FIGURE 8–13: Juan's Piece

Whole-Group Share

Remind students that they all had a chance to share their writing during talk time and that only a few students will get to share out to the entire class. Be sure not to pressure English learners at the preproduction stage of second language acquisition to share out loud to the entire group because they may not be ready. Let them hear their friends share, and that in itself will further help them develop language. Alternatively, you could ask the children if you can share their writing or their ideas. Even if the child is not comfortable conveying her ideas, she'll know that she is being recognized.

Carol Avery (2002) shares five rules for first graders to follow during a large-group share:

1. Look at the person who's talking.
2. Keep your hands still.
3. Be very quiet.
4. Listen carefully.
5. Think of any questions you have.

In addition, you should remind students that they want to let their classmates know what they like about their writing and what they notice about their classmates as writers. Develop your own list with your class about how to engage in the whole-group share.

Writing Workshop for Transitional and Self-Extending Readers Across All Levels of Second Language Acquisition

Transitional and self-extending readers are ready to move beyond drawings and simple sentences to creating texts with multiple sentences and varying structures. Though some English learners at this stage may still need to draw their ideas out first, our goal at this stage is to get them to write out what their drawings represent, the story that they want to tell as writers.

Minilessons

Transitional and self-extending readers have strong word work skills. This knowledge will transfer to their writing. These students will have a lot to say, so their writing will consist of multiple sentences and ideas. Minilessons should now begin to focus on how to organize those ideas more effectively. They need to learn how to stay on topic and how to use words more effectively to get their story across. The use of demonstrations and read-alouds will supply transitional and self-extending readers with models of how to write well. They will learn how to make their writing more exciting, more inviting for their audience.

As with emergent and early readers, minilessons for transitional and self-extending readers will come from a variety of sources as you get to know your students as writers. Figure 8–14 provides suggestions for specific minilessons. It is not an exhaustive list and should be used as a reference to support what you see and learn from your students as writers. Also, remember that your students at this stage can learn a lot from one another. Minilessons on how to engage in peer editing and peer revision will encourage community building, involving everyone in teaching and learning.

Independent Writing and Conferring

Transitional and self-extending readers will continue to build their endurance as writers, beginning by writing for twenty minutes and ultimately staying focused on a piece for thirty to forty minutes. Students will be reminded of classroom expectations for writing such as respecting other writers' thinking, knowing where and when to get materials, including reference materials such as dictionaries and thesauri, and monitoring their own writing process. Because these students are taking command of their writing process, you can begin to implement classroom management tools for individual writers. One example would be a writing process wheel on which students can express where they are in the writing process. (See Figure 8–15.)

Further, available paper should now include more lined paper choices rather than formats with large spaces for drawing. This sets

STRATEGIES	GRAMMAR, USAGE, AND MECHANICS
Selecting a topic	Word order in a sentence
Writing introductions: how to capture your audience	Using simple and compound sentences properly
Maintaining a consistent focus when writing	Identifying subject-verb agreement
Maintaining a logical sequence when writing	Spelling frequently used irregular words correctly (*was, were, said, because, says*)
How to show versus tell a story	Spelling one-syllable words with blends, contractions, and compounds correctly
Using sensory details	
Using adjectives, adverbs, and figurative language	Spelling basic short-vowel, long-vowel, *r*-controlled, and consonant-blend patterns correctly
Using vivid verbs	
Word choice: how to make our writing more dynamic	Capitalization rules for greetings, proper nouns, months, days of the week, titles, initials
Noticing overused words (e.g., *said, nice*)	Capitalization rules for holidays, geographical locations, historical periods, and special events
Establishing purpose and audience	
Writing a paragraph (topic sentences, supporting facts, conclusions)	Correct use of commas in greetings, dates, and series
Organizing ideas (within one paragraph or into multiple paragraphs)	Correct use of commas in locations and addresses
How to use reference materials (dictionary, thesaurus)	Punctuating dates, city and state, and titles of books correctly

FIGURE 8–14: Possible Minilessons for Transitional and Self-Extending Writers

new expectations for students as writers. Guide students through routines for writing on lined paper such as skipping lines to leave space for revising, writing only on one side of the paper to allow for moving text around, putting their name and date on every paper, and crossing out words instead of erasing so they can revisit old ideas later (Routman 2000, 293).

Independent writing time at this stage may involve peer revision and editing. Students will learn how to help each other improve their writing. To guide peer revision and editing, teachers can provide a checklist during minilesssons titled, "How Can I Help My Partner Improve His or Her Writing?" These peer sessions can be open, or through your minilesson you can ask students to look for something in particular.

FIGURE 8–15: Process Wheel

Talk Time

Talk time is not the time for peer revision and editing. That will take place during independent writing time. On days when your students have engaged in peer revision or editing, you do not need to give them talk time. They will have already shared their work as writers for the day. On all other occasions, students should get five minutes to engage in an open conversation about their writing with a partner.

Whole-Group Share

At the end of an independent writing session, when all students have already had a chance to share their writing with a partner, the teacher can select one or two students to share out something they did that day as a writer. Again, the teacher will select the students based on observations of students during independent writing time and talk time. Because many students at the transitional and self-extending stage will have longer pieces of writing, remind them to share out only a small part that they want the class to hear or the place in their writing where they tried something new as a writer.

Developing Writing, Developing Language

It is always wonderful to be able to see growth with a child's writing. Now we'd like to tell you about Isaac, an English learner at the late transitional stage of literacy development. When Isaac started second grade he was at the early production stage of second language acquisition (stage II). He spoke in simple sentences and could understand directions and social language. Isaac is an inquisitive child who loves to read in both English and Spanish. At home, his parents speak only Spanish. They encourage Isaac to read at home and though they do not have many books, his mother always reminds him to ask his teacher if he can borrow books from the classroom. Isaac's teacher is aware of the lack of books at home, so she too reminds him that he is welcome to take home books from the classroom library daily.

In the beginning of the school year, the class was working on developing personal narratives during writing workshop. The students had been collecting drafts about personal experiences they had shared with family and friends. One of Isaac's personal narratives is shown in Figure 8–16. In this piece we can see that Isaac had been developing his English language quickly. As mentioned before, when starting second grade, he was at stage II of SLA. This piece was written one month into the school year. When looking at his writing, you can see evidence that Isaac had moved on to the next stage of SLA, speech emergence. At this stage ELs are not ready for constant correction of their form or sentence structure because they are trying to develop their oral fluency and the confidence to try out longer stretches of language. Notice that Isaac seemed confident in trying out longer stretches of language. He wrote, "One buetiful day my dad came from his work with some tickits for us to go to the funnist sircis of all so we went." He was not worried about form; he just let his ideas about this special day at the circus flow. He connected a series of ideas together in a string of language—it was a nice day, his father came home from work, he had tickets to a circus, and the family went to the circus. Each of these ideas could be elaborated on, but at this stage in his language acquisition, Isaac was simply allowing his language to flow as he thought and heard it in his head. He also provided more details in his sentence than you would have seen at stage II of SLA, for example, words like *beautiful* and *funniest*.

Now, let's see his work and language development five months later. In conjunction with a unit of study on nonfiction in reading workshop, at this point in the school year, the class has been working on writing descriptive, informational pieces of writing. Isaac loves nonfiction and gets very excited about the things that he learns. He shares what he learns from reading informational texts with his parents at home. Even when reading the information in English, he talks to his parents about it in Spanish at home. This helps Isaac continue to develop his background knowledge about the information he reads as well as supports his continual language development of his primary language at home and his English language when reading and at school.

Isaac's teacher further supports his love for nonfiction. She has noticed that during reading workshop Isaac is reading a lot about owls. She pulls books from the classroom library, books from the school library, and Internet articles on owls for Isaac to read during reading

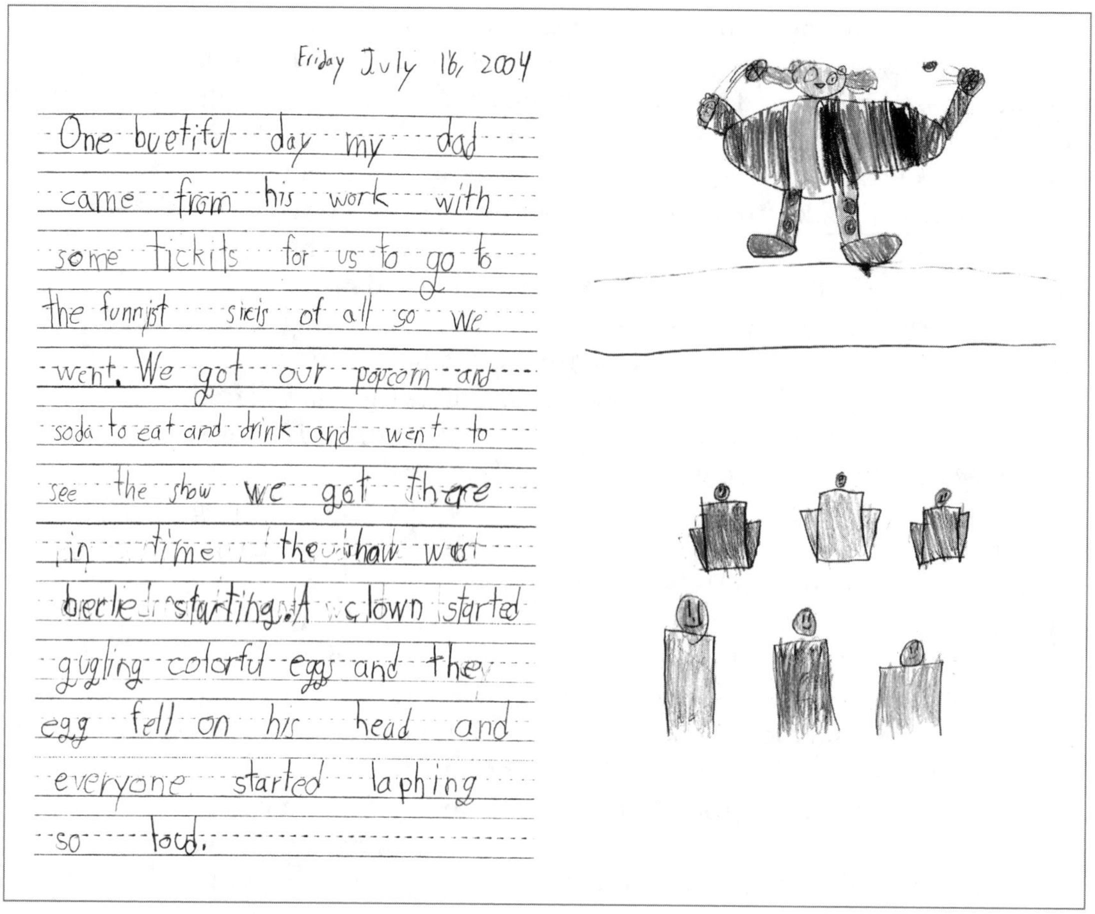

Friday July 16, 2004

One buetiful day my dad came from his work with some tickits for us to go to the funnist siceis of all so we went. We got our popcorn and soda to eat and drink and went to see the show we got thare in time the show was berlei starting. A clown started gugling colorful eggs and the egg fell on his head and everyone started laphing so loud.

FIGURE 8–16: Isaac's Piece

workshop and to take home. This research into owls has led Isaac to use owls as a topic for a descriptive informational piece during writing workshop. (See Figure 8–17.)

In this piece there is evidence that Isaac has been provided the proper support as a writer and is now at the intermediate fluency stage of second language acquisition (stage IV). He is able to present a great deal of detailed information about owls with elaborated ideas and text evidence. Cue words in sentences such as *because* and *the reason why* are clues that students are able to do this. Isaac can explain his abstract thinking in concrete ways. For example, he writes, "Owls are birds. they are warm blooded even in the winter. The reasin they are always warm blooded is because of its feathers." In these sentences Isaac gives information about owls, tells what type of animal they are and explains why, and tells what about them makes them birds. Another example of his language development can be seen when he writes, "Owls are masters of camaflage. The ear tufts of an owl is part of it's camaflage because it helps them look like a tree. It helps them get their prey. They eat mice and rats." Here not only does Isaac provide a complex-compound sentence when presenting information, but

(p. 1)

Owls live in trees. Owls live in the branches of trees not like chipmunks. The kind of trees are thie trees in the forest or jungle.
Owls are birds. They are warm blooded even in the winter. The reason

(p. 2)

they are always warm blooded is because of its feathers.
Owls have their ears forward. Their ears are covered with feathers but really hear well. The owls' ear on the right is higher than the left ear. The owls' ears dont hear some things.
Owls have huge eyes to help them see in the dark. It has to turn its

(p. 3)

entire head to look to the side.
Owls are masters of camuflage. The ear tufts of an owl is part of its camaflage because it helps them look like a tree. It helps them get their prey. They eat mice and rats.

FIGURE 8–17: Isaac's Owl Piece

you also see him using content-specific vocabulary words such as *camouflage* and *tufts*.

This rapid, ongoing, and successful development of Isaac's writing and language was possible for a variety of reasons.

- His parents and teacher encourage reading. He reads daily both in the classroom during independent reading workshop and at home.

- The teacher makes connections between reading and writing. She encourages Isaac to write about topics and ideas he is reading about during reading workshop.

- The teacher provides demonstrations of writing informational texts. During writing workshop, Isaac's teacher created her own piece on dolphins, her favorite animal. In his piece on owls, you see Isaac modeling the discourse he saw in his teacher's example as well as in texts he has been reading about owls. He attempts paragraph structures and uses vocabulary he has been exposed to when reading about owls.

- The teacher always adheres to talk time. Every day, Isaac's teacher allows the students to talk to one another about their writing. They share information and this helps develop their academic language. The daily opportunities to talk give them a sense of comfort and enjoyment in using oral language even when they are still trying to develop their English.

Isaac's development of language and literacy can be easily seen when looking at his two pieces of writing side by side (see Figure 8–18).

(on one page)	(on three pages)
One buetiful day my dad came from his work with some tickits for us to go to the funnist sircis of all so we went. We got our popcorn and soda to eat and drink and went to see the show we got there in time the show was berlie starting. A clown started gugling colorful eggs and the egg fell on his head and everyone started laphing so loud.	Owls live in trees. Owls live in the branches of trees not like chipmunks. The kind of trees are the trees in the forest or jungle. Owls are birds. they are warm blooded even in the winter. The reasin they are always warm blooded is because of its feathers. Owls have their ears forward. Their ears are covered with feathers but really hear well. The owls' ear on the right is higher than the left ear. The owls' ears don't hear some things. Owls have huge eyes to help them see in the dark. It has to turn it's entire head to look to the side. Owls are masters of camaflage. The ear tufts of an owl is part of it's camaflage because it helps them look like a tree. It helps them get their prey. They eat mice and rats.

FIGURE 8–18: Comparison of Isaac's Writing

Conclusion

Throughout the day students are working as writers. Their experiences outside the classroom provide ideas for writing; their experiences in class provide models of how to effectively share those experiences through written language. Writing workshop provides a context for students to try out written language. They receive minilessons on developing and expanding ideas, on how to write clearly, and on how to work as a community to develop writers. Further, providing lots of opportunities to talk about writing helps English learners continue to develop their academic language in a risk-free environment. Just as students need opportunities to read to improve their reading, they also need daily opportunities to write to improve their writing. In both cases, these opportunities are presented through a workshop model where students receive constant and consistent feedback to develop both literacy and language.

Professional Literature on Writing Instruction

Anderson, Carl. 2000. *How's It Going?* Portsmouth, NH: Heinemann.

Buss, Kathleen, and Lee Karnowski. 2002. *Reading and Writing Nonfiction Genres*. Newark, DE: International Reading Association.

Calkins, Lucy McCormick. 1994. *The Art of Teaching Writing*. Portsmouth, NH: Heinemann.

Calkins, Lucy et al. 2003. *Units of Study for Primary Writing: A Yearlong Curriculum*. Teachers College Reading and Writing Project. Portsmouth, NH: Heinemann.

Culham, Ruth. 2005. *6+1 Traits of Writing: A Complete Guide for the Primary Grades*. New York: Scholastic.

Fletcher, Ralph, and Joanne Portalupi. 2001. *Writing Workshop: The Essential Guide*. Portsmouth, NH: Heinemann.

Graves, Donald H. 2003. *Writing: Teachers and Children at Work*. Portsmouth, NH: Heinemann.

Pinnell, Gay Su, and Irene C. Fountas. 2000. *Interactive Writing: How Language and Literacy Come Together, K–2*. Portsmouth, NH: Heinemann.

Ray, Katie Wood. 1999. *Wondrous Words: Writers and Writing in the Elementary Classroom*. Urbana, IL: National Council of Teachers of English.

Ray, Katie Wood, and Lisa B. Cleaveland. 2004. *About the Authors: Writing Workshop with Our Youngest Writers*. Portsmouth, NH: Heinemann.

Ray, Katie Wood with Lester Laminack. 2001. *The Writing Workshop: Working through the Hard Parts (and They're All Hard Parts)*. Urbana, IL: NCTE.

Stead, Tony. 2002. *Is That a Fact? Teaching Nonfiction Writing in K–3*. Portland, ME: Stenhouse.

Guided Reading

It is through guided reading that teachers can show children how to read and can support children as they read. Guided reading leads to independent reading that builds the process.

—Irene Fountas & Gay Su Pinnell

What Is Guided Reading?

As a first-grade teacher, Ms. Mamdou has twenty-five students who range from emergent to transitional reading levels and from preproduction (stage I) to nativelike fluency (Stage V) in their second language acquisition. During reading workshop, students have ample time to read their just-right books independently and talk to their partners about their books. Each child is making steady progress, but Ms. Mamdou constantly wishes she could get to more of them each day. In read-aloud, the children are becoming strong listeners and talkers as they develop their comprehension skills. During shared reading, the students are engaged and chime in with her as she reads. She notices that it is becoming more difficult to spend extended periods of time meeting common needs during these sessions.

Ms. Mamdou's dilemma is one that is so typical in our primary classrooms. We provide experiences to model strategies and read *to* children. We consistently provide them with the critical time for independent practice with reading *by* themselves. In whole group, we even provide experiences when we read *with* the children through shared reading. In order to provide a balanced reading approach, we also need a time in which we can meet readers' needs in differentiated small groups where we read *with* children. Guided reading is the time when we are able to take all that we know about individual students through our conferring during reading workshop, group students according to need, and select a book that is slightly beyond their independent level in order to orient them to the next level of reading.

Because Ms. Mamdou's reading partnerships are matched by level, she reviews her conferring notes and often merges two to three partnerships together for a guided reading lesson. Most often, this is an efficient way to organize groups since these students are reading at similar levels. She doesn't combine more than six children together because that would make the small group too difficult to manage. Furthermore, it is not often that so many children have such similar needs at the same reading levels. While Ms. Mamdou meets with a guided reading group, she organizes the rest of the class in independent literacy activities that include independent and partner reading, independent writing, and word work activities across various levels and needs.

Foundations of Guided Reading

Guided reading is the time of day when teachers have a chance to work with a small group of students around a common need. Lessons focus on learning to read and equipping students with word-attack skills and reading comprehension strategies for independent reading. "The final goal of guided reading is not guided reading; it is to enable students to become independent readers who comprehend and analyze, problem-solve and self monitor as they read, and choose to read for pleasure and information" (Routman 2000, 140). Guided reading in conjunction with read-aloud and shared reading lessons prepare students for independence. Where read-aloud and shared reading are conducted in a whole-group setting, guided reading helps a teacher work more intimately with a small group of students as they develop their literacy and language abilities. Figure 9–1 lists the purposes of guided reading.

- To provide instruction that meets the individual needs of students in both literacy and language
- To help students develop strategies for independent reading
- To provide an enjoyable and meaningful context for learning to read
- To emphasize the purpose of reading for meaning

FIGURE 9–1: Purposes of Guided Reading

Context in Our Book

Guided reading is defined and understood in many different ways. Though there are common principles across definitions and methodologies, we present guided reading methods by reading levels. We believe that guided reading differs in purpose and methodology depending on students' reading levels. There are times when we might create a group for guided reading based on language development needs. While guided reading might feel more comfortable to teachers because we can get to more children in groups rather than working with one child at a time, it is important to remember that independence is the goal. We might be tempted to keep working with the most struggling readers in guided reading groups, feeling that we must *teach* them. However, we must provide all children with opportunities to transfer the strategies we have taught into independent practice.

Language Theory in Practice

The work of guided reading is explicit scaffolding for English learners. Students learn best when they are provided the support needed to meet the larger objective within their zone of proximal development (Vygotsky 1962). In particular, English learners will receive the proper language scaffolds in an intimate setting with the teacher and a few classmates. Listening to each other's responses, ideas, and oral language will help students learn from one another. "Language is also more context-embedded when the number of participants in a conversation is reduced. . . . Within the classroom, as well, when teachers can work with individuals or small groups of English language learners, they provide greater contextual support than when they work with the whole class" (Freeman and Freeman 1998, 77).

Students will feel comfortable in these small-group lessons because the group has been gathered to focus on a particular need. This can encourage greater participation and risk taking with oral language. It is important to keep these groups flexible and not fixed. The groups should change as the needs of the readers change. With early and transitional readers, this might happen quite often.

Guided reading offers teachers an opportunity to focus on the particular language needs of English learners. Lessons should be designed to take students forward in their oral as well as academic language. Just as with general guided reading, grouping of English learners should be flexible. Though at times you might have similar second language acquisition levels, those groups will change, depending on the need. You might even use your small-group time with ELs to provide a preview-review session. A *preview* is an opportunity for ELs to receive a comprehensible lesson on upcoming material for whole-group lessons. They will have the background knowledge and language skills needed to be successful with the whole group (*view*). You can provide *reviews* of lessons to ensure that the information was understood and learned. In a traditional preview-view-review model, the preview and review are actually conducted in students' primary language, while the teaching is in their second language. Yvonne and David Freeman (1998) present the success of that model in working with English learners. If you can use students' primary language for instruction, you will find greater success in literacy and language development. If this is not an option, front-loading concepts and language will still help students be more involved in the learning process.

What Does Guided Reading Look Like?

Key Elements (Across All Levels of Readers)

Guided reading can be implemented as a separate time of day, when the remainder of the class is engaged in learning centers (see Appendix F), or it can be incorporated during independent reading workshop as suggested by Calkins (2001). Some teachers choose to conduct guided reading during independent reading workshop because of time constraints. When students are reading independently, the teacher may choose to pull a small group of students together for a guided reading lesson rather than conduct individual conferences. This decision will come from conferences because as the teacher is observing and learning from her students as readers, there may be a few students who exemplify a similar reading behavior and need similar guidance as readers.

Assessing Students for Guided Reading

In order to provide successful guided reading lessons, a teacher must learn from the students. Assessment is key to ensure that the students are receiving the proper lessons. Assessments can include a running record with miscue analysis, conferring notes from reading workshop, and/or an analysis of students' performance on program-specific assessments.

Running Records

A running record is an analysis of a student's independent reading behaviors. The student will be asked to read a passage orally, and as he reads, the teacher will be noting his behaviors, what he says, and what he does while reading. Figure 9–2 provides examples of possible reading behaviors noted during a running record.

During a running record, the teacher and student will each have a copy of the text in front of them and as the student reads, the teacher follows along and makes notations on her copy. The teacher later analyzes the notations she made while the student read, looking at errors, strategic reading behaviors, and the level of text difficulty. The teacher will take a running word count (total number of words in the

- *Omissions*—The student does not read a word.[*]
- *Substitutions*—The child substitutes a word in the text for another word.[*]
- *Insertions*—The student inserts a word into the text. This is not a substitution because there is no word being replaced; it's simply an addition.
- *Repetitions*—The student repeats a word, a sentence, or a phrase for fluency or meaning.
- *Appeals*—The student does not know the word and asks for help.[*]
- *Wait time or hesitation*—The student pauses while reading.
- *Self-corrections*—The student misreads a word and then rereads it correctly.

[*]Indicates behaviors that count as errors.

FIGURE 9–2: Traditional Behaviors Noted During a Running Record

text) and count the total number of errors to determine the percentage of words read correctly. In mathematical terms,

$$\frac{\text{total number of words read} - \text{errors}}{\text{total number of words read}} \times 100 = \text{percentage of word reading accuracy}$$

This percentage will determine if the text is at a student's independent, instructional, or frustration level (see "Literacy Development Levels" in Chapter 2). These levels are helpful when selecting texts for guided, shared, and independent reading. For a more in-depth and practical guide to conducting running records, we recommend Marie Clay's *Running Records for Classroom Teachers* (2000). It is a great how-to guide with plenty of real classroom examples!

Miscue Analysis

While the running record gives us information such as accuracy rates and basic reading behaviors, that is not enough to inform us. A miscue analysis takes a running record even further. A miscue analysis will give you insight into the cueing systems a child uses when reading. Miscue analyses are conducted by analyzing the substitutions a child makes during a running record. Each substitution is analyzed for its acceptability based on syntax (structure—S), graphophonics (visual—V), and semantics (meaning—M) (see Appendix C). Figure 9–3 provides some insight into what a miscue analysis can help teachers understand about a reader. Again, to find out more information about how to conduct a miscue analysis, refer to Marie Clay's *Running Records for Classroom Teachers* (2000).

Conferring Notes

When conferring with students during reading workshop, the teacher will keep records of her work with individual students. During these conferences there will often be some similarities across readers. These readers can be pulled together for a small-group lesson to address their

- What kind of substitutions is the child making (S, M, V)?
- Do the substitutions interfere with the meaning of the text?
- Is the student relying on a specific cueing system when reading?
- Is there a pattern in the student's substitutions (e.g., the child tends to substitute words with other words that start with the same initial letter, indicating an overreliance on the visual cueing system)?
- What is the significance of the pattern? What other sources of information can I reinforce or introduce to the student?

Insignificant Miscues

- Mispronunciations based on dialect or accent
- Substitutions that do not affect meaning; that is, the word used maintains the meaning of the text

FIGURE 9–3: Miscue Analysis

common need. For teachers who keep conferring notes from the class on an entire sheet, it is easy to quickly identify which students have similar needs. For example, a teacher might find that four of her students are having trouble following texts with two lines. They are able to follow one line of text with their fingers, but seem to have trouble with the *return sweep* and continue pointing to each word on the second line of text as they read. This would be a group that the teacher can put together to read texts with two lines of print—just beyond what they are able to do independently. Alternatively, a teacher may find that six students have become stronger decoders and are ready to progress to books with less direct picture support. These children would benefit from a guided reading lesson to practice reading these harder texts. Often, these children will need to be reminded that they must still use the pictures to help them understand the words they are reading.

Program Assessments

Many teachers across the country are faced with the time-consuming task of administering frequent and lengthy assessments from their mandated reading programs. The teacher should analyze this data in ways that will inform his instruction. The teacher should take some time to look at broad class needs to set goals for shared reading lessons but also take a look at similar needs that groups of students may have, which can lead to guided reading and small-group strategy lessons.

Leveling Texts for Guided Reading

Once you have determined the need of the group, you must select the right materials to facilitate learning. Understanding how to analyze texts for their levels of challenge will help you select appropriate materials. When analyzing the complexity level of a text, keep the following in mind: contextual supports (e.g., pictures, accessible story line), amount of text on a page and layout, length of words and sentences, and types of sentences (including dialogue). We use the Fountas and Pinnell (1996) guided reading levels to select text for our guided reading groups. We find that their criteria for different levels are fairly consistent and used widely, which makes their system a practical choice.

For English learners, the literacy levels are only part of text selection. Teachers must also be aware of students' second language acquisition levels. Figure 9–4 provides suggestions of what to look for when selecting texts for students at different levels of second language acquisition. These guidelines are not meant to be limiting. For exam-

SLA LEVELS	CONTEXTUAL SUPPORT	VOCABULARY	SYNTAX
Preproduction	High visual support. Descriptive pictures.	Simple, high-frequency vocabulary.	Labeled pictures. Simple sentences with illustrations to support meaning.
Early Production	High visual support. Descriptive pictures.	Familiar concepts.	Simple sentences. Compound sentences with high visual support. Variety in types of sentences (telling, questioning, exclamatory).
Speech Emergent	Visual support for general comprehension.	Familiar concepts.	Simple and compound sentences. Dialogue.
Intermediate Fluency	Rich textual support with limited visual support to guide comprehension.	New words for known concepts and new concepts.	Complex and compound sentences. Dialogue.
Nativelike Fluency	Rich textual support; limited pictures or illustrations.	Content-specific, low-frequency vocabulary.	Complex and compound sentences. Variations in syntactic structures.

FIGURE 9–4: Text Supports for English Learners

ple, all ELs can benefit from visual support. So when the chart says "limited visual support," that does not mean you should avoid visual support. Rather, it means that because an English learner's ability to read and comprehend English text is higher at the intermediate and nativelike fluency stages, she may not rely on the visuals as much as she used to.

Structure of Guided Reading by Reading Levels

Emergent Readers

We find guided reading most effective with early readers because this method includes the integration of print strategies in reading. However, small-group work with emergent readers is integral to literacy instruction in different ways. For instance, we might pull together a group of students who are having some difficulty retelling their emergent storybooks. We could reread the text to these students or even have them act out various parts of the story in order to make the necessary connections to read it completely. Alternatively, we might want to gather a group of students who need more exposure to particular shared reading texts. Some emergent readers who are also in the beginning stages of second language acquisition may also need additional opportunities to hear the structure of the English language through familiar texts. These students may also benefit from repeating these lines after the teacher has modeled them.

Early Readers

We believe guided reading in addition to independent reading for early readers is central to their development as readers. It is important, however, to clearly note that we cannot substitute guided experiences for independent experiences during reading workshop. These students need support in word-reading skills and strategies while gaining meaning from text. Because they are just beginning their journey as independent readers (in this case, readers who can read the text on their own and comprehend what they are reading), they need guidance on how to integrate various sources of information in order to fully comprehend what they are reading. Students need to consider semantic, syntactic, graphophonic, and pragmatic sources of information simultaneously (see Appendix C). Figure 9–5 describes the teacher's and students' roles during guided reading.

Guided reading lessons should be conducted with groups of four to six students. The texts selected for guided reading should be at the students' instructional level, a level slightly above what they can read on their own, in order to provide some challenge so that you can teach strategies. When students get stuck when reading, it presents an opportunity to show them how to work through the challenge. However, if the book is too difficult, the student will not be able to gain meaning

ROLE OF THE TEACHER	ROLE OF THE STUDENTS
• Always introduce the text. • Listen to students' use of strategies and provide models and examples of additional strategies. • Provide a lesson that is within a group's ZPD so that learning can occur. • Provide the appropriate materials to meet the learning objective. • Use flexible grouping based on students' needs. • Make connections to their work as independent readers.	• Read the text softly. • Monitor their comprehension. • Share their thinking and problem-solving strategies as readers. • Listen to the strategies their classmates use as readers. • Use the strategies learned to read independently. • Ask for support when needed.

FIGURE 9–5: Teacher and Student Roles in Guided Reading for Early Readers

from the text and may become frustrated. This can inhibit learning and there will be so much to teach that the student won't be able to internalize the learning.

All guided reading lessons will include an introduction to the text, a reading by the group, a strategy lesson, and a follow-up activity. The introduction sets the context for learning, builds background knowledge, or introduces new knowledge to help students comprehend the story. Marie Clay talks about the importance of the book introduction: "Rich introductions to new stories make these stories easier to read at the first reading . . . with a high degree of successful processing" (1998, 172). The introduction is like a tour guide giving an overview of the area for those who have not visited before. The guide gives everyone the lay of the land, tells what challenges one might encounter along the way, and explains what one might look forward to in the midst of this journey. Fountas and Pinnell (1996) emphasize that 80 percent of the teaching in a guided reading lesson is accomplished through the introduction.

A book introduction is tailored specifically for a particular group of students and is how a story is scaffolded for students both linguistically and cognitively. Some ways to introduce the text include the following:

- *Picture walks*—Give a synopsis of the entire story through the illustrations.
- *Make connections*—Discuss the cover page, including illustrations and the title, and ask students to talk about how it reminds them of something they have experienced in their life or in other books.
- *Personal experiences*—Talk about the theme or story content and what it means to the students.
- *Summarize*—Provide a brief summary from beginning to end.

- *Analyze* how a text is structured.
- *Skim text* to give an overview of difficult words and/or concepts that readers might encounter.

Once the teacher gives the book introduction, the group will read the book independently at the same time. Most early readers will read aloud. Often students want to listen to each other and read chorally; however, it is important that they maintain their own pace and are truly reading independently. One way to set this up is to deliberately distribute the books in a staggered way, having some students begin their reading slightly before the others. This will allow you to listen to individual children read and be able to observe how they problem solve in the midst of reading. The strategy lesson at the end will depend on the group's needs, based on your observations during the reading. For this reason, it is important to observe carefully and take notes while children are reading. However, be open to looking for teachable moments when listening to the students read. Regie Routman shares that before jumping into a focused lesson such as working with words, the first thing she always says after the students have finished reading is, "Tell me about what you just read," to remind students that the purpose of reading is at all times for meaning (2003, 167). Following are some possible strategies to teach during guided reading:

- *Decoding*—Sound out a word using knowledge of letters and sounds.
- *Chunking*—Look for patterns within words.
- *Rereading*—Perhaps the context or the sentence can give you a clue about what the word is and means.
- *Using visuals*—Use the pictures or illustrations to determine an unknown word.
- *Reading with attention to punctuation*—Pause after periods; read exclamatory sentences differently than questions and telling sentences.
- *Reading with fluency*—Choral or echo read to hear what reading should *sound* like.
- *Chunking meaning*—Stop at the end of each page or few pages and summarize in your head what is happening in the text.

When you are listening to them read, take advantage of a teachable moment if you hear a student use a new strategy. This can lead to your strategy lesson or it can be shared in conjunction with what you had planned for the guided reading lesson.

After the strategy lesson, students can take their learning and practice on their own. They can reread the text for fluency, reread with a new focus, reread with a partner, reread the text during independent reading workshop, or write a response in a journal. The transcript in Figure 9–6 provides an example of a guided reading with early readers.

CLASSROOM TRANSCRIPT	REFLECTION
Introduction	
Today we are going to read a book called *Dizzy Lizzy*, by Lucy Lawrence. [Shows the students the front cover and points with index finger under each word as she reads the title]	Ms. Mamdou points to each word in the title deliberately and makes sure the children see the words because the students will need to be able to read them in the book.
This is Lizzy and in this book, she gets dizzy while she's playing in many different ways.	She wants to set the readers up for the different ways in which Lizzy plays. This book has few words and the picture support is not strong. The students will need to take what they know about letters and sounds, coupled with the context of the story, in order to read the story.
Have you ever felt dizzy? I know that if I keep spinning around in a circle, around and around, I get really dizzy—it's like the room is spinning and I almost fall down.	She poses the question in a rhetorical way because she doesn't want to entertain excessive comments that will detract from the lesson. She continues immediately with an example to get their minds around the idea of being dizzy, particularly since some of the students may not know what the word means.
Let's look at Lizzy doing different things and getting dizzy. [Turns to page 2] Look at Lizzy swinging.	It is fairly obvious on this page that Lizzy is swinging, so Ms. Mamdou does not pay particular attention to the entire sentence. She does want the students to be familiar with the pattern and structure of these sentences so she states, "Look at . . ."
[Points to next page] Look at Lizzy touch the sky [points to Lizzy extending her hand to the sky].	This is a difficult page as the picture support is low, so Ms. Mamdou reads it and draws attention to the picture. This is also a behavior that she wants the students to practice as they read.
[Simply turns through the next few pages without commenting]	These pages contain high picture support, so the teacher quickly bypasses them.
[Turns to page 6] Oh, look at Lizzy whizzing round [reads this page verbatim and points to *whizzing*].	Ms. Mamdou knows that the syntax and vocabulary here might be difficult for the students. In addition, the picture support is weak, so she points to Lizzy spinning around—"whizzing round"—a rope.
Lizzy is sure getting herself dizzy while she plays!	She wants to reinforce the idea of Lizzy getting dizzy so that the children can hold onto the meaning as they utilize their word-solving strategies while reading.
	(Continues)

FIGURE 9–6: Guided Reading in Action: Early Readers

You'll read this book by yourself and find out all of the ways Lizzy is getting dizzy.

[Distributes the books in a staggered way—first to the student on the left of her, then to the ones on her right, and so on until everyone has a book]

Ms. Mamdou makes sure each child reads independently so that she can listen to their reading. She does not want them to read chorally.

[Students read independently as Ms. Mamdou listens and writes notes.]

As she listens to each child, she notices that most of them are encountering some problems on the last page, which reads: "Look at whizzy, dizzy Lizzy!" The structure of this sentence is different from the other ones, which throws them off a bit.

[Many of the children read the last page: "Look at whizzing, dizzy Lizzy"].

[Ms. Mamdou tells students who are finished reading first to read the book again, looking for their favorite part.]

Some students will inevitably finish before others; however, the teacher cannot give the strategy lesson until they are all finished reading.

[After they are all finished] I noticed that the last page was a bit tricky for most of you. Let's all turn to the last page and look at the words carefully.

Ms. Mamdou decides that she wants to select the ending pattern of the words on the last page as her teaching point.

[She writes the word *whizzy* on a whiteboard. The students say "whizzing." She then underlines *zy* and writes *dizzy* right underneath *whizzy* so that the letters *zy* line up. Then she writes *Lizzy* in the same manner.]

The students know the word *whizzing* from a previous page and have simply transferred it to the last page. She takes this opportunity to teach them about word endings and decides to write the words on a whiteboard so the pattern is clear to the students.

Let's read the other words. [The students read the others correctly.]

When we read, we need to carefully look across the word at the ending as well. You guys are doing a great job of looking at the beginning of the word, but we must also look at the end to make sure we are reading the word correctly. [She then underlines the *zy* in *dizzy* and *Lizzy* as well.]

You will be able to keep this book in your book bag so that you can continue to practice reading it during reading workshop.

She wants them to continue to practice reading this book because it is slightly more difficult than the others in their bags. Also, it is important for students to have multiple exposures to the same text.

FIGURE 9–6: *Continued*

Transitional and Self-Extending Readers

Guided reading for transitional and self-extending readers can include a variety of lessons. Teachers might choose to teach or reinforce particular content (across subject areas), grammar lessons, morphology lessons, content-specific vocabulary lessons, book clubs, or extensions to shared reading or read-aloud lessons. Because strategy lessons can encompass all kinds of lessons, the text selection will be dependent upon the objective of the lesson.

When I was working with a second-grade teacher, she noticed that there was a small group of students who would always summarize when she asked them to talk about the books they had been reading. She was happy to see that they could provide descriptive summaries, but she also knew they were capable of thinking more deeply about text. She wanted to help them learn how to question the author's decisions throughout the text, how to see the bigger picture, and how to read between the lines. We decided to pull the students together for a guided reading lesson with a book the class had read during shared reading, called *Amazing Grace*, by Mary Hoffman. The story was at this group of students' independent level, meaning they could read and understand the story at a basic level on their own.

When introducing the text to the small group, the teacher reviewed what the class had discussed during shared reading. She talked about how the story is about a little girl who loves to use her imagination and act out different characters from books. The little girl tried out for her class play, in which she played Peter Pan.

The teacher then engaged the group in a say-mean-matter activity. Figure 9–7 shows what a say-mean-matter session looks like as well as what the students discussed during the guided reading lesson.

During a say-mean-matter task, students start at a very basic level of comprehension (what the text says), then move to inference and synthesis (what it really means), and ultimately move to a deeper understanding at the evaluation level (why it matters to them in their world). This is the beginning of critical literacy and becoming a proficient reader.

After the lesson, the teacher reminded students that when they read, they should think beyond what the story says to get a better understanding of why the story was written and what they can learn from it.

This example of a guided reading lesson using *Amazing Grace* reflects how different reading levels determine different needs and methods of guided reading. Children are now more proficient decoders and need to focus more of their attention on comprehension skills. With transitional and self-extending readers, the range of guided reading lessons is wider. The role of the book introduction is still important with these readers, however. In the book introduction to *Henry*

SAY: WHAT DID THE TEXT SAY?	MEAN: WHAT DID IT MEAN?	MATTER: WHY DOES IT MATTER?
Grace pretended to be a doctor with her mom and nana.	She likes to use her imagination.	It helps you be creative.
Grace's friend said she couldn't be Peter Pan because she was a girl.	She was mad because she is a girl and she wants to be Peter Pan.	That's not right to say what boys and girls can and can't do.
Raj said she couldn't be Peter Pan because she was black.	He was being mean because it doesn't matter what you are.	You shouldn't let people stop you from what you want to do no matter what they think about your skin color or if you're a boy or girl.
Grace's nana took her to see a ballet.	She wanted Grace to see that anybody can be the star no matter what he or she looks like.	You can be whatever you want to be if you work hard.
Grace tried out for the play *Peter Pan*.	She didn't care about what her friends said. She knew she wanted to be Peter Pan.	It never hurts to try out, because it's important just to try and work hard.
Grace was Peter Pan in the play.	She showed them. She was perfect for Peter Pan even if she was a girl or was black.	Perseverance [class vocabulary word at the time]: If you work hard and keep trying, you can be great too.

FIGURE 9–7: Say-Mean-Matter Activity for *Amazing Grace*, by Mary Hoffman

and Mudge: The First Book, shown in Figure 9–8, the teacher is orienting the students to a slightly more difficult series of books than they are accustomed to. Notice how this introduction is different from the example of *Dizzy Lizzy* with early readers. There is more emphasis on the complexities of the text.

In this example, the teacher is using the guided reading lesson to introduce the students to a new level and type of chapter book. The entire story is much longer than those in the previous episodic chapter books the children are accustomed to reading. Also, readers at this level often ignore the many pictures that are present on each page. This valuable source of information helps the reader better understand the story. The teacher has also noticed that although this group of readers focuses primarily on the words when they read, they don't often pick up on the subtle use of words that could help them infer what is happening in the text. This is an important transition in the level of texts they are now reading.

Today we are going to read a book called *Henry and Mudge: The First Book*. Notice that part of the title says *The First Book*, which means that there are many other books about Henry and Mudge, like there are many Fox books [a series they have been reading regularly]. In this first book, the author, Cynthia Rylant, introduces us to a little boy named Henry and his dog, Mudge. She tells us how Henry and Mudge first met and how they became such good friends. We are going to learn how their friendship first started!

Before we start reading, I want you all to look at the contents page. What do you notice? Yes, they are called "Henry" and "Mudge," and they almost make a pattern with the last chapter being "Henry and Mudge." The title tells you who the chapter will mostly be about. Different from your Fox books, each chapter in this book goes together. When you read the Fox books, each chapter was a story by itself, but in Henry and Mudge books, the chapters go together to tell the whole story. In *Henry and Mudge: The First Book*, the whole book is about who Henry is and how he and Mudge became friends.

The first chapter, "Henry," tells us about how Henry had no brothers or sisters and was lonely. He had no one to play with, so he asked his parents if he could have a dog. They almost said no, but they noticed how lonely he was and said OK instead. [Students often miss out on the subtlety of Rylant's use of the word *almost*.]

In the second chapter, "Mudge," Cynthia Rylant tells us how Henry searched and picked out Mudge. We also learn how Mudge grew from a puppy to a *big* dog. [Turns to a page where the pictures indicate the passing of time through the various sizes of dog collars]

I want you all to read the first two chapters: "Henry" and "Mudge." You will stop on page 13. Then we will talk about what you read.

FIGURE 9–8: Transcript of Book Introduction for *Henry and Mudge: The First Book*

Conclusion

Guided reading is an important part of the literacy day as it provides the scaffolds necessary for reading with students in small groups according to need. While it might seem effective to simply organize random small groups, this decision must be carefully planned. Group members must have similar needs in literacy and language. Teachers must select a book that is slightly beyond what students in the group can read independently. The book introduction builds a bridge to the higher-leveled text for the readers and must be tailored to the specific needs of these readers. A teacher does not give exactly the same book introduction each time she uses the same book. Guided reading is used regularly with early readers; however, transitional and self-extending readers do not need this practice as often because they are able to decode proficiently.

Professional Literature on Guided Reading

Calkins, Lucy McCormick. 2001. *The Art of Teaching Reading*. New York: Addison-Wesley.

Clay, Marie M. 2000. *Running Records for Classroom Teachers*. Portsmouth, NH: Heinemann.

———. 1998. *By Different Paths to Common Outcomes*. York, ME: Stenhouse.

————. 2002. *An Observation Survey of Early Literacy Achievement*. Portsmouth, NH: Heinemann.

Diller, Debbie. 2003. *Literacy Work Stations: Making Centers Work*. Portland, ME: Stenhouse.

Fountas, Irene. 2005. *Guided Reading: Essential Elements*. Portsmouth, NH: Heinemann.

Fountas, Irene C., and Gay Su Pinnell. 1996. *Guided Reading: Good First Teaching for All Children*. Portsmouth, NH: Heinemann.

————. 1999. *Matching Books to Readers: Using Leveled Books in Guided Reading, K–3*. Portsmouth, NH: Heinemann.

Goodman, Kenneth, Dorothy Watson, and Carolyn Burke. 1987. *Reading Miscue Analysis*. New York: Richard C. Owen.

Saunders-Smith, Gail. 2003. *The Ultimate Guided Reading How-to Book: Building Literacy Through Small Group Instruction*. Tucson, AZ: Zephyr.

Schulman, Mary Browning, and Carleen Dacruz Payne. 2000. *Guided Reading: Making It Work (Grades K–3)*. New York: Scholastic.

Wilde, Sandra. 2000. *Reading Miscue Made Easy*. Portsmouth, NH: Heinemann.

10 Word Work

Words mean more than what is set down on paper. It takes the human voice to infuse them with shades of deeper meaning.

—Maya Angelou

What Is Word Work?

Word work is a foundation for communicating and gaining meaning from oral and written language. It is the explicit and implicit study of the English language. Students learn how to decode, encode, and interpret parts or chunks of the English language. These chunks or smaller units of language include sounds (phonology), letters (orthography), words (semantics), and word parts (morphology) and how they are organized and used in the English language to convey meaning. Word work can be incorporated into many of the reading and writing components of a balanced literacy program. We provide some examples of this integration throughout this chapter. When children have a solid foundation in word work, they can better understand how to read and, more importantly, what they are reading.

Word work includes a variety of linguistic and interpretive skills. In their literacy development, children begin with an understanding of how print works (concepts about print) when they are read to and see their mom and dad or teachers reading the markings on the page. They continue their development as readers by then becoming aware of sounds (phonemic awareness) and eventually connecting those sounds to letters (phonics) to form words when reading and writing. Throughout their development as emerging readers students are continuously learning new words. From the time they are born, they are exposed to words and they quickly acquire oral language. They use these words to communicate with others but are not yet aware of how those oral sounds are written. That is the purpose of word work in school. Students are taught *how* words are created and that the same words they speak can be written and read. Children use their oral language to guide them through this process.

Concepts About Print

Children begin to develop literacy before entering school. They engage in numerous emergent literacy behaviors when they scribble on walls and read imaginary stories as they turn the pages of books. They are exposed to adults engaging with text such as magazines, newspapers, advertisements, bills, food labels, recipes, and email messages. All of these forms of text around the house provide models that text conveys meaning (Clay 1966). This knowledge is further understood when children are read to at home. They see how to handle a book and experience the purpose of books and how they work. They learn that there are pictures in books and other markings that they may not be familiar with yet, called letters. As they hear a story they see the connections between the pictures and the story. They see their mom or dad turning the pages in a certain way (from left to right) and that their parent stays on one page for a bit while telling the story. They do not know yet that the reason their parent doesn't turn the page right away is because he or she is reading the words to tell the story. Ultimately children will be made aware that those markings on the page are words made up of letters and that they are organized in a certain way to create sentences that tell stories. Understanding concepts about print will prepare children to attack books and understand the meaning behind the pictures and the text.

The challenge for teachers is in developing these concepts with a very diverse student population. Shirley Brice Heath (1983) explains that there is a great disparity in the home-literacy experiences of children from different socioeconomic backgrounds. Some students may enter school already aware of these concepts, some might even be reading, while others may not have had many experiences with books and print. For this reason, teachers will need to be explicit in demonstrating these concepts throughout the day.

Phonemic Awareness

Phonemic awareness is the ability of children to isolate, identify, and manipulate spoken sounds, called phonemes. It is a developmental skill in which children can initially identify individual sounds in isolation and eventually identify each sound in a spoken word. This knowledge of sounds will then help students learn the sounds of the English alphabet and ultimately serve as a foundation for phonics when they connect those sounds to letters when reading and writing. Marilyn J. Adams (1990) and Keith Stanovich (1986) found that phonemic awareness is a strong predictor of early reading success. Students who are instructed in phonemic awareness have a smoother transition to becoming beginning readers, who have the ability to decode words in and out of context. Phonemic awareness serves as a marker for extensive literacy opportunities (Cummins 2003).

For English learners, it is important to teach not only sound awareness but also the pronunciation and dialect of Standard English. Because many ELs are exposed to a variety of accents and dialects, it is the role of the teacher to be a model of what English sounds like.

Phonics

Phonics is the ability to match spoken sounds (phonemes) to their corresponding letters and letter combinations, called graphemes. It is the understanding that the sounds children hear have written counterparts.

There are two different approaches for teaching phonics: synthetic and analytic. In a synthetic approach, phonics is taught from part to whole. Children are asked to decode words by blending sounds together to read words. The words used for decoding practice are taught in isolation and typically practiced through the reading of decodable texts. Analytic phonics instruction focuses on the use of real stories and literature to teach phonics in context. It is considered a whole-to-part approach. Instruction takes place during shared reading, interactive writing, and word wall time. Students learn to find commonalities and patterns in words to understand how letters and letter combinations are transferred from word to word and text to text. These connections are then reinforced in guided and independent reading. There are many advocates who argue the advantages of one approach over another; however, we have found that teachers must be aware of both in order to make knowledgeable decisions about which approach works best for each different group of students they teach. It's most important to understand that the knowledge of phonics is a tool, one of four cueing systems (the graphophonic cueing system; see Appendix C) that children can call upon to attack challenging and unfamiliar words.

Instruction in phonics further helps children with encoding, or spelling. They use their knowledge of phonemic awareness and phonics to write words. When children write, it is a window into their internalization of letters and sounds. For example, when a child writes words that contain only the beginning and ending sounds, it is an indicator that they may need additional help with hearing medial sounds. This will lead to phonemic awareness activities that focus on medial sounds as well as phonics instruction on vowels. Analyzing student writing samples helps teachers plan and prepare for future phonics lessons. "Written English is based on the alphabetic principle and children need to understand that sounds and letters correspond" (Diaz-Rico and Weed 2002, 102). Phonics emerges best through students' writing and wordplay.

The work of phonics begins with the study of simple consonants and vowels for reading and writing one-syllable, consonant-vowel-consonant (CVC) words and continues with work on varied spellings for known sounds (such as digraphs, consonant blends, and vowel teams) and then moves to learning complex spelling patterns of multisyllabic words. Figure 10–1 includes a variety of sounds and spellings to help children become better decoders and encoders of the English language. It is not an exhaustive list but provides information on a variety of sounds and spellings that we use to read and write in the English language.

Consonants:

b, c (spelled c, k, -ck), d, f, g, h, j (spelled j, ge, gi, gy, -dge), l, m, n, p, q, r (spelled r, rr, wr), s (spelled s, ss), t, v, w, x, y, z (spelled z, zz, s)

Vowels:

Short vowels: a, e, i, o, u

Long vowels: a (spelled a, ai, ay, a_e, eigh), e (spelled e, ee, y, ie, e_e), i (spelled i, igh, i_e, y), o (spelled o, oa, o_e, ow, oe, ough), u (spelled u, u_e, ew)

Consonant Blends:

bl, br, cl, cr, dr, fl, gr, pl, pr, sl, sm, sn, st, str, tr

Digraphs:

ch, sh, th, -tch, -ng, -nk

Diphthongs:

oi, oy, ou, ow

R-controlled:

ar, er, ir, ur

Schwa:

aw, au

FIGURE 10–1: English Phoneme and Grapheme Connections

It is important for children to have phonics skills in order to be successful conventional readers; however, when children enter kindergarten, they also need to learn that meaning is derived from the print that they will eventually learn to decode. Children learn this through experiences in interactive read-aloud and emergent storybook reading. We caution teachers that as children understand how to decode (how to use their knowledge of letters and sounds to read), class time should be spent on reading. Jim Cummins shares "that phonics instruction drags out over too many years" and can be further developed through repeated opportunities for reading (2003, 9). In doing so, children will become better readers, writers, spellers, and speakers of English. Phonics is only one of many building blocks to becoming fluent readers and writers. And when children learn to become strategic decoders, word work should focus on phonemic analysis of complex spelling patterns and morphology. Morphology is further explained in "Vocabulary and Word Study."

Teachers can capitalize on English learners' primary language as a resource for learning English by making comparisons and noting commonalities and differences in the two language systems. For example, Spanish-speaking children learn that the long /e/ sound is spelled with an *i* in Spanish, but in English it is spelled with an *e* and other vowel combinations (see vowels in Figure 10–1). When this connection is explicitly taught to students, they will be able to apply spelling rules appropriately.

Vocabulary and Word Study

English learners are confronted with the challenge of learning basic communication skills (BICS) in conjunction with academic language (CALP). They are frantically trying to stay afloat, learning basic expressive phrases and words while learning new content area vocabulary words. These two monumental tasks require a great deal of knowledge in vocabulary and word study (phonemic, syllabic, and morphemic analysis). Stephen Krashen (2004) and Keith Stanovich (1986) have both expressed that one of the most effective ways for children to improve their vocabulary is through reading. When children read widely and often, they are exposed to a variety of words. They see many words repeated and this frequent exposure helps them comprehend and internalize the words, building their receptive vocabulary (words we can understand) and leading to a larger expressive vocabulary (the words we use when we speak and write). Many students' receptive vocabulary is greater than their expressive vocabulary. Though this is not necessarily a problem, it is important to further develop children's expressive vocabulary so that they can communicate more effectively. For example, sometimes when you are talking to someone or writing an essay, you might think to yourself, "Oh, what is the word—I can't think of the word for what I am trying to say," and you might talk your way around it. This can lead to very wordy speaking or writing. Many ELs will write out descriptions of what they are trying to say because they do not possess the vocabulary to express themselves more directly and succinctly. In our society, those with a greater expressive vocabulary are viewed as more intelligent. It is not always a correct assumption, but a sophisticated vocabulary is one sociocultural indicator of an educated person.

It is necessary in vocabulary instruction that children have opportunities to talk! Through talk they can practice basic communication while having discussions around texts that include exposure to and practice with academic language. In addition, students need time to transfer learned vocabulary to their expressive language (Beck, McKeown, and Kucan 2002). The most effective lessons are those that force children to learn and use new concepts and vocabulary words as part of daily conversations in the classroom, on the playground, and at home.

We do not recommend that you isolate vocabulary development from its application for real purposes because words learned out of context have little carryover into the daily lives of children (Clay 1991). In addition, direct instruction and dictionary work alone are *not* effective vocabulary instruction. Only about four hundred of the three thousand words learned a year are taught through direct instruction (Kame'enui et al. 1998; Stahl and Fairbanks 1986). The others are learned through engagement, exposure, talk, and practice.

Part of word study instruction for English learners should further include morphology. Children need opportunities to examine words and discover patterns in their structure (Bear et al. 2000). Morphology is the study of small units of meaning called morphemes that include roots, base words, and affixes (prefixes and suffixes). In learning morphology, students become strategic readers for meaning. When they come to an unknown word they can analyze chunks of the word to figure out its meaning. As many as 60 percent of rare and low-frequency words in the English language can be broken down into morphemes and understood (Lehr, Osborn, and Hiebert 2005). Take the word *unlock*, for example: A child may be familiar with *lock*, to close something so that it cannot be opened, but perhaps has not heard *unlock*. If she has learned that the prefix *un-* means the opposite, or not, she can think through the meaning of *unlock*. Figure 10–2 illustrates some components of morphology instruction.

To help you better understand these components of morphology instruction, Figure 10–3 provides examples of each.

Vocabulary and word work are *critical* for ELs in many ways. Many of them are learning English for the first time in school. They will need many opportunities to hear and practice English in school. Betty Hart and Todd R. Risley (2003) studied home oracy and found that children from homes rich in conversation learn about four times as many words by the age of four as children from less advantaged homes by the

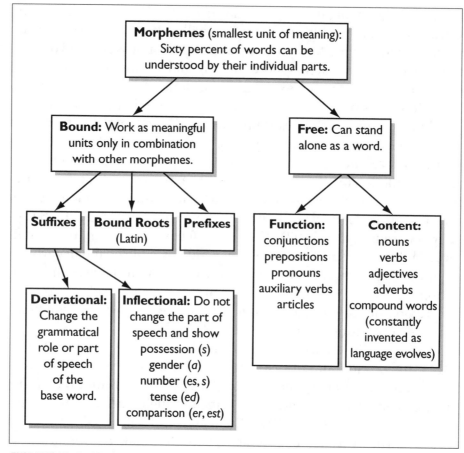

FIGURE 10–2: Morphology

BOUND MORPHEMES	
Suffixes	A morpheme added at the end of a word. Common suffixes taught in primary classrooms include *-ly -ful -ed -ing -s -es -er -est*
Derivational Suffixes	*teach/teacher* (changed from a verb to a noun) *write/writer* (changed from a verb to a noun) *lazy/lazily* (changed from an adjective to an adverb)
Inflectional Suffixes	Possession: *student/student's/students'* Gender: *alumni/alumna* Number: *car/cars, watch/watches* Tense: *skip/skipped/skipping* Comparison: *tall/taller/tallest*

FIGURE 10–3: Components of Morphology

Roots	Typically of Italian, Greek, and Latin derivation but a bit too challenging for primary students. For example:
	Root: *-ject* (meaning to throw)
	Possible words: *reject, subject, inject*
Prefixes	A morpheme added to the beginning of a word that changes the meaning of the word. Common prefixes taught in primary classrooms include

un-	*im-*	*poly-*	*tele-*
re-	*in-*	*bi-*	*semi-*
pre-	*multi-*	*di-*	*mis-*

FREE MORPHEMES

Conjunctions					
can't	*couldn't*	*shouldn't*	*wouldn't*	*haven't*	*aren't*
don't	*doesn't*	*isn't*	*hasn't*	*won't*	
I'm	*I've*	*we've*	*they've*	*you've*	

Prepositions						
into	*behind*	*between*	*above*	*below*	*over*	*under*

Pronouns						
I	*me*	*mine*	*he*	*she*	*it*	*we*
they	*them*	*their*	*you*	*her*	*him*	*his*
this	*that*	*these*	*those*			

Auxiliary Verbs (linking or helping verbs)						
be	*is*	*are*	*does*	*do*	*has*	*have*
can	*could*	*should*	*will*	*would*	*might*	*must*

Articles		
a	*an*	*the*

Nouns	Any person, place, thing, or idea, including proper and common nouns.
Verbs	An action.
Adjectives	Words that describe a person, place, thing, or idea (noun).
Adverbs	Words that describe an action (verb).
Compound Words	Two base words (free morphemes) put together to create a new word.

rainbow	*backpack*	*popcorn*	*newspaper*

FIGURE 10–3: *Continued*

same age. This is not to say that English learners are not from homes rich in oral language, but it is most likely not the English of school. ELs have to catch up and keep up with those English-only-speaking students who already come to school with a rich vocabulary base. What does help English learners is that they have learned concepts and cognitive language in their primary language and this will help them understand English (see "Second Language Acquisition" in Chapter 1).

Finally, because ELs are new to the language, they start with a very literal comprehension and interpretation of the language. The study of idioms and figurative language is important so that we don't confuse children. Think about the common expressions used in a classroom such as *cut it out* and *knock it off*. When English learners first hear these expressions, they think there is something you want them to cut out or something you want them to push off. There are some great picture books on idioms and figurative language for children listed in the teacher resource section near the end of the chapter.

Word Work Activities for Emergent and Early Readers at Different Levels of Second Language Acquisition

Concepts About Print

Sharing Labels (Print Awareness/Visual Literacy)
Ask students to bring in product or advertisement labels from home (or you can bring them in). These can include food labels from cans or jars, cereal boxes, advertisements for different products in catalogs or newspapers, and beverage labels. Break the students up into groups of four to five and have each child share his label with his group. The student should share what the label is from and what you can do with the product it came from or how to use the product. For example, a child might bring in a Nike advertisement with the famous Nike swoosh (it looks like a checkmark) and say, "This is for shoes. They make a lot of shoes for basketball and sometimes other clothes too." Another student may bring in the label for a can of soup and say, "This is soup; we eat it."

After each group member shares, the teacher can ask the student to tape her label to a class chart titled "Print in Our World." This chart will stay up in the room as a reminder of print and the understanding that print conveys meaning. This is a foundation for later understanding that letters and words are different forms of print but they serve the same purpose: to convey meaning.

This activity is helpful to English learners in many ways. The visual images convey meaning for the students using their common underlying proficiencies (see "Second Language Acquisition" in Chapter 1). Though they may not have the English to express their understanding of the label, they can still make sense of the image. They will still understand that these images convey meaning. Also, in sharing their label in a small group, even the students at the early production stage of second language acquisition can give a one- to two-word description. For example, if an EL at the early production stage of SLA was sharing the label, the student might say, "*Sopa*, eat." The student understands the concept that print conveys meaning, he feels successful as a participant, and he learns new vocabulary and syntax from his group share.

Making Letters
This activity has been done in many successful and enjoyable ways, including the following:

- Provide a large copy of individual alphabet letters and ask the students to trace each letter using their finger and then using a pencil. (Model for the students the direction in which to trace.)

- Provide a large copy of an individual alphabet letter and have students trace it by gluing beans, pasta, or seeds to it.

- Place sand in a small box and have students practice forming letters in the sand. (Model for the students the direction in which to form the letters.)

- Have the students write letters in the air. (Lead the students with the proper hand movement to form each letter.)

Alphabet Books
Have students create an alphabet book. For each page of the book, write the focus letter at the top of the page, leaving enough room on the page for pictures. Have students cut out pictures or words from a magazine that start with that letter and glue them to the page. Create a page for each letter as you study it, and in the end the students will have created a complete alphabet book. This can also be completed as a class book or done in small groups.

Shared Reading
Shared reading is an excellent time of day to provide direct instruction on concepts about print. Prior to beginning the story, point out the parts of the book (including author, illustrator, and title). While reading, point out words, sentences, and punctuation. Because the text used for shared reading is large enough for students to see, shared reading works better than read-aloud for developing print awareness and concepts about print.

Phonemic Awareness

The first two activities in this section, Listening Walk and Name That Sound, are helpful in developing students' awareness of sounds. These are useful as initial phonemic awareness activities because they help students begin to listen for distinct sounds and begin to match those sounds with icons, items, images, and meaning. The rest of the activities are specific phonemic awareness activities to develop an awareness of the sounds of the English alphabet. They will begin to develop in students the distinctive skills of isolating and manipulating sounds as a foundation for phonics instruction. These include activities in sound matching, sound isolation, sound blending, sound substitution, and sound segmentation. All are oral language activities that focus on having students listen for sounds.

After a shared reading experience with a text that contains common sounds or rhymes, such as a poem, riddle, chant, or song, the teacher can pull words from the text for further practice and reinforcement through the activities explained in this section. For English learners, teaching phonemic awareness in context when reading the text and from a context when doing follow-up activities is important (Hamayan 1994). This helps with comprehensible input, meaning learning will occur because the students can understand the language and information being shared.

Listening Walk

Take students out on a tour of the school, but tell them that they are going to take a tour of the sounds of the school. Pair the students up for the walk by SLA levels (see Figure 1–2). After walking a bit, stop and ask the students to close their eyes and just listen. After about fifteen seconds, ask them to open their eyes and tell their partner what they heard. Children will say things like, "Cars driving by, people talking, kids, doors closing, laughing." Write down some of the sounds the students share with their partners. Continue the walk around the school, with frequent stops and pair-shares. After returning back to the classroom, share the notes you took when listening to partnerships on the walk.

Name That Sound

Gather different items that create sound. These should be familiar classroom, home, or community items the students can relate to. Ask the students to close their eyes. Once all their eyes are closed, pull one item out and make a sound with it. Tell students to listen carefully to the sound and think about what is making the sound. Hide the object and tell them to open their eyes and tell a partner what they think the item was. After the students have had a chance to share with a partner, pull out the item and create the sound again, this time allowing the students to see the item while hearing the sound. Continue the activity with other items and sounds.

This activity can be done using a tape or CD of sounds, but it is more effective for English learners if the items are visible to them once they have made predictions so that they can connect each sound to an image. Students can also do the activity at home as a family project on the sounds of their house.

Sound Matching

Students listen for similar sounds across words. This can be done through the use of poetry, songs, and chants with alliteration. Teaching children rhymes such as "Peter Piper picked a peck of pickled peppers" exposes them to a sound, in this case /p/, helping them hear similar sounds across words. This can be followed up with thumbs-up, thumbs-down activities where you can say, "When you hear the /p/ sound in the words I read, put your thumb up; if you don't hear a /p/ sound, put your thumb down." The point is for students to listen for a particular sound and match the sound to words that contain the sound.

Sound Isolation

Students will be listening for sounds in a particular location within a word, including beginning, medial, and ending sounds. The teacher will ask students to listen for words that contain a sound at the beginning, middle, or end of a word. The thumbs-up, thumbs-down activity described under "Sound Matching" can also be used for Sound Isolation. After reading a poem, big book, song, or chant, pull out words that contain the same sound, for example, /m/. Ask the students to give a thumbs-up if they hear the /m/ sound at the beginning of the word. "OK, class, ready? I am going to say some of the words from our song and if you hear the /m/ sound at the beginning, I want you to put your thumbs up. If you don't hear the /m/ sound at the beginning, then I should see thumbs down. Ready, /man/ [the students' thumbs go up], /stamp/ [the students' thumbs go down]." Notice that the word *stamp* does contain the /m/ sound, but in this Sound Isolation activity, the students are listening for the beginning sounds only.

Sound Blending

The teacher asks students to blend sounds together orally to form words. This can include blending chunks of words and blending isolated sounds. For example, a teacher might ask the students, "What word am I making if I put these together, /ham/ [pause] /ster/?" The class would call out "Hamster." Or the teacher might separate the words to be blended by onset and rime, such as /c/ [pause] /at/ or /a/ [pause] /pple/. Another option is to blend the words by individual sounds, such as /c/ [pause] /a/ [pause] /t/. In all cases the purpose is to start showing students that by putting sounds together, they can form words. Again the words can come from a shared text experience.

Sound Substitution

In Sound Substitution the students are now going to manipulate sounds in words to form new words. After a shared text experience, select a word from the text such as *bat* and say, "If we changed the /b/ in /bat/ to /h/, what's the new word?" The class then calls out /hat/. Continue by changing other sounds in the word. Through practice with sound substitution, students hear how words are created from common sounds.

Sound Segmentation

Up until this point the phonemic awareness activities have asked students to listen for sounds and express in some way either verbally or through gestures if they heard the sounds. Students were also asked to manipulate sounds provided by the teacher. In Sound Segmentation, it is now the students' job to identify the individual sounds in a word. The teacher simply provides the word and asks the student to orally express each sound in the word. For example, if the teacher says "stick," the student should reply /s/ /t/ /i/ /k/. This is the most difficult phonemic awareness skill for many students because it requires careful attention to each and every sound in a word. Students with good sound segmentation have an easier time when writing because they can hear the sounds and will match letters to those sounds. As students start to learn phonics (the letters that correspond to the sounds they hear), they will start to write letters. The more sounds they hear, the more letters they'll write. This leads to strong phonetic spellers.

Sound Bingo

Create a set of bingo cards with pictures only. As the caller, call out sounds one at a time. Students are to mark pictures that contain the sound in them. For example, if the caller says /m/, and the students' bingo card contains a picture of a man, they can mark that square. To help prolong the game, let the students know that they have to mark every square on their card to win.

Phonics

Carousel

In this activity students will practice writing words that contain a given sound-spelling combination. Place a number of chart papers around the room, each containing a particular sound-spelling pattern. For example, if you have been studying the long /a/ sound and its various spellings, write each different spelling for long /a/ on a chart. You would then have five charts around the room, one with *a*, another with *ai*, another with *ay*, another with *a_e*, and a challenge one with *eigh*.

Divide the class up into groups of four or five, assign a recorder for each group, and provide each group with a different color marker. Each group will begin at a different chart around the room. When you say "go," they will write down as many words as they can think of that contain the sound-spelling pattern written at the top of the chart paper. Give the groups about three to five minutes to write and then flash the lights and say, "Rotate." The groups rotate in a clockwise direction to the next chart. When you say "go," they will repeat the activity with the new sound-spelling in front of them. Remind them to read all the words written on the chart thus far because they cannot repeat a word.

Once all groups have had a chance to rotate to each chart, ask the recorders to bring the charts and their markers up to the front, and have the other children gather on the rug or at their desks. Review the charts with the class, crossing out any words that used the wrong spelling for long /a/. The students enjoy working together, they review their sound-spelling patterns, and they engage in a lot of talk as they move from one chart to the next. Though it is not necessary, you can further motivate the students by giving them a goal. For example, you might say, "If as a class you come up with one hundred words total, you will get a class point." They also like to compete against other groups, so providing each group with a different color marker allows them to count how many words each group got.

Making Words

Provide students with a familiar scene, for example, a picture of a playground. Provide letter cards to each student and tell them to start by pulling out the letters *m*, *a*, and *n*. Ask them to place the letters in order to spell the word *man*. Once they have done that, ask them to point to the man in the picture. Then tell the students, "Let's take the letter *m* in *man* and change it to an *f*. What is our new word?" The class calls out, "Fan." Ask the class to find the fan in the picture. Continue to guide the students through the lesson, then ask them to work with a partner to make other words for things they see in the picture.

This activity is similar to traditional word making activities that involve substituting letters to form new words or working with word families; however, what helps English learners contextualize their learning and make meaning from the isolated words is connecting them to an image. The pictures can come from coloring books, picture books, original drawings, anthologies, magazine advertisements, or posters.

Spell Down

When engaging in a Spell Down activity, students learn to focus on sounds and their spellings. It is a sound-by-sound spelling of a word. For the word *chips*, they would write:

ch
chi
chip
chips

Notice that the *ch* was written together because it is one sound. This helps students with their spelling. They learn to think about each of the sounds they hear in a word and know that they must connect the sound to a grapheme (spelling). This can be done in class to introduce the concept, but it is most effective as a homework assignment for spelling so that class time can be used on other phonics activities.

Search and Find

Break students up into groups of four or five. Provide each group with a large piece of construction paper or chart paper and magazines, newspapers, scissors, and glue. On the chart paper write a sound-spelling pattern. The group is to find words or pictures that are spelled with their given sound and spelling. You can give each group a different sound and spelling or have the entire class work on one as review. At the end of the lesson, each group will share out their poster. Put these up around the room as future resources for students.

Sight Words

Shared Reading

During shared reading, when children have visual access to the text, select a high-frequency word to review with the class. Ask students to come up and point to the high-frequency word as it appears in the story. You can then place the word on a word wall or high-frequency word list for future reference.

Free Voluntary Reading

Children will learn sight words through exposure. The more they read, the more they will see the words. Since many sight words are not phonetically spelled, the frequent exposure to the words will help with not only reading and comprehension but spelling as well. Encourage families to read to their children at home and provide them with a list of high-frequency words to practice.

Vocabulary and Word Study

Lingo Bingo

Using words you have been working on in class, provide students with a list of words and a blank bingo sheet. Students will select words from the list to create their own bingo card. You should have a set of bingo caller cards that contain the definition of each word on one side and a picture of the word or a representation of the word on the other side. As you read the definition, the students can see the picture. The picture helps English learners connect the oral definition with meaning. The game is played out like a regular bingo game: you read a word and its definition, and students mark that word on their cards.

Memory Game

Using words you have been studying as a class, create a set of cards that contain a word on one card and a corresponding picture on a different card (the back side of each card should be blank). In partnerships the students will place all the cards upside down on their tables or the floor. On his turn, one student will turn over two cards, trying to match a word card with its corresponding picture. If the student is successful, he keeps the cards and takes another turn. If he is not successful, he turns the cards back over, and it becomes his partner's turn.

Figure 10–4 provides teachers with a variety of possible literacy goals for developing students' word knowledge.

Concepts About Print	Recognize/identify logos and words in the environment.
	Recognize their name.
	Recognize the first letter in their name.
	Understand that printed materials provide information.
	Write the letters of the alphabet using the proper formation.
	Recognize and name all uppercase and lowercase letters of the alphabet.
	Match oral words to printed words.
	Identify letters, words, and sentences.
Phonemic Awareness	Recognize rhyming words.
	Recognize and track sounds.
	Identify the number of sounds heard in words with two to three sounds.
	Separate words into beginning or ending sounds.
	Produce rhyming words in response to oral prompts.
	Blend consonant-vowel-consonant (CVC) words orally.
	Distinguish initial, medial, and final sounds in single-syllable words.
	Distinguish long and short vowel sounds in orally stated single-syllable words.
	Add, delete, or change target sounds in order to change words (*cat/fat*).
	Segment single-syllable words into their components.

(Continues)

FIGURE 10–4: Language and Literacy Goals for Emergent and Early Readers

Phonics	Know letter names.
	Match all consonants, vowels (short and long), and consonant blends to their sounds and be able to blend those sounds into words.
	Read common and irregular sight words.
	Use knowledge of consonant and vowel digraphs, schwas, and *r*-controlled letter associations to read words.
	Read compound words and contractions.
	Read common word families.
Vocabulary and Word Study	Identify and sort common words into basic categories.
	Describe common objects and events.

FIGURE 10–4: *Continued*

Word Work Activities for Transitional and Self-Extending Readers Across All Levels of Second Language Acquisition

Phonemic Analysis

Students look for commonalities, or patterns, across words to inform their reading and writing. All phonics activities we described for emergent and early readers can also be used with transitional and self-extending readers. The difference would be in the phonics spelling patterns used for the activities.

Word Sorts

Provide students with a set of words. In partnerships, ask the students to sort the words based on their spelling. After they have sorted the words, students will share other words they know that contain the same spelling pattern. Sample word sorts are available in Appendix G.

Four Corners

Fold a large piece of chart paper into fourths. In the inside corner of each square, write one of the spellings for a selected phoneme. For example:

ai	a
a_e	ay

Arrange the students into groups of four and place a poster in the middle of the group. Each student will be writing in one of the corners at the same time as the other group members write in their squares. When given a signal, the students will write words they know that contain the sound and spelling indicated in their square. After three to five minutes, call time and have each group rotate the paper once clockwise. Each student will begin by silently reading the words the previous group member wrote, and when you give a signal, the student will write additional words that she knows contain the sound and spelling. The activity will continue until the chart has rotated to each group member. Once the charts have been filled, each group shares their chart with the class.

Syllabic Analysis

Helping students understand how words are formed can further help them with pronunciation, reading, and spelling. Students should be taught what syllables are and how they are organized. Syllabification rules and generalizations are as follows:

- All syllables are organized around a vowel *sound*.
- There is only one vowel *sound* in each syllable.
- When the vowel sound is long, the syllable break follows the vowel. This is called an open syllable.
- When the vowel sound is short, the syllable break will follow the consonant or consonant blend that follows the vowel. This is called a closed syllable.
- When two consonants come between two vowels in a word, divide syllables between the consonants (*bor-der*).
- Keep blends together when there are more than two consonants together (*mon-ster*).
- When two vowels are together that do not represent a long vowel or a diphthong, divide syllables between the vowels (*po-em*).

Practice with syllabification will help students decode and pronounce multisyllabic words. Let's try the word *nobody*. Students may think it is separated *no-body*, but the proper syllabic separation would be *no-bod-y*. When sounding the word out, I know to pronounce the first *o* long because it is an open syllable and the second *o* short because it is a closed syllable, closed off by the consonant *d*. Because the *y* is an open syllable as well, it should be pronounced as a long vowel. In studying the letter *y* students will learn that the *y* can make the long *e* or long *i* sound. As words get longer and longer in children's text from second grade on, syllabification will become very useful when reading.

Morphemic Analysis

Teaching children how to use their knowledge of roots, base words, prefixes, and suffixes can help them understand unfamiliar words.

Word Sorts

Provide students with a set of familiar words that contain common prefixes. In pairs, they should separate words by similar prefixes and talk about what each of the prefixes means. After they have done so, they can share additional words they know containing the same prefixes with their partner. This can also be done for words with similar suffixes, roots, and base words.

Find Your Morpheme

Divide the class up into groups of three. Give one group prefixes, another group suffixes, and the last group base words and roots. Each member in the group should have her own unique morpheme. Ask the students to stand around the room and when you give a signal, they must find a morpheme that will make a word with theirs. For example, a student holding the word *pack* might pair up with a student holding the prefix *un*. Together they make the word *unpack*. A root or base word may have more than one prefix or suffix attached to it. Once everyone has paired up, quickly have each morpheme pair state their word and what it means. Then give the signal again and have the students go around and find another morpheme to pair with to make a word. Again have them share their word and what it means. Repeat the procedure, giving students a chance to find different morpheme pairs.

Word Play

Activities and direct instruction on morphemic analysis help students become strategic readers who use their knowledge of word parts to make sense of unknown words and maintain comprehension. Wordplay, on the other hand, serves a different purpose. It provides repeated exposure to words in an enjoyable way. Wordplay helps with retaining words and developing greater receptive and expressive vocabularies.

The first five activities in this section are actually modeled after real board games. They are games that involve wordplay in a variety of different ways. The descriptions explain how the games serve as vocabulary activities but do not necessarily follow the exact rules of the popular board game. We are not suggesting you go out and buy these games; rather, create your own versions with words that are unique to your class needs.

Watz-It

Have students create word cards that depict a visual representation of given vocabulary words. They should write the word on one side and draw a visual of the word on the other side. After the class has made a set of word cards, collect the cards and divide the students up into two groups. Line the students up into two lines facing each other. Stand at the end of the lines, say "go," and show the first two students in line the picture side of a card. The student who guesses the word first will win the card for his team. After the first two students are done, they go to the end of the line, and the next two are up. The game continues until the cards run out. The team with the most cards is the winner. As the year goes along, continue to add new Watz-It cards to the deck for future game play. Students can also play the game in small groups or partnerships once the deck gets large enough.

Tri-bond

Create a set of word cards that contain three words on one side and the larger concept they all fit within on the other side. For example:

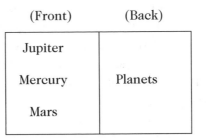

Have students work in partnerships. One student will read out the front side of the card and her partner has to try to figure out the concept. Again the words and concepts should be words that the class has been studying across the subject areas. As the year progresses, continue to add more and more Tri-bond cards to the set.

Blurt It

Using words you have been studying as a class, create a set of word cards with a word on one side and its definition on the other side. In this game, you read a definition aloud and the students have to guess the vocabulary word. This is a great game to get students to remember the words, not just understand them. As with the other games, this can be played out as a class in two teams or in small groups and partnerships. Continuously add words to the game throughout the year.

Vocab Pyramid

The cards created for this game are similar to the cards used for Tri-bond, with a concept on one side and words on the other, except the purpose of this game is very different. In this case students use elaborative descriptions and definitions to describe the individual words associated with the concept. Take a look at this sample card:

(Front)	(Back)
Mammals	1. dolphin 2. lion 3. person 4. dog 5. bear 6. elephant 7. deer 8. giraffe 9. cow 10. cat

In partnerships or in small groups, one student will be the clue giver. This student will show her partner or group the front of the card only. Then she will provide definitions, descriptions, gestures, or sounds that will help the other student(s) guess the words on the back side. For example, using the previous sample card, the clue giver might say, "This animal lives in the ocean and is really smart." When the group guesses a word correctly, the clue giver provides clues for the next word. This continues until the group has guessed all ten words. To make it more challenging, give students a time limit for each card. A good time limit is anywhere from thirty to sixty seconds. The use of the concept on the front of the card helps bring forward students' schema on the topic to contextualize their guesses.

Secret Word

In pairs, one student has a set of word cards with one word on each card. His partner is not allowed to see the words. The student holding the words will provide a one-word clue for his partner to guess the secret word. If his partner does not get the word from the first clue, the partner can ask for additional one-word clues. But keep in mind, only one-word clues can be given each time. Set a goal for the partnerships; for example, tell them to try to figure out the secret word in less than three clues. After a set of ten words has been played, have the partners switch roles. This game is much more difficult than the previous ones because students have to have a pretty good understanding of the secret words to be able to describe them with only one word. As the class studies new concepts and learns new vocabulary words across content areas, create more Secret Word cards and add them to the existing set. This will help students practice words throughout the year, not just when studying a unit.

Riddles (Hink-Pinks)

Students must develop riddles whose answers are two words that rhyme. For example, a chubby feline is a *fat cat*. This is a tricky but enjoyable activity for students, and they can work in pairs to develop their hink-pinks. Once they have developed anywhere from one to five hink-pinks, collect the riddles and share them with the entire class. It may help them make sense of what you are asking them to do if you create some of your own first as practice. You can also find hink-pinks online; just type "hink-pinks" into your favorite search engine.

Word Detective

Set aside a bulletin board in your room titled "Words, Words, Words." As you study new vocabulary words throughout the year, have students add words to the bulletin board. But they should not just write the words out and put them up on the bulletin board; the rule is that they have to find the words in their daily lives. This can be from magazines, newspapers, or flyers from home or it can be written documentation of how someone outside of the classroom used the word. This ongoing collaborative activity helps take word learning beyond the classroom. You want students to be aware of words everywhere. Give them a goal: tell the students that once they fill the board, there will be a special word party or an afternoon of word games.

Figure 10–5 provides teachers with literacy goals for developing students' word knowledge.

Phonemic Analysis	Recognize and use spelling patterns with diphthongs and special vowel spellings (such as *-eigh*, *-ough*, and *-augh*).
	Decode regular multisyllabic words.
	Know and use complex word families.
Syllabic Analysis	Apply knowledge of basic syllabification rules when reading multisyllabic words.
Vocabulary and Word Study (Including Morphemic Analysis)	Understand the meaning of simple affixes.
	Use knowledge of prefixes and suffixes to determine the meaning of unknown words.
	Identify simple multiple-meaning words.
	Understand and use antonyms, synonyms, homophones, and homographs to determine the meaning of words.
	Use sentence and word context to find the meaning of unknown words.
	Use a dictionary to learn the meaning and other features of unknown words.
	Understand and use idioms and figurative language, including similes and metaphors.

FIGURE 10–5: Language and Literacy Goals for Transitional and Self-Extending Readers

Conclusion

Word work involves the study of sounds, letters, and meaningful units (morphemes) of the English language. Students need direct instruction and practice with how the English language is organized to develop literacy. In understanding concepts about print, phonemic awareness, and phonics, students build a solid foundation for learning to read. Once equipped with these tools, they can decode and encode words to make sense of oral and written language. To further develop their comprehension of the English language, students need frequent exposure to words for retention and lots of opportunities to talk and use words. This will help students develop their receptive and expressive vocabularies to communicate more effectively.

Teacher Resource Books to Support Word Work Instruction

Cassie's Word Quilt, by Faith Ringgold
Suddenly! by Colin McNaughton
The Boy Who Cried Fabulous, by Leslea Newman

Idioms

Parts, by Ted Arnold
More Parts, by Ted Arnold
Even More Parts, by Ted Arnold
The King Who Rained, by Fred Gwynne
A Chocolate Moose for Dinner, by Fred Gwynne
A Little Pigeon Toad, by Fred Gwynne
In a Pickle and Other Funny Idioms, by Marvin Terban
Punching the Clock, by Marvin Terban
My Teacher Likes to Say, by Denise Brennan-Nelson and Jane
    Monroe
My Mommy Likes to Say, by Denise Brennan-Nelson and Jane
    Monroe
Weighty Word Book, by Paul M. Levitt and Elissa S. Guralnick

Puns

Otter Nonsense, by Norton Juster

Homophones and Homonyms

Sue Threw the Goop Through the Hoop (Homophone series), by
    Amanda Rondeau
*How Much Can a Bare Bear Bear? What Are Homophones and
    Homonyms?* by Brian P. Cleary

Similes and Metaphors

Quick as a Cricket, by Audrey Wood
Mad as a Wet Hen, by Marvin Terban
As Silly as Knees, as Busy as Bees, by Norton Juster
You Dance Like an Ostrich! by Sylvia Tester
What Did You Say? What Did You Mean? An Illustrated Guide to Understanding Metaphors, by Jude Welton

Phonemic Awareness

Listening Walk, by Paul Showers
Clara Caterpillar, by Pamela Duncan Edwards

Professional Literature on Word Work

Bear, Donald, Marcia Invernizzi, Shane Templeton, and Francine Johnston. 2000. *Words Their Way: Word Study for Phonics, Vocabulary, and Spelling Instruction*. 2d ed. Upper Saddle River, NJ: Prentice Hall, Pearson Education.

Beck, Isabel L., Margaret McKeown, and Linda Kucan. 2002. *Bringing Words to Life: Robust Vocabulary Instruction*. New York: Guilford.

Cunningham, Patricia M. 1995. *Phonics They Use: Words for Reading and Writing*. 2d ed. New York: HarperCollins College.

Greenwood, Scott C. 2004. *Words Count: Effective Vocabulary Instruction in Action*. Portsmouth, NH: Heinemann.

Sinatra, Richard. 2003. *Word Recognition and Vocabulary Development Strategies for Literacy Success*. Norwood, MA: Christopher-Gordon.

Snowball, Diane, and Faye Bolton. 1999. *Spelling K–8: Planning and Teaching*. Portland, ME: Stenhouse.

Concluding Thoughts

*T*he life of a teacher is like the never-ending story; no matter how much you read, there is another chapter to follow with new ideas and new ways of teaching and learning. Every year as a teacher you are presented with the challenge of getting to know and teach a new group of individuals with unique needs. The students come with different learning styles and different experiences and so you will need an instructional program that allows for individual growth while maintaining high expectations for all. This requires a great deal of knowledge and reflective practice on the part of a teacher.

We wrote this book with no intention of prescribing a reading program to anyone, because it is you the teacher who knows your students best. You know what their needs are, what excites them, and how to meet their unique individual needs. Instead we wanted to present a comprehensive view of what it means to develop proficient readers, writers, and speakers of the English language by discussing the *essential elements* of literacy. These essential elements are guides for reflection as you work tirelessly to develop highly literate students. We hope you will take time to ask yourself how your current reading practices and programs are helping you meet your students' needs. For example, do your students have daily opportunities to "understand and use words to convey and receive meaning" (essential element #5) or "form ideas and communicate them purposefully and effectively" (essential element #8)? If not, then we hope you will think about how the methods we present can help fill the gap in your instruction so that students are provided a holistic reading program; a program that develops thoughtful, independent readers and writers.

One of our greatest concerns as educators was how this element of quality and holistic instruction is implemented with second language learners. We worried and unfortunately saw through our work with teachers of English learners that the students were receiving instruction that emphasized only a few of the essential elements. For example, we saw teachers spending most of the instructional day on phonics and decoding, not allowing English learners to explore real text and apply their knowledge of phonics. Phonics is important and is part of a holistic program, but it is only one piece. We wanted to highlight the importance of providing English learners with the type of reading program that expects high levels of English literacy.

All of the methods presented and the classroom examples shared were developed with attention to diversity. They provide the scaffolds for children to develop as individuals. When teaching *to*, working *with*, and encouraging learning *by* students, you help provide students with the proper supports for learning. Our ultimate goal in all lessons is independence and it is important to consistently keep that in mind. Even when we engage in interactive read-aloud or shared reading, we are thinking about how these experiences will support the students in independence.

As you close this chapter in the never-ending story of teaching and learning, we hope you open the next chapter with the same optimism and passion as when you began your journey. And we hope that we have helped better inform your practice to ensure that all of your students are given the ultimate gift as a student, the gift of opportunity! We see this book as the beginning of a conversation in your journey in providing your English learners with meaningful literacy and language experiences. We hope that you seek out companions along this journey because it is through professional reflection and dialogue that we can all improve our practice.

Appendix A : Academic Language Functions and Forms

LANGUAGE FUNCTIONS	POSSIBLE SENTENCE FRAMES (FORMS)	CUE WORDS	
Agreeing and Disagreeing	I agree with . . . but . . . I believe . . . was right when he said . . . but . . . I disagree with . . . when he said . . . I don't agree with . . . I think . . . I think . . . was wrong when he said . . . I agree with . . . however, . . .	Agree Believe Think Right Wrong	But However Disagree Wrong In favor
Expressing Likes and Dislikes	I like . . . I want . . . I love the way . . . I enjoy . . . I don't like . . . I dislike . . .	Like Enjoy Love Adore	Dislike Hate Do Don't
Identifying	It has . . . It looks like . . . It feels like . . . It sounds like . . . It tastes like . . .	Sensory Words: Looks Feels Sounds	Tastes Smells (Location)
Refusing	I will not . . . I do not want to . . . He/she did not want to . . . I wouldn't . . . I didn't . . . I am not going to . . .	Not Wouldn't Didn't Shall not	Won't Will not Cannot Can't
Sequencing	First . . . then . . . lastly . . . At the beginning . . . next . . . finally . . . In the beginning . . . in the middle . . . in the end . . . First . . . second . . . third . . . last . . .	Ordinal Words: First Second Third Beginning Middle	End Finally Next Then Later Last(ly)
Wishing and Hoping	I wish . . . If only I . . . Maybe I can . . . I hope . . . If I had . . . then . . .	Hope Wish Maybe If . . . then	Want Perhaps Crave
Comparing	. . . is . . . but . . . is not. . . . has . . . but . . . does not. . . . can . . . however . . . . . . can . . . whereas . . . cannot. Though . . . can . . . , . . . cannot.	But Whereas However Can/cannot	Is/is not Different As opposed to

Drawing on the work of: Halliday, M. A. K. (1970) and Gibbons, Pauline (1991).

LANGUAGE FUNCTIONS	POSSIBLE SENTENCE FRAMES (FORMS)	CUE WORDS	
Classifying	. . . belongs in this category because . . . . . . is part of this group because . . . I organized the . . . by . . . You can group these together because . . .	Belongs Part of Group Order	Organize Sort Together
Explaining	. . . is . . . because . . . The reason for . . . is . . . He/she was . . . for example . . . I would like to clarify that . . .	Is/is not Because For example	Make clear Such as Clarify
Warning	Don't . . . because . . . Be careful not to . . . Watch out for . . . Stay away from . . . because . . . I warned you not to . . .	Don't Be careful Watch out Caution Stay away	Inform Advise Notify Alert Warn
Hypothesizing	I think . . . because . . . I believe . . . because . . . Maybe . . . is . . . because . . . Perhaps . . . is the reason that . . . It's possible that . . .	Think Believe Perhaps Maybe	Assume Possible Imagine
Planning and Predicting	I think . . . is going to happen because . . . Perhaps he/she will . . . Maybe he/she will . . . because in the text it said . . .	Think Believe Perhaps Maybe	Expect Guess See coming
Commanding	Begin by . . . First you will . . . then . . . Start by . . . then . . . finally . . . Before you begin . . . then . . . I order you to . . .	Start/begin Then/next/finally Order Demand	Command Will Should Do not
Reporting	It all began when . . . The incident/event took place . . . It is/was about . . . What happened was . . . The real story is that . . . It all started because . . .	Tell State Describe Story Details Happened Report	Testify Give an account Convey Inform Recount Inform Event/incident
Expressing	I would just like to say . . . I find . . . I was thinking . . . I just had a thought . . . I have an idea . . . I am sure that . . . I realize now that . . .	Think Idea Thought Find/found Sure/unsure	State Communicate Put across Say Realize
Obligating	You have to . . . because . . . He was forced to . . . because It was necessary because . . . You must . . . or else . . .	Must Force Necessary	Require Make Mandatory
Evaluating	I would have to disagree with . . . because . . . I agree that . . . but . . . I think . . . I decided that . . . Based on what happened, I believe . . .	Agree Disagree Decided Accept	However Further Furthermore Think

LANGUAGE FUNCTIONS	POSSIBLE SENTENCE FRAMES (FORMS)	CUE WORDS	
Expressing Position	I support the idea/position that . . . because . . . I would agree that . . . I side with . . . because . . . I do not believe that . . . because . . . In my opinion . . .	Support Agree Disagree Opinion	View Side with Position
Expressing Obligation	I must . . . I feel I have to . . . I believe it is my responsibility to . . . I should . . . because . . .	Must Obligated Should Responsibility	Duty Commitment Requirement Have to
Inferring	I believe the author is trying to say that . . . Even though it doesn't say so in the text, I think . . . The more I think about this passage, I realize . . . After reading this page, I think that . . . I suppose the author is trying to say that . . .	Infer Believe Think Thought	Assume Understand Suppose Conclude
Suggesting	I would recommend . . . After listening to/reading . . . I suggest . . . I would advise you to . . . I propose . . .	Propose Advise Recommend	Suggest
Criticizing	I don't think he/she should . . . because . . . I dislike the way . . . He/she should not have . . . I disapprove of the way in which . . . I commend him/her for . . . I admire how . . .	Disapprove Dislike Approve Praise	Admire Commend Congratulate Applaud

Bloom's Taxonomy

COGNITIVE COMPETENCE	WHAT A CHILD IS ABLE TO DO	CUE WORDS FOR GENERATING QUESTIONS AND STIMULATING THINKING
Knowledge: Recall information.	• State major ideas. • Identify, name facts and details.	list, define, tell, describe, identify, show, collect, examine, quote, name, who?, what?, when?, where?
Comprehension: Understand and interpret in one's own words the meaning of information presented.	• Understand information. • Interpret information. • Make predictions. • Make comparisons. • Identify and interpret cause and effect.	summarize, describe, discuss, compare, contrast, predict, associate, say more, interpret, why did?, what made?
Application: Translate knowledge across contexts.	• Use information to understand new situations. • Solve problems using known skills, strategies, and information.	apply, demonstrate, explain, show, illustrate, relate, change, modify, imagine, if?, could?
Analysis: Break down information into smaller meaning units to understand the intention, ulterior, or possible meanings.	• Distinguish between facts and fiction. • Identify inferences. • See patterns. • Identify hidden or inner meaning.	analyze, select, separate, organize, arrange, rearrange, classify, categorize, connect, compare, explain, infer, why?, should?
Synthesis: Create an original view, idea, or opinion from meaningful units.	• Identify a structure or pattern. • Create new or alternate meanings. • Generalize meaning from known or given facts. • Draw conclusions.	synthesize, combine, modify, rearrange, substitute, formulate, hypothesize, compose, revise, envision, design, create, rewrite, generalize, what if?
Evaluation: Make judgments about the validity of ideas or information.	• Discriminate and assess ideas, theories, information. • Make informed decisions. • Be critical consumers of information. • Support arguments and ideas with evidence. • Recognize objectivity versus subjectivity. • Assess subjectivity.	evaluate, assess, critique, decide, measure, determine, judge, discriminate, explain, support, recommend, convince, conclude, would?

Appendix C

Cloze Procedures for Teaching Cueing Systems

CUEING SYSTEM	TEXT EXAMPLE	DISCUSSION
Graphophonic: Letters/sounds omitted.	Sandra went to the p___ and played on the swings.	In this example, the student can use what she knows about the sound (phoneme) /p/ represented by the letter (grapheme) *p* to make a guess that the swings were at the park. Keep in mind that the child may have used what she knows about swings (semantics) to guess that the word was *park*; however, without using her graphophonic understanding of the letter-sound correspondence of *p* as /p/, the student could have said *house* because people do have swings at their homes. So you can see here how semantics helps the student think about the missing word, but the use of her graphophonic cueing system helps confirm her prediction. Other cueing systems are also involved, but in a cloze where letters and sounds are omitted you can draw attention to the graphophonic cueing system.
Semantic: content, meaning deleted.	Sandra ate the red _____ that fell from the tree.	In this example, the student can use what he knows about red things that grow on trees to figure out the unknown word. Keep in mind he may also use his syntactic cueing system to anticipate a noun following the adjective, but the meaning derived from what grows on trees can confirm what the word is. By deleting content words, you are highlighting the semantic cueing system.
Syntactic: word structure, part of speech omitted.	Sandra _____ home from school.	In this example, the student can use what she knows about verbs and sentence structure. What would make sense in this sentence? What would sound right? She could say *ran*, *walked*, *skipped*, *jumped*, *hopped*, and so on to decipher the unknown word. She may then use her knowledge of graphophonics to confirm her selection.
Interrelated: graphophonic, semantic, syntactic.	Sandra toppled off the bed.	As fluent readers we use all of our cueing systems to read. In this example, the student can use what he knows about sentence structure to determine that the unknown word is a verb (syntax), his knowledge of what can happen from a bed (semantics), and his knowledge of how to sound out the word *toppled* (graphophonic) to decipher the underlined word.

Describing the Setting

The story takes place_____

_____

It looks like_____

_____

You can hear _____

_____

You can see _____

_____

You can almost taste _____

_____

You can almost feel _____

_____

_____

Name _____ Date _____

Describing

| Character Name: | What did they see?
What did they say?
How did they feel?
What did they do? | Character Name: |

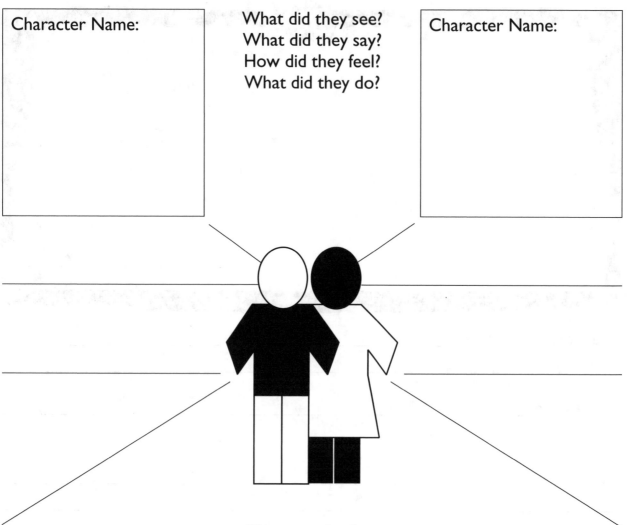

Character Analysis

Likes and Dislikes

My favorite character was _____
_____

because _____
_____

My favorite scene in the story was when
_____

because _____
_____

My least favorite character was_____
_____

because _____
_____

My least favorite scene in the story was
when _____

because _____
_____

Reporting

Top Story: _____

Setting

It happened on . . .

In . . .

Characters

Present at the scene were . . .

Theme or Main Idea

It will be remembered as . . .

Plot

It all began when . . .

Name _____ Date _____

Planning and Predicting

Title: _____

Author: _____

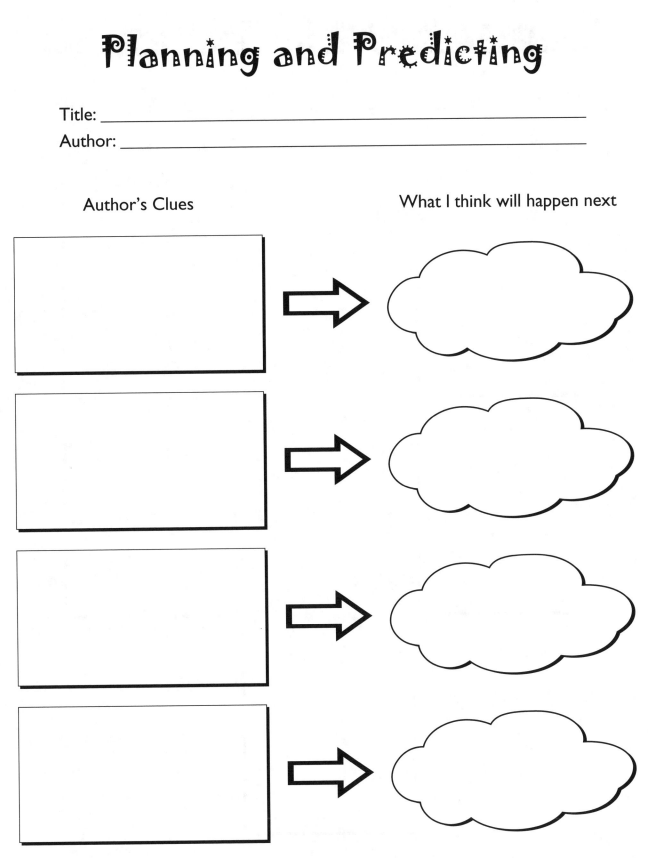

Author's Clues   What I think will happen next

Name _____   Date _____

Commanding/Giving Instructions

Process/Activity: _____

Start by . . .   Then . . .

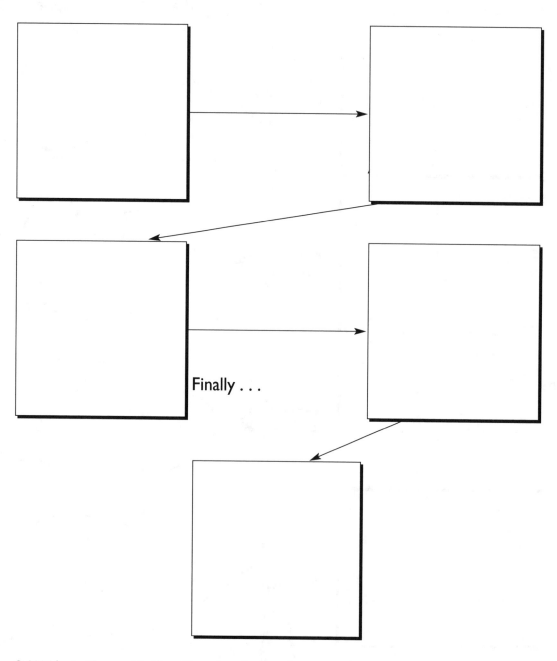

Finally . . .

Name _____   Date _____

Defining

Formal dictionary definition

The larger concept it fits into is . . .

Word

In my own words it means . . .

The context we are using it in is . . .

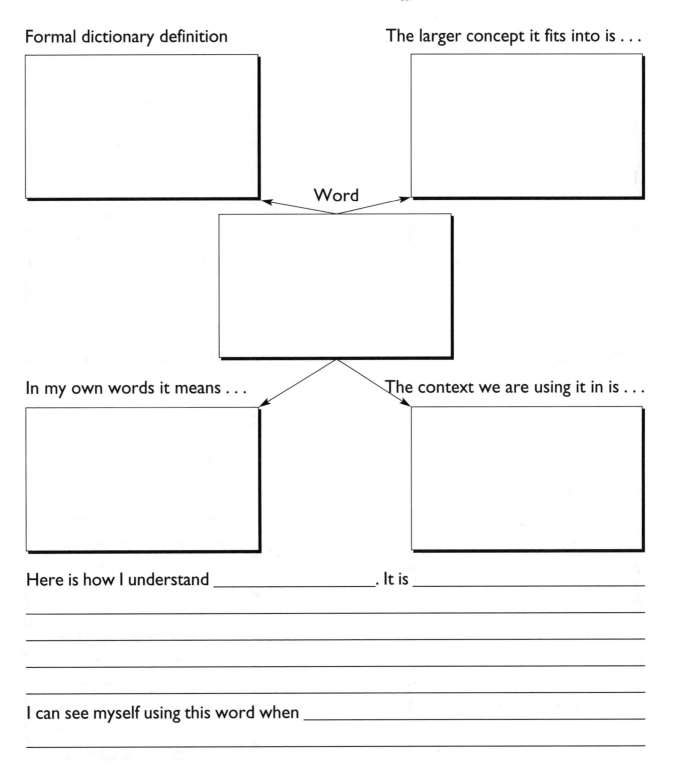

Here is how I understand _____ . It is _____

_____

_____

_____

I can see myself using this word when _____

_____

Name _____   Date _____

Inferring and Justifying

Book Title: _____

Text Support

Text Support

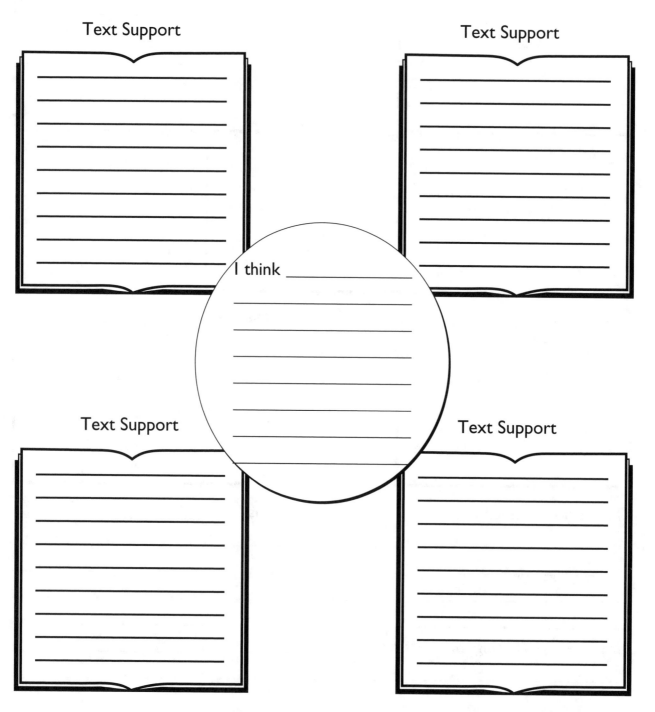

I think _____

Text Support

Text Support

Name _____ Date _____

Synthesis

Title: _____

Author: _____

The story was about . . .

```
_____
_____
_____
_____
_____
_____
_____
_____
_____
```

It was really about . . .

```
_____
_____
_____
_____
_____
_____
```

Classifying and Categorizing

Category: _____   Category: _____

Items to Sort

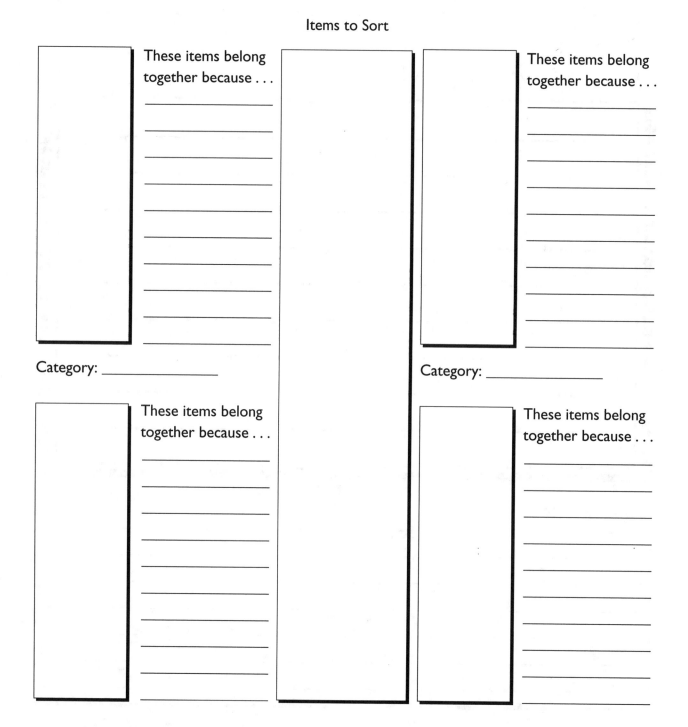

These items belong
together because . . .

_____

_____

_____

_____

_____

_____

_____

_____

_____

These items belong
together because . . .

_____

_____

_____

_____

_____

_____

_____

_____

_____

Category: _____   Category: _____

These items belong
together because . . .

_____

_____

_____

_____

_____

_____

_____

_____

_____

These items belong
together because . . .

_____

_____

_____

_____

_____

_____

_____

_____

_____

Name _____ Date _____

Inquiring/Questioning

Title: _____ Author: _____

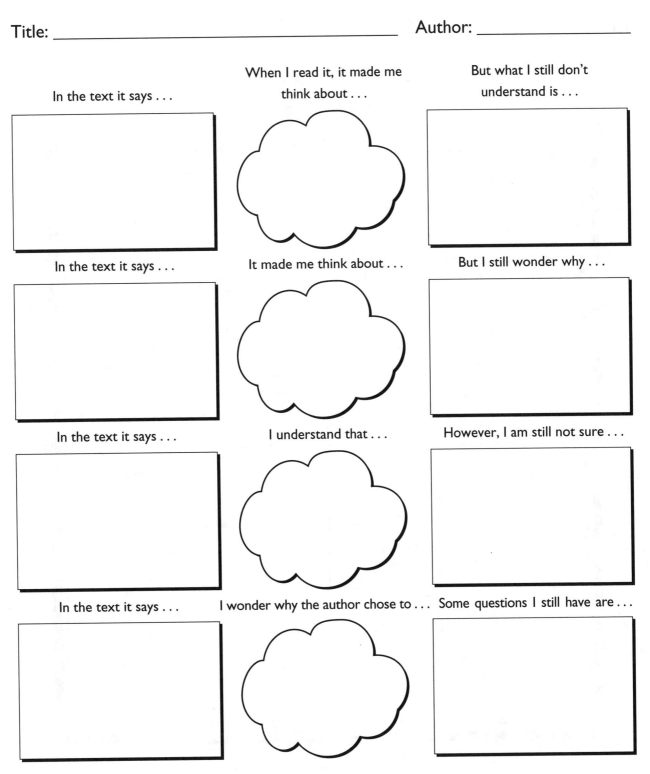

In the text it says . . .

When I read it, it made me think about . . .

But what I still don't understand is . . .

In the text it says . . .

It made me think about . . .

But I still wonder why . . .

In the text it says . . .

I understand that . . .

However, I am still not sure . . .

In the text it says . . .

I wonder why the author chose to . . .

Some questions I still have are . . .

Name _____ Date _____

Analysis

Title: _____ Author: _____

Characters' Actions in the Text

What did it mean?

_____

_____

I believe the author chose to include this part in the story because . . .

 E

Literary Genres

LITERARY GENRE	DEFINITION	CHARACTERS	PLOTLINES	SETTING	THEMES/MOTIFS
Realistic Fiction	Consists of stories that take place in modern times Characters are involved in events that could happen	Ordinary people, real animals	Real-life experiences with problems to solve Unfolding dramas with probable predicaments	Real places (home, school, community)	Changes/challenges Adventure/survival Identity/growing up Moral values
Mystery	A story line is gradually revealed Characters use deductive reasoning and research skills to solve the mystery	Sharp-witted and intriguing characters, private detectives, police, thieves, eyewitnesses	Reviewing a problem or crime Series of clues to follow (footprint, tracks, secret codes)	Dark, remote places (haunted houses, alleys, hidden stairways) Mysterious places (graveyards, shipwrecks, attics)	Good versus evil "Whodunits" Solving problems
Fantasy	Fiction that contains elements that are not realistic, such as talking animals and magical powers	Elves, ghosts, spirits, giants, goblins, personified animals, toys	Begins in reality and moves to fantasy Time warps Supernatural events	Imaginary or future worlds Unusual places	Quests, adventures Back to the future Struggles between good and evil
Fable	Legendary, supernatural tale. Narration demonstrates a useful truth, especially in which animals speak as humans	Cunning animals (clever fox, deceitful wolf), personified animals	Straightforward; moral explicitly stated at the end	Nondescript backdrop for action Animals' natural habitats	Moral lessons Universal truths
Fairy Tale	Story about magical creatures Narration provides strong plot development	Nobility (king, queen, prince, princess), heroes and heroines, common people (peasants), giants, dragons, dwarfs, trolls, ogres, wicked witches, sorcerers, magical objects, supernatural beings	One-dimensional (good/evil, industrious /lazy, brave/cowardly) Often begin with "Once upon a time . . ." Happy endings (living happily ever after)	Villages Castles Countryside Humble cottages Enchanted forests	Rags to riches Magical wishes Abandonment Good and bad luck

Genre	Definition	Characters	Plot / Actions	Setting	Themes
Folklore	Includes fairy tales, fables, myths, legends, and tall tales that were passed down over the years	Ethnic and racial groups, wise people, tricksters, magical objects	Plot advanced by journey, spell, sleep; Highly predictable and brief; Positive, uplifting endings	Usually general; Places around the world	Insights into human predicaments; Ordinary lives of folk people; Explain beliefs, values, customs
Legend and Tall Tale	Story, sometimes of a national or folk hero, which has a basis in fact but also includes imaginative material	Folk heroes, real and imagined heroes, larger-than-life heroes	Describe a series of extraordinary events or guests; Actions that reveal what happened	Imaginary places; Unexplored territories; Known locations	Focus on how things come to pass; Natural phenomenon explanations; Humor and human imagination
Myth	Legend or traditional narrative, often based in part on historical events, that reveals human behavior and natural phenomena by its symbolism; often pertaining to the actions of gods	Greek and Roman gods and goddesses, Mother Earth, natural phenomena, mythical beasts	Supernatural incidents leading to explanations of nature or civilization	Imaginary kingdoms; Unexplored territories	Origins of the world; Creation stories; Human nature

Learning Center Activity Cards

ART CENTER

1. Think about our theme:_____.

2. Cut out pictures or words from the magazines that relate to our unit theme.

3. Make a collage of your clippings.

LISTENING CENTER

1. Listen to the story.

2. Use the index cards to write down any words you thought were challenging.

3. Read the words together as a group and come up with a definition for the word on the back of the index card.

4. Review the words by playing Blurt It.

READING CENTER: STORY STRETCHER

1. Sequence the pictures provided for the story.

2. Add two of your own scenes using the blank picture cards.

3. Rewrite your new story.

WORD WORK

1. Read the sentence strips.

2. Use the index cards to write words that will make sense in the blank spaces.

3. Reread the sentences with the new words.

4. Try to find more words that would fit in the blanks.

WRITING CENTER

1. Select a picture from the basket.

2. Write a story about your picture.

ART CENTER

1. Pick a nonfictional book from the library.

2. Write down 5 new facts you learned from the book.

3. Make a bookmark of the main idea.

ASKING QUESTIONS

1. Pick a picture from the box.

2. Use your question words to write 5 questions about your picture.

3. Repeat steps 1 and 2.

SOCIAL STUDIES

1. Think of a job from our community.

2. Create an advertisement for the business.

3. Use the newspaper to help you create your advertisement.

WRITING CENTER

1. Pick a book from the classroom library.

2. Read the book.

3. Pick one of the characters in the story and write a friendly letter to the character.

WORD WORK

1. Read the story provided.

2. Underline the adjectives in the story.

3. Replace each adjective with a synonym.

4. Reread your story.

5. Replace each adjective with an antonym.

6. Reread the story. How has it changed?

WORD WORK

1. Read the words below.

2. Separate the words by part of speech.

3. Separate the nouns as singular or plural.

4. Write sentences using all the words. (Clue: You can use more than one of the words in each sentence.)

quickly	Mr. Mora	beautiful	he	ran
Ivette	car	they	table	thin
she	dirty	Jose and Yaxive	it	you
smart	we	socks	new	riding
huge	walk	has	jump	talk
frantically	slowly	carefully	loudly	quietly

READING CENTER

1. Select and read a fairy tale from the classroom library.

2. Using the paper provided, draw or write what happened in the beginning, middle, and end of the story.

3. Add a new ending to the story.

READING CENTER

1. Select a book from the classroom library.

2. Read the book you selected.

3. Compare two characters from the story.

WHAT'S THE STORY?

1. Pick a picture from the box.

2. Write a paragraph about the picture.

3. Repeat steps 1 and 2.

Appendix G

Word Sorts

WORD SORT

cow	saw	loyal	ouch
August	joy	cloud	coin
spoil	owl	ground	crawl
couch	because	boy	down
point	toy	howl	join
law	shout	oil	draw
flower	oink	author	mouse

DIPHTHONG WORD SORT

with	ring	wish	wrong
string	watch	mother	wink
cherry	hang	wash	chat
bath	crash	stitch	that
should	cheese	sank	bang
champ	short	math	song
witch	ink	long	hatch

Works Cited

Adams, Marilyn J. 1990. *Beginning to Read: Thinking and Learning About Print*. Cambridge, MA: MIT Press.

Allen, Janet. 2000. *Yellow Brick Roads: Shared and Guided Paths to Independent Reading 4–12*. Portland, ME: Stenhouse.

Allington, Richard L., and Patricia M. Cunningham. 2003. *Classrooms That Work: They Can All Read and Write*. 3d ed. Boston: Pearson Education.

Arnosky, Jim. 1995. *I See Animals Hiding*. New York: Scholastic.

Avery, Carol. 2002. *. . . And with a Light Touch: Learning About Reading, Writing, and Teaching with First Graders*. Portsmouth, NH: Heinemann.

Bear, Donald, Marcia Invernizzi, Shane Templeton, and Francine Johnston. 2000. *Words Their Way: Word Study for Phonics, Vocabulary, and Spelling Instruction*. 2d ed. Upper Saddle River, NJ: Prentice Hall, Pearson Education.

Beck, Isabel L., Margaret McKeown, and Linda Kucan. 2002. *Bringing Words to Life: Robust Vocabulary Instruction*. New York: Guilford.

Bloom, Benjamin S. 1984. *Taxonomy of Educational Objectives*. Boston: Allyn and Bacon with Pearson Education.

Calkins, Lucy McCormick. 1994. *The Art of Teaching Writing*. Portsmouth, NH: Heinemann.

———. 2001. *The Art of Teaching Reading*. New York: Addison-Wesley Educational.

Cambourne, Brian. 1988. *The Whole Story: Natural Learning and the Acquisition of Literacy in the Classroom*. Auckland, NZ: Ashton Scholastic.

Cambourne, Brian, and Jan Turbill. 1991. *Coping with Chaos*. Portsmouth, NH: Heinemann.

Cameron, Ann. 1989. *The Stories Julian Tells*. New York: Knopf.

Chomsky, Noam. 1959. "A Review of B. F. Skinner's Verbal Behavior." *Language* 35: 26–58. Reprinted in Chomsky, Noam. 1965. *Aspects of the Theory of Syntax*. Cambridge, MA: MIT Press.

Clay, Marie. 1966. "Emergent Reading Behaviour." PhD diss., University of Auckland, NZ.

———. 1991. *Becoming Literate: The Construction of Inner Control*. Auckland, NZ: Heinemann Education.

———. 1998. *By Different Paths to Common Outcomes*. Portland, ME: Stenhouse.

———. 2000. *Running Records for Classroom Teachers*. Portsmouth, NH: Heinemann.

Cummins, Jim. 1984. "Wanted: A Theoretical Framework for Relating Language Proficiency to Academic Achievement Among Bilingual Students." In *Language Proficiency and Academic Achievement*, edited by Charlene Rivera, 2–19. Avon, England: Multilingual Matters.

———. 1991. "Interdependence of First- and Second-Language Proficiency in Bilingual Children." In *Language Processing in Bilingual Children*, edited by Ellen Bialystok, 70–89. Cambridge, MA: Cambridge University Press.

———. 1992. "Language Proficiency, Bilingualism, and Academic Achievement." In *The Multicultural Classroom: Readings for Content-Area Teachers*, edited by Patricia Richard-Amato and Marguerite Ann Snow, 16–26. New York: Longman.

———. 2003. "Reading and the Bilingual Student: Fact and Friction." In *English Learners: Reaching the Highest Level of English Literacy*, edited by Gilbert Garcia, 2–33. Newark, DE: International Reading Association.

Diaz-Rico, Lynne T., and Kathryn Z. Weed. 2002. *The Crosscultural, Language, and Academic Development Handbook: A Complete K–12 Reference Guide*. 2d ed. Boston: Allyn and Bacon.

Dutro, Susana, and Cecilia Moran. 2003. "Rethinking English Language Instruction: An Architectural Approach." In *English Learners: Reaching the Highest Level of English Literacy*, edited by Gilbert Garcia, 227–58. Newark, DE: International Reading Association.

Farrell, Thomas S. C. 2006. *Succeeding with English Language Learners: A Guide for Beginning Teachers*. Thousand Oaks, CA: Corwin.

Fountas, Irene C., and Gay Su Pinnell. 1996. *Guided Reading: Good First Teaching for All Children*. Portsmouth, NH: Heinemann.

———. 2001. *Guiding Readers and Writers Grades 3–8: Teaching Comprehension, Genre, and Content Literacy*. Portsmouth, NH: Heinemann.

Freeman, Yvonne S., and David S. Freeman. 1998. *ESL/EFL Teaching: Principles for Success*. Portsmouth, NH: Heinemann.

Genishi, Celia. 1998. "Young Children's Oral Language Development." ERIC Digest. ERIC Clearinghouse on Elementary and Early Childhood Education. Retrieved from www.readingrockets.org/print.php?ID=28.

Gibbons, Pauline. 1991. *Learning to Learn in a Second Language*. Portsmouth, NH: Heinemann.

———. 2002. *Scaffolding Language, Scaffolding Learning*. Portsmouth, NH: Heinemann.

Graves, Donald H. 1994. *A Fresh Look at Writing*. Portsmouth, NH: Heinemann.

Halliday, M. A. K. 1970. "Language Structure and Language Function." *New Horizons in Linguistics*, ed. by John Lyons, 140–165. Baltimore: Penguin Books.

Hamayan, Else. 1994. "Language Development of Low Literacy Students." In *Educating Second Language Children: The Whole Child, the Whole Curriculum, the Whole Community*, edited by Fred Genesee, 278–300. Cambridge: Cambridge University Press.

Handheld Education. 2004. "Specially Designed Academic Instruction in English." Retrieved from www.handheldeducation.com/readingscene/abc/SDAIE.html.

Hart, Betty, and Todd R. Risley. 2003. "The Early Catastrophe: The 30 Million Word Gap by Age 3." *American Educator*. Washington, DC: American Federation of Teachers. Retrieved from www.aft.org/pubs-reports/american_educator/spring2003/catastrophe.html.

Heath, Shirley Brice. 1983. *Ways with Words*. New York: Cambridge University Press.

Holdaway, Don. 1979. *The Foundations of Literacy*. Gosford, NSW: Ashton Scholastic.

Kame'enui, Edward, Douglas W. Carnine, Robert C. Dixon, Deborah C. Simmons, and Michael D. Coyne. 1998. *Effective Teaching Strategies That Accommodate Diverse Learners*. Upper Saddle River, NJ: Pearson Education.

Keene, Ellin O., and Susan Zimmermann. 1997. *Mosaic of Thought: Teaching Comprehension in a Reader's Workshop*. Portsmouth, NH: Heinemann.

Krashen, Stephen D. 1981. *Principles and Practice in Second Language Acquisition*. English Language Teaching series. London: Prentice-Hall International.

———. 2004. "Free Voluntary Reading: New Research, Applications, and Controversies." Retrieved from www.Free_Voluntary_Reading-Krashen/FVReading1-Krashen.pdf.

Lancome, Julie. 1993. *Walking Through the Jungle*. Cambridge, MA: Candlewick Press.

Lehr, Fran, Jean Osborne, and Elfrieda Hiebert. 2005. "A Focus on Vocabulary." Research Based Practice in Early Reading Series, ES0419. Honolulu: Pacific Resources for Education and Learning.

Liu, Jun, and Jette G. Hansen. 2002. *Peer Response in Second Language Writing Classrooms*. Ann Arbor: University of Michigan Press.

Lyle, Susan. 1993. "An Investigation into Ways in Which Children Talk Themselves into Meaning." *Language and Education* 7 (3): 181–87.

Mooney, Margaret. 1996. *Reading to, with, and by Children*. Katonah, NY: Richard C. Owen.

Parkes, Brenda. 2000. *Read It Again! Revisiting Shared Reading*. Portland, ME: Stenhouse.

Peregoy, Suzanne F., and Owen F. Boyle. 2005. *Reading, Writing and Learning in ESL: A Resource Book for K–12 Teachers*. 4th ed. Boston: Allyn and Bacon with Pearson Education.

Routman, Regie. 2000. *Conversations: Strategies for Teaching, Learning, and Evaluating*. Portsmouth, NH: Heinemann.

———. 2003. *Reading Essentials: The Specifics You Need to Teach Reading Well*. Portsmouth, NH: Heinemann.

Rylant, Cynthia. 2004. *Henry and Mudge and the Wild Goose Chase*. New York: Simon and Schuster.

Sibberson, Franki, and Karen Szymusiak. 2003. *Still Learning to Read: Teaching Students in Grades 3–6*. Portland, ME: Stenhouse.

Snow, Catherine, Susan Burns, and Peg Griffin, eds. 1998. *Preventing Reading Difficulties in Young Children*. Washington, DC: National Academy Press.

Stabb, Claire. 1986. "What Happened to the Sixth Graders: Are Elementary Students Losing Their Need to Forecast and to Reason?" *Reading Psychology* 7 (4): 289–96.

Stahl, Steven A., and Marilyn M. Fairbanks. 1986. "The Effects of Vocabulary Instruction: A Model-Based Meta-Analysis." *Review of Educational Research* 56: 72–110.

Stanovich, Keith. 1986. "Matthew Effect in Reading: Some Consequences of Individuals' Differences in the Acquisition of Literacy." *Reading Research Quarterly* 21 (4): 360–407.

Sulzby, Elizabeth. 1991. "Assessment of Emergent Literacy: Storybook Reading." *The Reading Teacher* 44 (7): 498–500.

Trelease, Jim. 2001. *The Read Aloud Handbook*. 5th ed. New York: Penguin.

Vygotsky, Lev S. 1962. *Thought and Language*. Cambridge, MA: MIT Press.

Index